OPERA

Robin May has had a life-long interest in the theatre and opera and was an actor for ten years. He contributes regularly to *Look and Learn* on the arts, history and America, and has written many books in these areas, including *Operamania, Theatremania, The Wit of the Theatre, Who's Who in Shakespeare, Concise Encyclopedia of the Theatre, Wolfe's Army, The Wild West*.

TEACH YOURSELF BOOKS

By the same author

Operamania
Theatremania
The Wit of the Theatre
Who's Who in Shakespeare
A Companion to the Theatre
Concise Encyclopedia of the Theatre
Who was Shakespeare?
Wolfe's Army
The American West, etc.

OPERA

Robin May

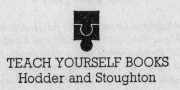

TEACH YOURSELF BOOKS
Hodder and Stoughton

To Jane, suffering seriously from operamania

First Impression 1977

Copyright © 1977
Robin May

ISBN 0 340 21847 9

Printed and bound in Great Britain for Hodder and Stoughton
Paperbacks, a division of Hodder and Stoughton Ltd,
Mill Road, Dunton Green, Sevenoaks, Kent,
(Editorial Office; 47 Bedford Square, London WC1 3DP)
by Hazell Watson & Viney Ltd, Aylesbury, Bucks

Contents

Introduction

This book is intended as a companion for the opera-goer, especially the newcomer to this art form. Basically, it is a history of opera, with a prelude that discusses the particular problems of performance, and with an appendix of operatic terms and definitions of words such as *tessitura* and *castrato*, which also contains short essays on some more general terms, such as singers and stage design.

It would be foolish to claim too much for the book, because only in the opera house, preferably with an experienced and sympathetic guide, can opera really be discovered. But discovery – which may originally be triggered off by a record, a broadcast, or a television programme – is not enough, even with a good companion. The world of opera can seem alien to a newcomer, however much he or she enjoys a first experience.

Not everyone can become an opera-lover in the fullest sense, but, as many discover, opera-going can be exciting, enjoyable and deeply moving. The chief aim of this book is to help increase the enjoyment and excitement by providing background knowledge. It would be idle to pretend that the author has not taken a personal stand on some subjects, notably on operas of the second rank that so enchant ordinary opera-lovers, but so often apparently cause the austere to suffer; but essentially this is a book that stresses informed opinion about an art that for many thousands round the world is the greatest of them all. It can rarely be the most perfect – the problems and expense of staging opera prevent that happening frequently – but for many it is infinitely the most satisfying.

R.M.
Wimbledon, 1976

I

Prelude—in the Opera House

Despite the inroads of inflation, opera houses are still standing and still used. Some are elegant; some, like Covent Garden, are beautiful enough to make a newcomer gasp and to make a 'regular' purr with pleasure every time that he enters the auditorium; some are merely functional.

The entertainment within them is the subject of this book, especially its long history and its composers, for, however stellar the singers, the men who have provided them with the music to sing are the ones who matter most. Sometimes, as we shall see, the singers got the upper hand to a dangerous degree, sometimes the balance was right.

But just what is an opera? Simply, it is a play set to music, usually a drama or comedy written for the purpose. There is in fact no simple explanation of opera, however, for it ranges from works full of set pieces like duets and elaborate songs called arias, linked by accompanied and declamatory 'recitative' passages, to works with plenty of spoken dialogue; and there are many variations in between.

Opera gives a composer a marvellous opportunity to communicate more emotions and thoughts in a single moment than a playwright can, quite apart from the 'heightening' effect music can have in raising the emotional temperature. An actor can, say, ask for a glass of wine and hope to convey to the audience something more than the simple request to the person he is addressing, but all he can use is a look or a gesture or a strong vocal inflection. With a composer's help a singer can ask for wine in such a way that we know that he is thinking of his mother at home, or his girl friend, or that his mind is actually on someone he has just stabbed. Alternatively, the singer can express this while remaining silent because the composer will be repeating an earlier theme. Or four singers can sing together and yet express exactly what each of them is thinking, as in the famous quartet in the last act of *Rigoletto*.

Of course, the disadvantage of singing is that, despite these possibilities, which are not beyond the scope of quite ordinary composers, it cannot get across continuous, dense thoughts as readily as drama can. There are not so many words in an opera as there are in a play, because opera takes its time with the words. Opera-lovers are more than contented because they find the proceedings thrilling and satisfying, but not surprisingly, as we shall see, battles over the relative importance of words and music have been going on throughout operatic history.

Ultimately, it is the sheer emotional punch of opera that so many find so exciting, along with the pleasure of listening to fine music which can clothe even unlikely stories and make them seem masterpieces of drama. In some countries, like Germany and Italy, opera is so much part of the scene that many are exposed to it from their youth, but in Britain and America, with no long tradition of opera-going by mass audiences, the barriers of suspicion still linger.

Some think it odd to sing rather than speak the words 'I love you'; but to hear a thrilling tenor sing the words will make the listener realise how much more *effective* it is to sing it in a theatrical context. Singing and dramatic poetry – blank verse such as Shakespeare used so matchlessly – may seem 'unnatural' ways of behaving; but are they? For those who love them they are more 'real' than ordinary life because they express all human feelings in such powerful and beautiful form.

But the only true place to find the secret of opera's magic is in the opera house.

For many, the most dazzling of all is Là Fenice in Venice, where in 1851 Verdi dared not give the music of 'La donna e mobile' to the tenor until the very last moment, and where all the theatre staff were sworn to keep its melody secret, for fear that it would reach the rest of the city before the première of *Rigoletto*. He was right. Almost moments after an opera finished in that enchanted theatre, gondoliers were likely to be singing its melodies on the Grand Canal.

Some opera houses are in the open air. Santa Fé's is roofed by the bright stars of the New Mexican sky, while the greatest of all temples of song in the sight of heaven is the Verona Arena, where 2 000 years ago blood used to flow to make a Roman holiday. Night after night in high summer for the last half-century, 25 000 have gathered to glory in opera, and older Italians present recall a time when Italian opera was the national passion, before it was surpassed by football and the cinema.

Happy the opera-goer who is introduced to the art in such glamorous circumstances, or at Salzburg, or – if he or she is that rare being, a born, not made, Wagnerite – at Bayreuth. Happy the operatically virgin Briton or American who, finding himself in Parma for the food, comes upon the opera house where the most demanding operatic audience in the world lives and breathes opera throughout the winter season.

In Parma, errand boys can actually be heard whistling Verdi and Puccini (as peasants all over Italy could do up to a generation ago), and *all* classes can be found in the Teatro Regio. It is People's Art as it once was in all Italy throughout the nineteenth century, when the most popular arias were literally the pop music of the day. Parma's partisan public has been known to hound a singer to the station, abusing and even threatening him with violence for his shortcomings in the music of their hero Verdi, born nearby. Toscanini was actually born in the town. Taxi-drivers have on occasion refused to stop for a failed tenor, porters have refused to handle the baggage of such a wretch. But a success in the cauldron of the Teatro Regio, where Gigli was discovered, and the divine Tebaldi began her career, is a triumph indeed.

In Italy, even though opera is no longer as popular as eating and loving and films and sport, it is still part of the national life. So it is in both the Germanys, which, all told, boast some hundred opera houses. It is of exceptional interest even to those Viennese who never enter their world-famous State Opera. Prague, where *Don Giovanni* had its première, is only one of a number of operatic centres in Czechoslovakia, and the trip round Europe could be extended. But in Britain and America, for all the growing number of opera-lovers, and the remarkable wealth of talented singers, opera is not in the blood and the bones of the people. The Italian of the 1970s, even if he rarely goes to an opera, knows many of its melodies by heart; the German who reaches maturity without ever having entered an opera house is an exception. In these countries, and others, like France, with a long operatic tradition, there is no need continually to defend opera, its traditions, its audiences, its opera houses, and its subsidies.

Meanwhile both America and Britain have different versions of the same problem: subsidies for opera are not yet totally inadequate in Britain, but at the time of writing, inflation is rapidly making them so. In America, where millionaire opera patrons are less thick on the ground than once they were, the idea of having *any* subsidies for the arts is only just beginning to catch on. The leading opera house, the Metropolitan, New York, lurches from crisis to crisis as regularly as the British economy.

Opera is the most expensive form of theatrical art, for even with less-than-stellar casts, it is nearly always more elaborate than ballet, its nearest cost rival, and the demand for a full symphony orchestra on hand is not a problem that affects the 'straight' theatre. Its justification, like that of the other subsidised arts, is that a civilised nation should provide its citizens with a chance of experiencing, and rejoicing in, great art. Arguments can rage about what exactly great art *is*; but when subsidies are under discussion it is generally agreed to be an eminently worthwhile part of our cultural heritage. The individual can rebel against certain judgements, but Beethoven, Shakespeare, Wagner, Rembrandt and lesser masters are not likely to be diminished.

As for availability, in the case of opera there is more outside

London than is generally realised, especially now that Scottish Opera and the Welsh National Opera, apart from brilliant seasons on their home ground, do so much touring – even into 'foreign' England, where the English National Opera also tours. The situation is less good in America, despite the many universities where opera is presented. In between the great centres like New York, Chicago, San Francisco and half a dozen others there are some wide open spaces, operatically as well as geographically.

Only in exceptional circumstances will great art appeal to a majority: Shakespeare in Elizabethan England, opera in nineteenth-century Italy. In the former, a succession of thrilling new plays, and an audience that responded to dramatic poetry and strong story lines were the keys; in Italy, the line of glory from Rossini to Puccini, a long earlier tradition, a love of singing and – again – strong story lines, all made for an operatic paradise. An additional factor was patriotism, for as we shall see, patriotism and Verdi were strongly linked.

Elsewhere considerable minorities respond and responded to opera. But honesty compels even the partisan to admit that the operatic public in Britain, growing annually as it is, and filling the theatres night after night, is a small minority of the general theatre public in a land where the theatre itself is a minority art. That hundreds of thousands go to the opera every year in Britain is certain; so is the fact that many of that number are going time and time again.

For these reasons it is only right to enter the opera house in this book through the ears and eyes of a newcomer to an alien art form, a newcomer who hopefully longs to love opera, but has been used to absorbing the steely realism of the camera, TV or film, and plays where men and women do not erupt into song and continue to do so until the final curtain. Many a newcomer has to get used to song as the instrument of communication, and hardly the sort of singing that he is used to in today's pop music.

Let us assume that our newcomer has not had the benefit of having first been indocrinated by a friend, then brought by him to the opera house. Let us assume he has suddenly acquired a ticket, or passed Covent Garden or the Coliseum and decided to drop in. That the chances of just dropping in and finding a cheap seat available are not good should perhaps be stressed, but it is sheer myth that tickets are never obtainable. Booking in advance, having obtained the advance programme, is the answer; even so you may be unlucky for, say, a Sutherland performance, because 30 000 people will want the 13 000 or so tickets available for the six performances.

It is an accepted fact that the British working class as a whole do not go to the theatre, many feeling apparently that 'it is not for the likes of us'. The Welsh apart, how much more, therefore, must they feel that opera is not for them – opera, which fills many middle-class folk with deep suspicion. Television makes occasional valiant efforts to convince them otherwise and remarkable viewing figures have been achieved, but only in the opera house is an opera-lover made. Many ordinary British soldiers discovered this for themselves in Italy at the end of the Second World War. They got the essential message – that opera is there to be enjoyed.

Meanwhile our newcomer has managed to get a seat and is inside the opera house. What will he find before the curtain goes up?

Indoctrination by the invincibly ignorant will have told him that the theatre will be peopled by the rich in full evening dress (see almost any film or TV play in which there is a 'night at the opera' scene). In fact, except at Glyndebourne in Britain, where evening dress is 'recommended', anything goes. There are certainly some rich people to be seen, for inevitably prices are now so high that some seats are beyond normal means. But many who occupy the better seats are not wealthy, merely such keen opera-goers that they save their money to afford good seats. By way of contrast, just think how much 'ordinary' people pay out weekly on pop records and albums, and of the multi-million business which pop supports.

More daunting than the sight and sound of the rich (less in evidence anyway at the Coliseum and in the regional theatres) is the feeling of the newcomer that he is an outsider, a feeling that can make even the sophisticated feel uneasy. Cliques can be heard arguing the rival merits of singers, conductors, composers and directors, or exchanging operatic gossip, which may well make our newcomer feel not only an outsider, but that he is surrounded by that dread tribe, the élitists. Actually, the cliques are usually groups of opera-maniacs, some of whom enjoy noisily showing off their knowledge, or lack of it. But they can be enough to make the outsider feel inferior even before the curtain goes up and will probably spoil his intervals as well if he is unlucky.

The performance begins.

Two types of newcomer are at once at a distinct disadvantage, however good the performance. They are the tone-deaf – the author's inspirational history master was unable to detect any difference between 'God Save the King' and 'Rule, Britannia'! – and those lost souls who do not like the human voice raised in song, however beautifully. The latter at least may enjoy a beautifully staged performance, though they may decide that the *genre* is not for them. Fortunately, neither they nor the tone-deaf are many in number: some claim to be tone-deaf who cannot sing in tune, which is not the same thing at all.

But our newcomer suffers from neither of these afflictions, and, if he is or has been lucky enough to be faced with, say, Callas and Gobbi in *Tosca*, directed by Zeffirelli at Covent Garden in 1964; Cortubas, Benelli, Bruscantini and Geraint Evans in *Don Pasquale* in 1974, also at the Garden; the Coliseum *Carmen* of the early 1970s; a night of perfection at Glyndebourne; the legendary *Così fan Tutte* of Scottish Opera in 1967, etc, there would be no need, from his point of view, to continue this chapter any further. He would have been hooked.

He certainly would have been by Domingo in *Cavalleria Rusticana* and *Pagliacci* at Covent Garden in 1976. But opera, by its very nature, by the searing demands it makes on its performers theatrically and musically, is seldom perfect; indeed it is the most regularly flawed of the theatre arts and always will be. That its theatrical standards are infinitely higher in many countries than in the 1930s and before is undeniable, but they are rarely as good as those of the average reputable theatre company. It is a miracle that standards *are* so high, with jet-age stars arriving at the last moment and with large repertoires and continually changing casts, but even in usually excellently-run companies, like those in Britain, 'dud' nights can occur which are liable – unfairly but undeniably – to put off a newcomer for life. It may be grossly unfair for someone to write off opera as an art form on the strength of a single visit, but it happens.

The potential obstacles to opera conversion include the following: choice of opera, standard of singing, standard of acting, quality of production and the appearance of singers. The last of these, together with the standard of acting, are the likeliest hazards. It is no use for opera-lovers to deny these things, though the 'canary-fanciers' among them, who think of little but the singing, would claim that they do not matter. This is heretical rubbish.

The great operatic composers have always thought that acting matters. Verdi, in his old age, leapt up on to the stage to show Tamagno, his first Otello (and something of a stick), how he wanted the part played; Bizet desperately tried to get the ladies of the Opéra-Comique to behave like cigarette girls during the rehearsals of the original *Carmen*; Benjamin Britten publicly demanded singers who can act; and Wagner, the theatre in his veins as well as music, was brilliant at getting his casts to realize his theatrical dreams.

Our newcomer, alas, may see some bad or, indeed, abysmal acting on this first crucial visit, but there is a good chance that he will be pleasantly surprised. More and more singers, encouraged by the new generation of producers (British opera houses have not yet followed the theatre's switch to the word 'director'), are learning how to act, relax and look as if they belong on the stage. A Boris Christoff is a rarity, but then so is a Laurence Olivier. So, at the other end of the scale, are singers who just stand around.

There is, incidentally, a legend that operatic acting is different from 'straight' acting. It is not. It is true that the Wagnerian actor spends much of his life motionless on steep slopes, and that his calf muscles need to be strong, but then the style of acting in a Greek tragedy is on the monumental side compared with farce and comic opera. There are different styles of acting to suit different plays, but, ultimately, only two categories: good and bad.

Let us assume our newcomer can face the singer-actors' work without blenching. But what about their looks and size? The instinct of the opera-lover is to proclaim – rightly – that the number of good-looking singers today is legion, but it would be idle to claim that tenors (especially) all look like Franco Corelli and Placido Domingo, or that the average singer playing a hero or heroine looks ideal at short range. But the average size of singers has altered dramatically over the last decades.

Bernard Levin, in an article in *The Times* of January 23, 1976, headed 'Fat ladies are phantoms of the opera now', rightly stressed the disappearance of real heavyweights. Also rightly, he noted that those who state that opera singers in general are fat only prove that they never set foot in an opera house. *Never?* Levin was honest enough to admit that some are in the old tradition (though even in the past many were slim and good-looking). His article was written as Londoners were enjoying yet again the magnificent Brünnhilde of the marvellous Rita Hunter, claimed by an adoring Levin as 'the stoutest singer of the first rank the operatic stage has ever seen'. He also reminded his readers of the immortal night when Jessye Norman, a superb black soprano built, unlike her glamorous black fellow super-stars, Shirley Verrett and Grace Bumbry, on heroic lines, entered the dressing-room of the equally heroic Hunter. It was the occasion of the latter's first Brünnhilde. Cried Norman: 'Hiya, skinny!'

The chances are that if our newcomer experienced these ladies, or that other Juno-esque super-star, Monserrat Caballé, or the vast charmer with a huge, thrilling silver-trumpet of a voice, the tenor Pavarotti, he would be bowled over like the rest of the audience. But it must be admitted that he could hit a lesser cast that looked, in the main, unattractive. All the more reason to hope that a friend has chosen his first performance for him. As for the tenors, they are still a rare enough breed in the top class for audiences to make allowances, and happy would be the newcomer to opera in 1974 who at Covent Garden could experience in swift succession the following: Domingo as Radamès and Rodolfo, Ugo Benelli as Ernesto in *Don Pasquale*, Alfredo Kraus as the Duke in *Rigoletto* and José Carreras as Alfredo in *Traviata*. Even on the Wagnerian front a great Siegfried has arisen who actually looks and acts the titanic part: Alberto Remedios.

The other obstacles that our newcomer faces are easier to comment upon without accusations of special pleading. The choice of opera depends on the musical tastes, if any, that he already has. Just as the theatre ranges from *Oedipus Rex* to farce, so opera embraces *Götterdämmerung* and *L'Élisir d'Amore*. If our friend already likes eighteenth-century music, nothing could be more suitable for him than a good performance of *The Marriage of Figaro*, preferably in English. But the safest first choices tend to be *Butterfly*, *Bohème*, *Tosca*, *Traviata*, *Aida*, *Rigoletto*, *Cavalleria Rusticana*, *Pagliacci* and *Carmen*.

With the single exception of *The Flying Dutchman*, Wagner should not be the newcomer's introduction to opera, and even the *Dutchman* is not ideal. That rare being, the born Wagnerite, already referred to, is the exception. It is criminal to expose a novice to *Tristan und Isolde* and Heaven help our newcomer if he wanders in to it. Later it may become, as it for so many, an emotional experience almost without equal in the theatre, from which it can take days to recover, if, indeed, one wishes to. But a first *Tristan* – or any other supreme Wagnerian masterpiece – experienced without at least some 'homework', and an ear already receptive to mid- and late-nineteenth-century music, is for many sheer torture.

So let us hope our newcomer has walked into, say, *Bohème*. This brings us on to the standard of staging. Theatre folk and regular play-goers tend, even now, to be critical of operatic production, despite the fact that so many of the leading directors –

Peter Hall, Visconti, Strehler, Zeffirelli, John Dexter – often stage opera. The honest opera-goer has a problem here. He knows that the finest productions are equal to any in the 'straight' theatre. Mentioning only those of some of the directors listed above, Hall's *Figaro* and his Monteverdi and Cavalli productions at Glyndebourne can be honestly described as perfection; Visconti's work with Callas, his legendary *Don Carlos* at Covent Garden in 1958 and other European triumphs, are part of operatic history; Zeffirelli's *Tosca* has already been mentioned, but this is only one of his masterpieces. It was he who turned Joan Sutherland – as Lucia di Lammermoor – into a notable actress, in that part, at least.

There are at least a dozen other first-rate opera directors, some specialists, some imported from the theatre, but all are fated to watch or to hear of their productions running down over the years until they are sometimes altered out of all recognition. Cast changes may occur almost at once. Good house producers can keep the standard high, just as stellar guest artists can electrify everyone into making history in an old production, but the problem remains, especially in theatres with a vast repertoire. Only in festival conditions – like Glyndebourne and Bayreuth and a few more – can the visitor expect by right to see the productions of the highest quality. Elsewhere it is often – if we are expecting opera of truly high standards, and not a mere concert-in-costume – a matter of luck. Let us hope our newcomer is lucky.

Finally we come to the standard of singing, the heart of the matter. Some may say that other problems have been avoided in this chapter – the 'slowness' of opera dramatically compared with a play, women playing men's roles, characters who take a remarkably long time in dying simply so that they can sing about it (as if everyone died swiftly in 'real life'). But these and other facts of operatic life can take their place in the body of the book, while the standard of singing cannot. Our newcomer has enjoyed the overture and is waiting anxiously to hear the singers.

Again, he may be unlucky. It would be possible to strike a

performance where the soprano screeches, the tenor bleats, the mezzo hoots, the bass wobbles – vocally – and only the baritone and the chorus give pleasure. Just after the war, when the infant Covent Garden company was born and was expected to achieve high standards instantly by those who remembered the international (and ill-staged) short summer seasons up to 1939, there were some vocally vile evenings, especially in the tenor department. Only the very demanding would say that such saddening happenings are still in vogue today. Naturally, opera-goers disagree on voices. The art of Callas is as controversial today as the art of Olivier, witness the profound disagreements over his Othello. And, on a lower level, a soprano who may seem adequate to one, may be a painful experience for another.

This brings us back to the original point that ideally newcomers should not be loosed on opera without friendly guidance. The old hand can take a rough evening in his or her stride and gain something, perhaps much, from it. Not so the newcomer to the auditorium. Let us wish him well. Let us hope that the first visit, as so often happens, triggers off a strong desire for a second, then a third. For our newcomer will soon discover that his fellow opera-goers are passionately addicted, so much so that 'operamania' is the logical word to describe their condition. The more honest of them will admit that only occasionally is a performance unflawed; but they are not in the opera house to seek perfection. They are there because they find that the combination of music and song, drama and design, makes opera not the bastard art that some of its diminishing number of detractors in Britain and America claim that it is – there are scarcely any to be found in Italy and Germany – but the ultimate experience in art. Like life, it is not perfect, but, also like life, it has everything.

2

From Monteverdi to Mozart

One night in 1645, a young Englishman, John Evelyn, went to the opera in Venice. Fortunately, he was already keeping a diary, less racy than his friend Samuel Pepys was later to write, but informative enough, not least about his night out.

It was scarcely surprising that he found himself in an opera house. Opera was less than half a century old, but Venice, where the first public opera house had opened in 1637, was so obsessed by the new art that its citizens kept building new theatres to house it.

Evelyn saw *Hercules in Lydia* by Giovanni Rovetta:

. . . to the Opera, where comedies and other plays are represented in recitative music, by the most excellent musicians, vocal and instrumental, with variety of scenes painted and contrived with no less art of perspective, and machines for flying in the air, and other wonderful notions; taken together, it is one of the most magnificent and expensive diversions the wit of man can invent.

He then commented on the excellent singers, including 'an eunuch', and was held 'by the eyes and ears till two in the morning.'

No excuse is needed for that quotation, which is as fascinating as it is historically important. It is particularly fascinating today.

As late as the 1950s the operatic music of the early seventeenth century was virtually unknown, along with the names of most of the composers. Even the towering genius Monteverdi was such a stranger to the opera house that the 1954 edition of Kobbé's *Complete Opera Book* – as opposed to the 1976 one – had no entry on the passionate and now greatly-loved master-piece, *L'Incoronazione di Poppea* (The Coronation of Poppea). In the 1970s, *La Calisto* by Cavalli, Monteverdi's pupil, was seen by millions on TV. A decade ago he was not even an 'Interesting Historical Monument'.

This resurgence of interest in the very beginnings of opera makes the task of the historian much simpler, because growing numbers of ordinary listeners now know that for all the changes that the art has experienced since the first opera was produced in Florence in 1597, the heart of the matter was reached almost at the outset.

It is reasonable to state boldly that opera was literally in-vented in 1597 as a result of the meetings of a group of Floren-tines – poets, musicians and intellectuals – who used to gather in the houses of two noblemen, Giovanni de'Bardi and Jacopi Corsi. They were known as the *Camerata* (society) and in-cluded Vincenzo Galilei, father of the great astronomer, and Jacopi Peri, a Roman-born composer and singer, whose *Dafne* ranks as the first opera.

Naturally the *zeitgeist*, or climate of opinion, had to be right for such a birth, just as it had to be right in Elizabethan England for a Marlowe, then a Shakespeare, to appear. If the latter had been born only fifty years earlier his fame would not be a tenth of what it is, for at that time there was no blank verse (which first appeared in print in 1557), the language had not reached the fluid perfection of the late sixteenth century, and there were few professional actors and no playhouses, let alone the heady Elizabethan atmosphere that stimulated sea-dogs and poets alike.

Similarly, the Camerata did not exist in an artistic and intel-lectual vacuum; but whereas the history of drama, ballet music and song can legitimately be taken back to the primitive dances of mankind, opera, offshoot of music, song and drama, came

about by a happy accident. The American critic, Oscar Sonneck (1873–1928) noted the following:

> No historical subtleties will ever succeed in proving that
> opera really existed before the Florentine Camerata stum-
> bled on it. All the undercurrents of their time might have
> been converging towards opera, yet of themselves they
> would not have led to opera without the new element of
> dramatic musical speech.

It is fascinating to recall that Elizabethan England was as
musical as Rennaissance Italy. Poetic drama might have had a
rival if there had been a Mermaid Tavern Camerata. As it was,
opera in Britain was to follow an erratic, mainly unsatisfying,
course, as we shall see.

And what were the 'undercurrents' of which Sonneck wrote?
They are interesting enough, but need not detain us long. One
otherwise admirable history of opera devotes over 100 lines of
text to the subject and a mere 15 to Puccini, friend of most
opera-goers and all opera managements alike.

From around the tenth century AD dramatic scenes were
given at major festival times in Christian churches and these
became so popular that by the twelfth century they had
reached the market-place and been taken over by trade guilds.
These Mystery Plays on Biblical themes flourished in most
parts of Europe, including Italy, especially in the thirteenth and
fourteenth centuries. An Italian offshoot was the *Sacra Rap-
presentazione*, a kind of acted and costumed oratorio, which
gradually became entirely sung, and in Italian, not Latin. The
music used is not known, but one may claim the form as a link
with opera, though it was not enough to trigger off a new art.

Claims have been made that madrigals and masques were
direct ancestors of opera, the former because some were in
narrative form, the latter – written for special and very expensive occasions – because they were mixtures of song, dance,
drama and often stunning spectacle. But although the madrigal
and the masque were popular in England they did not lead to
opera. Nor did the interludes between the acts of Italian plays,

though some had orchestral accompaniments. It cannot even be claimed that the Italian love of the human voice and the sheer vocal talent available led to opera, for with the Camerata the *word* was to be of crucial importance. The long 'battle' between words and music in opera began with words in the ascendant.

The members of the Camerata were revolutionaries, for they dared to challenge polyphony and the restraints it involved. They resented the fact that in contrapuntal music the words were often distorted, degraded, made inferior to the notes, and their inspiration was the drama of Ancient Greece, the civilisation that most inspired them and their scholarly and artistic contemporaries.

In fact, though music played a key role in Greek drama, no one knows either the sound of the scores or just how the words were spoken. The masks worn by the actors certainly helped projection, but how much cast and chorus declaimed, or spoke, or on occasion sung, cannot even be guessed at.

Like all enthusiasts the Camerata sometimes went too far. Galilei announced as early as 1581: 'For all the height of excellence of the moderns' practical music, we do not hear or see the least evidence of its accomplishing what ancient music accomplished.' More practically, they busied themselves experimenting with a single voice singing freely to a simple accompaniment – a lute or harpsichord – the music only supporting and increasing the effectiveness of the words. This was a logical development from the belief that the Greeks had recited much of their parts to music, and it ensured that the thoughts and emotions of the poet could not be blanketed by sound, as in contrapuntal madrigals. Just how much it actually helped in the first opera, *Dafne* in 1597, is unknown, as Peri's music is lost. But in 1600 came Peri's *Euridice*, again with a text by his fellow member Rinuccini, and the score of this survives.

Another of the 'moderns', Caccini, also composed a *Euridice* and published *La Nuove Musiche* (The New Music) in 1602. Those who know these early scores have stated that the words – the libretto – of each of them are of more significance than the music, which was important not so much in its own right as in heightening the effect of the poetry. No doubt this was also due to the fact that the composers were not particularly distinguished. But they had prepared the way for genius, for opera was fortunate to discover a Marlowe and Shakespeare in one person, Claudio Monteverdi (1567–1643). Monteverdi's *Orfeo* (1607) did what *Tamburlaine the Great* did for Elizabethan drama but with a passionate humanity that Shakespeare had and Marlowe lacked.

Monteverdi was thirty-nine when his *La Favola d'Orfeo* (The Legend of Orpheus) was produced at the Accademia degl'Invaghiti in Mantua, the Chancellor of the Mantuan Court, Alessandro Striggio, providing the libretto. Already an established composer, Monteverdi had been in Mantua – where the painter Rubens also was – from 1590, and was to remain there until 1612, the year before he went to Venice as Maestro di Capella of San Marco. He had published more than a hundred madrigals by 1607 and these show how he had gradually changed from polyphony to choral declamation, so that when the Camerata had set the scene for him, he was able to effect not so much a revolution as a transformation which remains one of the supreme miracles of opera and music in general.

In his vocal line, as stunning as Marlowe's 'mighty line', but so much more emotional, he slipped naturally from *recitative* (declamation) to *arioso* (half-way between recitative and aria) and *aria* (an air), and in so fluid and masterly a fashion that its expressiveness remains unsurpassed. In the Monteverdian revival of the 1960s this vocal line came as a total revelation to those who had assumed that his operas were deadly dull or actually unperformable.

In *Orfeo*, superb examples of the line include the hero's joyous *Rosa del Ciel*, a rapturous hymn to love, the Messenger's description of the death of Euridice, and Orfeo's lament, 'Tu se'morta, mia vita'. The score is also rich in choruses, dances and songs. Exactly how it sounded in 1607 is a mystery that remains a battleground for scholars, and for the 'realisers' who decide what orchestral detail we shall hear. Raymond Leppard, who more than any other has given Monteverdi back to opera-goers, claims that the first listeners heard 'a dazzling web of sound', and his case is strengthened by the impressive list of instruments used, which can be found in Kobbé's *Complete Opera Book* and elsewhere, and which included trombones, cornets and trumpets. The singers were expected to add ornaments, like the instrumentalists. Monteverdi's ornamented version of Orfeo's song to Charon survives to prove what was expected of his cast, while the chord-playing continuo instruments – organs, cithers, chitarrones, clavicembalos, a harp, and bass gambas – did not, states Leppard, merely play simple chords. Other more austere realisers believe in more simplicity than Leppard, but what remains in any version is Monteverdi's matchless vocal line enhancing and transfiguring fine words.

The balance was right, for he had achieved a great opera in which the music was the senior partner, but the words were not subservient. At the first performance the audience had librettos 'so that everyone . . . might be able to read the story which was being sung'. It is of interest that Striggio wanted a tragic ending, with Orfeo being torn to pieces by Thracian women at an orgy, after his laments for his lost love had driven them to a frenzy. Instead of this traditional ending to the story, it was made to finish happily.

There followed a stream of operas, most of which have vanished. The famous Lament from *Arianna* (1608) survives and we have the short dramatic cantata, *Il Combattimento di Tancredi e Clorinda* (1624) with its evocation of a battle. And there are two more operas, both dating from after the opening of the first public opera house in Venice in 1637 – *Il Ritorno d'Ulisse in Patria* (1641) and *L'Incoronazione di Poppea* (1642).

The glories of the former were finally revealed at Glyndebourne in 1972 by the superb Monteverdian team of Leppard, Peter Hall and John Bury, but it did not shake the latter's position as the composer's masterpiece (unless a lost marvel is one day found). *Poppea*, the love story of Nero and the mistress who becomes his Empress, is a totally amoral story, for all that the composer was in holy orders in Venice. It is one of the greatest of Italian operas, fit to rank with Verdi at the height of his powers, and it seizes its audience's emotions not only more strongly than *Orfeo* can, but more than any opera, perhaps until the coming of Mozart. Its felicities include a sweetly sensuous love duet, the first great one in opera, which brings the final curtain down. Shortly before it, Poppea's Nurse enjoys a scene of self-congratulation on her rise to 'ladyship' in which Monteverdi's music is as genuinely humorous and colloquially swift as Verdi's *Falstaff*. And what could be more striking or truly operatic than the nobility of Seneca's death scene, followed by a cynical outburst of joy by Nero and Lucan when they learn of his suicide?

Before turning to lesser men it should be noted that those who, with reason, state firmly that Monteverdi was no revolutionary, cannot dispute that he was a major operatic inventor. The loss of so many works, the fact that it cannot be proved exactly how the surviving ones sounded – we have little more than the vocal and bass lines of *Poppea* – cannot hide his genius, nor the fact that he was father of *bel canto* and *buffo*. The former literally means 'beautiful song' or 'beautiful singing', a combination of tone, smooth phrasing and vocal technique all required by his operatic vocal line, while *buffo*, from the Italian for 'puff' or 'gust' means comic. It is possible that he was the first to use *pizzicato* as an addition to orchestral colour, and he invented the throbbing *tremolo* effect with its increase of feeling and excitement. If he did not invent recitative, his own was a sublime example for future composers, although they were to neglect it to the point of almost fossilising the art he had made so potent.

At first operas were not given regularly but were staged for special occasions in front of select groups of the nobility and clergy. The first opera house was the Teatro San Cassiano in Venice which was opened by Benedetto Ferrari (1597–1681), a composer-playwright. This was such a success that by mid-century there were five opera houses in Venice and by 1700 as many as sixteen, by which time all classes had been flocking to enjoy opera for many decades.

Since the late sixteenth century, Italy had led the world in stage and theatre design, although it is true that Elizabethan drama, where the word had unique importance, developed its own unique solution to theatre architecture, a solution much admired in our own anti-proscenium-arch times.

Before the first proscenium arch appeared at the Teatro Farnese in Parma in 1618 – giving a picture-frame effect – it had seemed that the Italian theatre was destined to follow classical lines. The famous Teatro Olimpico at Vicenza, built by 1584, had a semi-circular auditorium not unlike a Roman theatre. Parma's actors used the whole depth of the stage, and at both theatres, and other permanent structures, the most complex and spectacular effects were possible. Scenery could be changed by sliding one painted piece in front of another, and backcloths also could be changed, while rollers and winches were used to produce moving seas. Trapdoors were exploited and chariots and clouds could be made to appear and disappear by being lowered or raised from above. Lighting, too, was introduced, not just to illuminate, but also using candles and lanterns to contribute to the atmosphere.

The first opera houses inherited these techniques and developed them so well that the seventeenth century became an age of virtuoso scenic effects. The boxes that surrounded the auditoriums of the first opera houses were, along with the proscenium arch and the air of splendour in even modestly-sized theatres, to affect theatres, 'straight' and operatic, until our own times. 'Going to the theatre' for the average person means going to buildings directly or indirectly influenced by the Italian opera houses of more than 300 years ago.

The wealthy sat in the boxes, following their librettos – if they wished to – by candlelight; the humbler citizens sat in the pit, which was then, as elsewhere until the nineteenth century, the whole of what we now call the stalls. The few pits that are left today are a row or two at the back of the stalls. Every box had its withdrawing room – the SS. Giovanni and Paolo theatre which saw the first *Poppea*, had five tiers of twenty-nine boxes – and the opera houses rapidly became centres of social and political life in the city.

The spectacle that John Evelyn saw was typical and it should be noted that these theatres were perhaps no larger than Glyndebourne, where Peter Hall and John Bury have brought back a modern conception of seventeenth-century visual magic to performances of Monteverdi and Cavalli.

The cost of these commercial performances was considerable, especially as the Venetians had become used to spectacle on every occasion. Casts therefore tended to be kept to not more than eight with the chorus either abandoned or turned into virtual 'walk-ons'; but this was soon to alter as opera became even more popular and spread throughout the country. It reached Naples in 1651 and Palermo in 1658, and was soon truly established all over Italy. Meanwhile, 360 different operas were produced by 66 composers in Venice between 1637 and 1700.

After an initial spate of operas on classical legends and myths, history became a popular subject. However, as the century wore on, few plots were as clear as *Poppea*'s. An opera about Hercules produced in 1662 had 33 singing characters, which can hardly have made for clarity.

That opera remained brilliantly viable in its own right after Monteverdi's death has been proved by the resurrection of works by his pupil Cavalli (1602–76), whose *L'Ormindo* (1644) and *Calisto* (1651) have given enormous pleasure at Glynde-bourne. In 1660 he wrote *Ercole Amante* (Hercules in Love) for the marriage of Louis XIV to Maria Theresa of Austria, the ballets being composed by Lully. Even more prolific was Marc Antonio Cesti (1623–69), who was less interested in dramatic truth than Cavalli, sacrificing the precious birthright of recitative to a procession of popular songs, although these at least were good ones. But Venice was soon to give way to Naples as the centre of opera, and there opera was to become more dominated by the voice than at any time since, to such a point, as we shall see, that the slur heard to this day about opera when divorced from theatrical truth, 'concert-in-costume', was only too accurate a description.

Of the nations other than Italy who were to enrich the operatic world with a genuine tradition, only France achieved real success in the seventeenth and early eighteenth centuries. Elsewhere, the Italians were masters of their own art. Opera had crossed the Alps by 1618, Vienna becoming second in importance only to Venice itself, not least because the architect Ludovico Burnacini, a superb theatre builder and equally renowned master of stage baroque, was in his prime in the second half of the century. Soon any self-respecting German court had its Italian company, which included composer, librettist and designer as well as musicians and singers. An Italian opera was heard in London in 1705 (Franceschini's *Arsinoe*, Queen of Cyprus) and an Italian troupe reached Russia in 1731, while the Italians had conquered Amsterdam, Brussels, and Warsaw before 1700. A century after opera had gone 'public' its conquest of Europe was virtually complete.

French independence

France, though not unaffected by the Italians, was not swamped by them, not least because it was the birthplace of classical ballet. That birth cannot be dated precisely like that of opera, but in 1581 a performance was given to celebrate the wedding of the Duke of Joyeuse and King Henry III's sister-in-law that was highly significant for the future of French opera as well as ballet. *Le Ballet Comique de la Royne* combined not only spectacle and music but also dancing, mime, solo and choral song, and a properly resolved plot. In other words, the performance was far more genuinely theatrical in the fullest sense of the word than the entertainments currently being staged on occasions in Italy. The subject was the Circe story, the music was composed by Frenchmen, Lambert de Beaulieu and Jacques Salmon, and the whole was directed by the Italian de Belgioso, who had tactfully become de Beaujoyeulx. From all this stemmed not only Ballet de Cour which was to become the French opera-ballet, but also, more important (even an opera-lover must admit), the art of classical ballet.

De Belgioso may have changed his name, but there was no keeping the Italians out, especially when one of them, Mazarini, became first a Cardinal of France, then the Prime Minister, from 1642 until his death in 1661. Giacomo Torelli, the great scene-painter and stage engineer, was brought from Venice, Cavalli gave his *Serse* in Paris and, crucially, Giovanni Battista Lulli (1632–87) came to France from Florence and changed his name to Lully.

It is hard to imagine how Lully could fail in life, even if he had been tone-deaf. Reaching Paris at the age of 14, this born intriguer rose from scullion to a position of power rare in the history of art, a Diaghilev who was also a dancer, violinist and creative artist.

Lully soon commended himself to the dance-loving young king and this, plus his talent and energy, brought him real power. He became master of court music in 1662 and two years later began collaborating with Molière, composing incidental music and opera-ballets, a partnership that lasted until 1671. Then his even more productive partnership began with the poet, Phillipe Quinault (1635–88), which resulted in some 20 operas including *Alceste*, *Thésée* and *Armide*, all of which were in the repertoire for a century.

Meanwhile, the Académie Royale de Musique, later the Opéra, had been founded in 1669. Its director, the poet Pierre Perrin, together with the composer Robert Cambert, produced *Pomone*, a great success which ranks as the first French opera. However, when the Académie ran into trouble, Louis turned to Lully, making him the virtual dictator of opera in Paris. Quinault was a more than worthy partner for him, a fine poet of the school of Corneille. Unlike the Italians, who had switched to historical characters for their operas after initially choosing classical themes, Lully and Quinault were against using actual characters, preferring mythology or, sometimes, pastoral themes of medieval chivalric literature for their plots, and this convention was to last more than a century.

Lully was his own superb director and choreographer. He set the French language brilliantly in his recitatives, while his '*airs*', the French versions of arias, were simple and tuneful and never as elaborate as the Italian ones of his day; indeed the aria has never played so important a role in French opera as it has in Italian. Some of his tunes he repeated several times in an opera, an early *leitmotiv* technique, and his brilliant orchestra, larger than was usual, allowed him to experiment in sounds. His 'French Overtures', soon to be copied elsewhere, began in dignified fashion as the courtiers went to their places, including Le Roi Soleil himself, then an allegro proclaimed coming glories. He deserved all his fame, and it was a cruel fate that allowed him to die from an abscess sustained when he hit his foot instead of the floor with the staff he used for time-keeping.

The greatest of his successors was Jean-Phillipe Rameau (1683–1764), who made his name when he was 50 with his first opera, *Hippolyte et Aricie* (1733). His reputation as the father of the modern theory of harmony and as a composer who at his finest ranks with Bach and Handel, his great contemporaries, is somewhat awesome, and those who do not know his operatic music might be forgiven for not realising how entertaining it is. His most famous operas are *Les Indes Galantes* (The Courtly Indies) (1735), *Castor et Pollux* (1737) his masterpiece, and *Zoroastre* (1749), the first of which was revived with enormous success at the Paris Opéra in 1952.

Rameau's music is elegant and expressive and his recitative is more flexible than Lully's. He made classical French opera more dramatic and exciting than it had been and breathed new life into baroque music. Yet this master found himself derided by Parisian partisans of Italian music in the *Guerre des Bouffons*, to which we shall return when charting the runaway success of Neapolitan comic opera.

England: a missed opportunity

It is sometimes claimed that the English genius for dramatic poetry explains the fact that opera failed to gain a foothold in the seventeenth century; yet it is possible that if it had not been for the Civil War and the period of Puritanical hostility to the arts that followed, England's operatic history might not have been so essentially frustrating.

So enraptured by music were the Elizabethans that despite their devotion to polyphony, they swiftly took the new monodic style of singing to their hearts, and so up-to-date were they that copies of Caccini's *Nuovo Musiche* apparently reached England before its publication in 1602. Though Anglicised operas did not follow hard on Venetian ones, the Jacobean masques, more elaborate than Elizabethan ones, and with major poets like Ben Jonson and James Shirley contributing, were first cousins of the opera-ballet. They were performed mainly by amateurs – courtiers – but Jonson and the great Inigo Jones, who had travelled in Italy and whose imagination had been fired by Italian stage technique, were highly professional men of the theatre. So was Sir William Davenant, possibly Shakespeare's son, certainly stage-struck and with the talent and organising ability to match. He was the Poet-Laureate in succession to Ben Jonson. In 1639, he was granted a licence to build a theatre in which to 'exercise musick, musical presentations, dancing, or any other the like.'

Before it could be erected, the war clouds loomed. In 1642, the Puritans had the theatres closed and the buildings pulled down. There was no longer time for masques at Court, and Davenant joined the Royal Army, in which his bravery earned him his knighthood.

After many adventures, including being sentenced to death and being saved by John Milton and others, the undeterred Davenant decided to revive the theatre during Cromwell's régime. The Protector liked music, which, in fact, had not been banned, and Davenant cleverly persuaded the authorities that the recently invented art of opera was a respectable revival of the classical arts. In 1656 he presented *The Siege of Rhodes*, with singers, not outlawed actors, performing at Rutland House on a small, makeshift stage. He wrote the book for this 'Representation of the art of Prospective in Scenes and the Story sung in Recitative Musick', and the music – now lost – was by Henry Lawes, Matthew Locke and Captain Cooke. The story was based on reasonably recent history, the siege of 1522, which in itself was a novelty.

When the King was restored in 1660, he turned to Davenant and Sir Thomas Killigrew to re-establish the theatre. But what happened next belongs to theatrical, not operatic history. True, Davenant's 'improved' versions of Shakespeare had operatic elements, including the (to us) notorious *Macbeth*, 'being dressed in all its finery, as new clothes, new scenes, machines, as flying for the witches; with all the singing and dancing in it.' But we are left with only two works that may be called operas, John Blow's charming pastoral, *Venus and Adonis* (1684), starring one of Charles II's mistresses, Mary Davies, as Venus and their daughter as Cupid; and Henry Purcell's masterpiece, *Dido and Aeneas* (1689 or 1690).

Purcell (*c*. 1659–95), went on to write music for some 40 plays, some, like *Dioclesian* and *King Arthur*, *The Fairy Queen* and – from Shakespeare – *The Tempest*, being partly operatic. But with the principals speaking, not singing, they are disqualified as operas, unlike *Dido*, which is a true opera in every way.

Performed by young ladies attending the Chelsea school of Josias Pratt, *Dido* lasts an hour. Dramatically superb, it is musically enchanting and, with Dido's great lament, 'When I am laid in earth' and the final chorus, sublime. It is standard practice to reflect on *Dido*'s uniqueness and what it might and should have led to; standard and inevitable, for not until Britten, more than 250 years on, was the torch truly taken up again in England. Yet Purcell and John Dryden, his finest collaborator (though not on *Dido*, which was written by Nahum Tate), wanted to create a school of English opera. Circumstances, and the composer's early death, foiled them.

Fifteen years after Purcell's death George Frideric Handel (1685–1759) arrived in England. He was the greatest of *opera seria* composers. That unfortunate *genre* will be described later in full, but Handel's story belongs at this point. England loved him as it has loved no other serious composer, and the fact that his genius virtually smothered native talent and encouraged a lamentable line of oratorios was no fault of his.

'We cannot expect modern music-lovers to accept as an opera something designed as a "concert-in-costume" for an audience only half listening,' wrote Stanley Sadie in his biography of Handel; but he went on to point out the pleasures that can be got from the operas, provided that the opera-goer does not judge the result by how closely they stick to Wagnerian and Verdian dramatic principles. And their impact is lessened by the absence of the *castrati* from opera for nearly 200 years. These eunuchs – 'martyrs to music', as Philip Hope-Wallace has called them – had the combined range of tenors and sopranos, astonishing power, and also the flexibility of the female singer. They were the super-stars of their age, an age that lasted from Monteverdi to the 1820s, and longer in Vatican circles.

Melodically, Handel's operas are as rich as one expects from a great tunesmith, but only his most ardent supporters can deny that they lack sustained drama. Handel, no revolutionary, worked in the stunted conditions of the day and with grossly over-powerful singers, though he did his best to combat them, once threatening to throw a soprano from a window. The fashionable *da capo* aria, however beautiful, was unoperatic, containing two parts, the first being repeated with ornaments, after which the singer, by convention, left the stage. There were few trios or quartets, and the librettos, inspired or hack, were of supreme unimportance. Yet before turning to his (ironically) more dramatic oratorios, Handel produced opera after opera which contained tunes of glory.

Born in Halle, Handel's first operas, *Almira* and *Nero*, were given in Hamburg. He worked in Italy and again in Germany before the journey to London and fame, finding his unique

German-Italian voice which was first heard – in a London already obsessed by *opera seria* – in *Rinaldo* (1711). Its melodies were soon the delight of the town. His more notable operas include *Radamisto* (1720), *Giulio Cesare* (1724), the lead being taken by a castrato, and the often thrilling *Tamerlano* (1724) which has a magnificent death scene. *Rodelinda* (1725), like *Tamerlano*, had a tenor hero and was the opera that started the German Handel revival in the 1920s after being given in Göttingen.

The operas continued to come fast, including *Admeto* (1727), *Riccardo Primo* (1727), the fine *Orlando* (1733), the even finer *Alcina* (1735), and *Serse* (1738), whose languid opening, 'Ombra mai fu', was to be turned into quasi-religious 'classical' pop – Handel's *Largo*. His last opera was *Deidamia* (1741), but some of his oratorios, most notably *Samson* and *Semele*, have been successfully staged. The change to oratorio was mainly brought about by intrigues against him, and the opposition of some singers and composers, plus the success of *The Beggar's Opera* (1728). A delightful man, Handel suffered more than his share of slings and arrows for all that he was his adopted country's musical darling. Once he wrote an English piece, the pastoral *Acis and Galatea* (1718), so delightful that one can only regret his dedication to *opera seria*.

The Beggar's Opera, to John Gay's text, and with music gathered from popular ballads by John Christopher Pupusch, who also composed additional music, has been constantly revived (and even heavily adapted by Brecht in his *Threepenny Opera*), but only in its own day could it make a full effect. In one splendid entertainment it mocked operatic conventions, including bad librettos and falsely happy endings, rivalry amongst singers, notably in a notorious quarrel between La Cuzzoni and La Bordoni and their partisans, politicians in general and Sir Robert Walpole in particular (Macheath is partly a satire on him).

Other ballad operas of a less sensational nature followed, including *Thomas and Sally* (1760) and *Love in a Village* (1762), both by Thomas Arne of 'Rule, Britannia!' fame, who also composed an 'Italian' opera, *Artaxerxes* (1762), translating a text by the century's busiest librettist, Metastasio, into English. These and others made a modest but pleasant contribution to the lighter operatic stage, but Doctor Johnson's notorious description of opera as 'an exotick and irrational entertainment', which has caused so much embarrassment to opera-lovers down the years, was directed at the Italian opera of his day with some justification. The great, though unmusical, Doctor, had no objection to English opera (see *Lives of the Poets, Life of John Hughes* a now forgotten poet and dramatist). Nor did other eminent figures including Addison – who jealously attacked Italian opera when his own had failed – Fielding, Garrick and Sheridan, who wrote the delightful *The Duenna* (1775) with his father-in-law, Thomas Linley, compiling and composing the music. Well over a hundred ballad operas were written in eighteenth-century Britain, and that they were more plays-with-music than operas does not lessen this pleasant achievement.

Opera Seria rampant

Meanwhile, *opera seria* remained enormously popular in Europe. Handel's operas apart, even the names of most of the operatic dinosaurs of the period are forgotten. This was the supreme age of the 'canary-fancier', a breed not extinct today, for whom nothing matters but the voice singing suitable song, the music taking second place to the admittedly considerable art of the singer. Tortuous librettos, heroic or mythological plots, and the deadening formality, not least of the *da capo* arias noted above, all helped make the *genre* lose contact with reality and with life itself. Audiences in the undarkened auditoriums – a feature of all theatres until the late nineteenth century – were so used to chattering as they waited for arias that the *pasticcio* (pie), a string of arias loosely threaded by recitative provided by an available hack, was invented to pamper them.

Naples was the chief culprit, though much must be forgiven

it as *opera buffa* became a joyous art form there. The city became the operatic centre of Italy in the second half of the
seventeenth century, and from there composers, orchestral
musicians and, especially, singers set out to conquer Europe.
Lowest of the low were the librettists, who got less employ-
ment than they might have because of the fertility of Zeno
(1668–1750) and Metastasio (1698–1782), both Italians, who
provided enough librettos to keep a score of major and many
minor composers in business.

Neither of these were hacks. Zeno was influenced by Corneille and Racine and tried to observe the unities of time, place
and action. He also cut down on scenic extravagance, the one
fault that could be laid at the door of the Venetian school, and
he cut the number of characters down to what it had been in
opera's earliest days. Cherubini, Pergolesi, Scarlatti and Vivaldi
were among those who used his librettos. Metastasio only
wrote some thirty librettos, but these were set to music innumerable times. They were poetic enough to attract the great,
including Handel, Gluck and Mozart. Metastasio in particular
greatly influenced the structure of the *opera seria*, though the
father of Neapolitan opera was Alessandro Scarlatti (1660–
1725). His first opera was, *Gli Equivoci nel Sembiante* (Mistaken
Identities, 1679) and his finest, *Mitradate Eupatore* (1707),
which, like his single comic opera, *Il Trionfo del Onore* (1718),
is sometimes performed.

It is important to stress just how high the standard of singing
was at this time. The aspiring artist studying in Naples, Venice
or Bologna, was expected to study from ten to twelve years. He
was also expected to improvise his *coloratura* and *cadenzas* like
a true musician. That many singers were also vain and spoilt,
and that opera was infinitely harmed by the existence of *opera
seria*, should not make them culpable: they were fulfilling a
public need, as were the composers.

Opera seria's popularity increased still further because of its
value as a status symbol at court. Native German composers
stood virtually no chance before the onset of the fashionable
Italians. There were German composers, but they were mainly

forced to write in the Italian style, even in Berlin, where Frederick the Great, flautist and military genius, opened his opera house in 1740. Vienna, however, was the headquarters of the *opera seria* business (the word is deliberate). Theatres were often of great beauty, notably the Residenztheater, Munich, designed by Cuvilliés and opened in 1753.

Though orchestral sound came a poor second to the castrati and other stars on stage, the orchestra was gradually assuming the form we know today. The basis of Lully's orchestra had been a famous body of strings, including the *vingt-quatre violins du Roi*, renowned throughout musical Europe. Orchestral colour was otherwise occasional: trumpets and drums at suitable moments, flutes or oboes for pastoral charm. Rameau's orchestra was larger, employing bassoons, and horns came in, at first for 'hunting' colour, then as part of the texture. Clarinets were introduced from the 1770s, finding an early and still supreme champion in Mozart, while trombones began to add solemnity. Their first immortal moment – in *Don Giovanni* – sounded less powerful than today, the instruments then being softer-toned.

It should not be thought that *opera seria* did not have its vocal detractors before Gluck's reforms, but before describing the attacks on its imperfections, a happier phenomenon must be examined.

Opera Buffa triumphant

As if to make amends to the founding fathers of opera and their high ideals, Naples, having done so much harm to its well-being by promoting *opera seria*, nurtured *opera buffa* until it became a glorious entertainment. As has been noted, its germ was to be found in Monteverdi, but it was Neapolitan composers and playwrights who first decided to add entire comic scenes at the end of acts.

These blessed interludes were originally connected with the ponderous, if tuneful, matter that preceded them, but gradually they became small independent operas – *intermezzi* – which were performed between acts. Unlike other forms of comic opera – so far we have only touched on English examples – these were true operas, which were to culminate years later in the melodic champagne and brilliant fireworks of Rossini. For the dialogue was sung in recitative, the notes and rhythms freely and swiftly following the verbal accentuation to a minimal musical accompaniment, whereas rival forms of comic opera usually used spoken dialogue. However pleasant the result – and the average standard of speech by singers is not pleasant – it is essentially a negation of opera. And at a time when ensembles and even duets were at a discount in *opera seria*, *opera buffa* revived them, and gradually the no-holds-barred finale came into being.

To fertilise the *opera buffe* the everyday bustle of ordinary people, their lives, loves, hopes and fears, were put to operatic use and so were the stock characters of the old, improvised *commedia dell'arte* routines, which themselves had culminated in the plays of Goldoni and Gozzi. The former's comedies were used time and again by librettists, and he helped matters by living from 1707–93 and writing over 200 plays himself.

The most famous of the early *opera buffe* was *La Serva Padrona* (The Maid Mistress), first given in 1733 in Naples, its composer being Giovanni Pergolesi (1710–36). Given as an intermezzo in his *Il Prigonier Superbo*, it reached Paris in 1746, where, as we shall see, it caused more than a sensation. The opera, which tells how Serpina, a servant girl, lures her master into matrimony, has only three characters, the third being a mute servant.

The sparkling music makes Pergolesi's very early death seem particularly poignant, but there were many less-remembered composers in this *genre*, many of whose works were written in the local dialect. Most of these *opera buffe* are now forgotten, but one of them was the most famous of its time, *La Buona Figliuola* (The Good Daughter) by Niccolò Piccinni (1728–1800), based on Samuel Richardson's novel, *Pamela*. Not only is this a most skilled work musically, but its characterisations are compassionate as well as amusing, thus anticipating Mozart rather than Rossini.

Better known by far today is *Il Matrimonio Segreto* by Domenico Cimarosa (1749–1801), which is based on the play by Colman and David Garrick, *The Clandestine Marriage*. The opera was a late example of *opera buffa* and one which still holds the stage. It was first given in 1792 in Vienna, where the enraptured Emperor Leopold II requested that the cast repeat the performance after they had been fortified by supper.

Just 40 years before this double first, *La Serva Padrona* was given in Paris by an Italian troupe, an event that caused far more stir than its première there in 1746.

A school of comic opera already existed in France, stemming from groups of players in fairs. These had incurred the jealousy of the Opéra, the Comédie-Française and the Comédie-Italienne, to such an extent that they were forbidden to sing or speak. So they fell back on mime, with banners on which were words for their audiences to sing. From these entertainments stemmed *opéra comique*, for finally the great companies and the outsiders merged and in 1762 the Opéra-Comique and the Comédie-Italienne merged as well. Meanwhile, Parisians had enjoyed *pièces en vaudevilles* in the fair theatres, not unlike *The Beggar's Opera* and *pièces à ariettes*, with parodies of Italian opera such as nineteenth-century operetta kings were later to produce as well.

La Serva Padrona speeded the process up and set off a battle between partisans of the Italian and French styles of music. The great but now ageing Rameau was the chief target of the very vocal Italian partisans, whose leader was the philosopher, Jean-Jacques Rousseau. He flatly stated that only Neapolitan opera was worth listening to and his own amateurish but influential *Le Devin du Village* (The Village Soothsayer) (1752) imitated an Italian intermezzo. He and his colleagues and those who followed them made *opéra comique* essentially French. It was not necessarily comic, this mixture of song and dialogue, for *Fidelio*, serious and sublime, ranks as an *opéra comique* by French standards. But a stream of writers and composers produced a line of elegant, unrhetorical works, notably those by François Philidor (1726–95) and especially the Belgian André Grétry (1742–1813), whose operas included *Zémire et Azore* (1771).

As for the original battle, fought chiefly between 1752 and 1754, the champions of *opera buffa* were known as *bouffonistes* and the traditionalists as *anti-bouffonistes*, and they fought the *Guerre des Bouffons*. The Italophiles won because of the sheer high spirits and humanity of their imported product, which was soon to be absorbed into the French tradition started in the fairs. So it came about that *opéra comique* was far more realistic than *opera buffa* – not 'better' or 'worse' but different. Each suited its own nation admirably.

Germany, destined to become one of the twin pillars of opera, was almost swamped by the Italians, or by Italian-inspired native composers for most of the eighteenth century, though earlier it had seemed that a native school might have developed. The most notable composer was Reinhardt Keiser (1674–1739), with Hamburg as the operatic capital. Middle-class and working-class characters appeared in his works, singing and speaking in Low German, while the better-remembered Georg Philipp Telemann (1681–1767) also wrote German operas before the Italians finally submerged native talent for a time.

Around 1750 their supremacy was challenged by the *Singspiel*, a German version of English ballad opera and French *opéra comique*. Mozart was, as we shall see to bring the popular *genre* to a glowing climax, just as he was to redeem *opera seria* in two blazing masterpieces. As for his great predecessor, Joseph Haydn (1732–1809), he wrote a number of operas for the theatre at Esterhazy Castle, 15 of which survive, but most of them were more Italian than German. *Lo Speziale* (The Chemist) a comic opera, is not unlike a *Singspiel*, however. His best-known work – and none is regularly given – is *Il Mondo della Luna* (The World on the Moon), from a Goldoni play. Anyone who loves Haydn cannot fail to respond to this charming piece, first given in 1777.

But by now there was a great master in his prime a reformer, a redeemer of opera. He is more honoured today in the text book than in the opera house to which he so emphatically belonged. Born in Erasbach in 1714, he died in Vienna in 1787 and he ranks as opera's second founder. His name was Christoph Willibald Gluck.

The reformer

It is Gluck's misfortune to be like Willy Loman in *Death of a Salesman*: 'He's liked, but he's not – well-liked'. Even his reputation as a great reformer is qualified by the fact that the works against which he rebelled are largely forgotten. None of his operas is regularly given. Perhaps even the finest of them, undeniably containing sublime inspiration, have failed to gain wide acceptance because they lack obvious melodic appeal.

He was reasonably well-educated musically. Handel's alleged comment that his cook knew more about counterpoint than Gluck can be countered by the fact that Handel once employed a highly musical cook called Gustavus Waltz.

His first opera was in conventional mould, an *opera seria*, *Artaserse* (1741), to a Metastasio libretto. Settling in Vienna, he began to rebel against the conventions of *opera seria* with its all-powerful singers but over 20 years went by before he was able to cast aside the conventions used in *Artaserse*. During those years he wrote Italian operas – he was never to write a German one, though he was German-born of Bohemian descent – and set some French *opéras comiques* and a dramatic ballet, *Don Juan*, to music.

By now his musical characterisation had reached far beyond Metastasian confines, ready for his first masterpiece, *Orfeo ed Euridice* (1762) to a libretto by another reformer, the poet, Ranieri da Calzabigi (1714–95). His two most famous pieces of music come from this opera, the aria 'Che faro senza Euridice' (What is life without Euridice?) and 'The Dance of the Blessed Spirits'. In *Orfeo* Gluck found the 'beautiful simplicity' for which he had been striving, using accompanied recitative exploiting singers and chorus, but limiting the power of the singers. Deep human emotions were on display in a master-piece that linked drama and music in a way understood by the early masters and deliberately forgotten in the ensuing Metas-tasian years. A castrato male also sang the lead, though in 1774 Gluck rewrote it for a tenor in the Paris production. Today, more often than not, it is a famous contralto part. Perhaps the most famous singers in the role have been Pauline Viardot in 1859 (in Berlioz's revision) and Kathleen Ferrier.

In 1767, Gluck took his reforms a stage further in *Alceste*, which had a Calzabigi libretto again, and contained a preface of exceptional importance. It was not the first of its kind, for Gluck had been influenced by Francesco Algarotti's *Essay on the Opera* (1755), a cry for a return to the principles of the Camerata. But Gluck, the established composer, was writing from strength in his call for music that served poetry and kept the singers in second place.

His later operas included *Paride et Elena* (1770), *Iphigénie en Aulide* (1773), his first French opera, and *Armide* (1777). *Iphigénie* set off a typically Parisian feud with Niccolo Piccinni (1728–1800), though their supporters rather than the com-posers themselves were to blame. Gluck wrote *Armide* setting out to be 'more of the poet and painter than the musician', but the opera was not a success; then an impresario had both com-posers write *Iphigénie en Tauride*. Although by now, Piccinni had begun to follow Gluckian principles, his opera (1781) could not match Gluck's (1779), which was a huge success and, for many, the composer's masterpiece. In the same year *Écho et Narcisse* failed, after which Gluck virtually retired.

Two stories have come down to us about *Iphigénie en Tauride*, both well worth the telling. Someone remarked to the Abbé Arnaud on the many fine moments in it, but the Abbé said there was only one. 'Which one?' asked the man. 'The entire work!' was the reply. More significant operatically was the orchestra's reaction to the passage where Oreste was singing, 'Le calme rentre dans mon coeur' (The calm returns to my soul). The players could not understand why Gluck had pro-vided an agitated accompaniment at that point. 'Go on all the same,' cried Gluck. 'He lies. He has killed his mother!'

The première of the opera was a total triumph; indeed, when Achilles sang his warrior's song, every officer in the theatre is said to have leapt up and drawn his sword. It must surely have been a great night for the many followers of the French tradition and Rameau, for Gluck was far closer to it in spirit than were the Italian supporters. Yet he stands alone in the age before Mozart, for even though he was less technically skilled than some less important composers, he had the heart of the operatic matter in him. Swords are not drawn for him today; the cheers, if any, are respectful; but Gluck, who is said to have had some of his finest inspirations when seated at a piano in a field, with a bottle of champagne on either side, is at least loved by some and respected by all who know his achievement.

Mozart

The greatest art borders on the miraculous, or so many mere mortals must feel, and the history of opera provides a number of miracles, including the short, matchless career of Wolfgang Amadeus Mozart (1756–91). It was opera's good fortune that so much of his most personal music was poured into his work for the theatre. The unblessed who merely salute him as a great composer but who do not truly respond to him or, indeed, any late-eighteenth-century music – and this includes many opera-goers – might be stunned by the claim of Alfred Loewenberg (and others) that the scope and variety of Mozart's work has never been surpassed, not even by Wagner or Verdi; but the operas themselves support the claim. Bigger orchestras, more advanced orchestration do not automatically mean better art – or worse.

Mozart had certain advantages: a unique musical gift; a remarkable flair for the theatre; a very gifted librettist, Lorenzo da Ponte (1749–1838), for three of his supreme masterpieces; and the luck to be born when the symphony orchestra – whatever later additions it acquired – had reached maturity. He was not a revolutionary, but then neither was Shakespeare, to whom he was compared by Goethe. Both created worlds of characters drawn in the round, some of whom are heroic or villainous, but who are never the Heroes and Villains who so often appear in opera. Both were ambivalent, artistically all things to all men, yet with boundless sympathy for their creations.

Mozart was born in Salzburg where his father was Kapellmeister to the Archbishop. As the most remarkable of all musical prodigies, and with an accomplished musician for a father, his fabulous childhood makes a good story; but too much cannot be claimed for our concern, his early operas, except that because they are by Mozart they must be of interest if only as portents of things to come. The first, *La Finta Semplice* (The Simple Prentice) was written in 1767 at the suggestion of the Austrian Emperor that he should write an Italian opera, and was given at Salzburg in 1769. There followed *Bastien et Bastienne* (1768) to a German text; *Mitridate, Rè di Ponto* (1770), an opera which had a huge success in Milan, with Mozart conducting from the piano (where composers then supervised proceedings if they did not play first violin instead); *Ascanio in Alba* (1771); and *Lucia Sillo* (1772). Both these last also opened in Milan and the latter shows signs of the true Mozart breaking through at times.

There followed *La Finta Giardiniera* (The Disguised Gardener's Girl, 1775), which was acclaimed in Munich. It has charming moments and the characterisation is a distinct advance on earlier works. *Il Re Pastore* (1775) is a step back, being a mere succession of arias, but *Zaide* (1779), though unfinished, is a *singspiel* that foreshadows the later German masterpieces.

Then came greatness with *Idomeneo* (1781), which after an initial triumph in Munich and later performances after his death, virtually vanished until modern times when it was given in Germany between the wars. The turning-point in England was Glyndebourne's production in 1951 under Fritz Busch and Carl Ebert, since when, without becoming a runaway success, its modest popularity and great reputation have remained constant.

Idomeneo is a passionate *opera seria* that did not so much transform the almost extinct *genre* as enrich and transcend it. It would be wrong not to recall Gluck's reforms and their influence on Mozart, but the greater composer created a world in which the audience becomes deeply involved. It is a true music-drama.

Die Entführung aus dem Serail (The Abduction from the Seraglio, 1782), is a *singspiel* a world away from the tragic king of Crete. There is a youthful, unbuttoned rapture about this score that Mozart never tried to repeat, an unsophisticated joy that makes this musical play with its spoken dialogue greatly loved. Osmin, the mock-villainous head of the Pasha's harem, is a major comic creation, whose duet with Pedrillo is surely the jolliest hymn to Bacchus in art or life. Blonde, the English maid, is the first of Mozart's devastating charmers, the Pasha is one of the few superb spoken parts in opera, the hero Belmonte has some lovely music, and the heroine Constanze an aria, 'Marten aller Arten' (Torture me and flay me) that, although a throwback to a more static, undramatic tradition, is nonetheless an electrifying dramatic coloratura aria which, with the right singer, conquers every audience.

Three minor works followed, one of which, *Der Schauspieldirecktor* (1786) (The Impresario,) pleasantly pokes fun at the world of opera. The same year came perfection with *Le Nozze de Figaro* (The Marriage of Figaro), based on the play by Beaumarchais which had caused such a sensation in France in 1784. It was far too revolutionary for the Emperor of Austria: Figaro, the poor writer turned barber and valet, has at least one speech – to the Count – which directly challenges the principle of a nobility ruling by the privilege of birth, not talent. But Mozart persuaded da Ponte to collaborate with him and the dissolute Abbé prepared a brilliant libretto with the criticism of the aristocracy implied, not stated.

The Italian musicians in Vienna, led by Salieri, hoped for a failure, but the Emperor decided that the season should start with *Figaro*. At rehearsals Michael Kelly, the Irishman who created Curzio and Basilio, described how Mozart was the inspiration of all. 'I shall never forget his little animated coun-

tenance, when lighted up with the glowing rays of genius – it is
as impossible to describe it as it would be to paint sunbeams.'
And the première was a sensational success, though the fickle
Viennese were soon taking other works to their heart. *Figaro*'s
real rise to immortality dates from its Prague performances in
1787, where Mozart enjoyed a total triumph – 'Here they talk
about nothing but Figaro,' he wrote. 'Nothing is played, sung
or whistled but *Figaro*.' Prague remains one of the most musical
cities in Europe to this day.

Describing perfection is daunting, for too many superlatives
can blunt effect. *Figaro*'s musical construction is flawless, and
its dramatic construction almost equally so, for the plot, even
when it becomes dense, is almost always clarity itself, as well as
utterly satisfying. It is a genuinely funny opera, hugely entertaining, especially when the audience hears it in their own
language. Its melodies are irresistible – Figaro's 'Non pi andrai'
and Cherubino's 'Voi, che sapete' may be cited amongst a dozen
others because they happen to be known far beyond the ranks
of opera-goers – but even more significant than that is the way
they explore character. No one, surely, has so concisely portrayed a youth who has just discovered the heady delights of
love and sex as Mozart when he composed 'Non so piu' for
Cherubino; and like Shakespeare, he could breathe vivid life
into even a tiny part, as with Barbarina's lament for a lost pin!

Like some, though not all, the greatest comedies – and unlike
Rossini's admittedly delectable *Barber* – *Figaro* is also a deeply
moving, compassionate work. The cheerful Rosina of the
Barber is now the neglected, betrayed wife of her once ardent
Almaviva. She plays her part in the comedy situations, but she
lives in our minds in her two great arias, 'Porgi amor' and 'Dove
sono' ('God of love' and 'I remember days long departed' in the
Dent translation).

The pace of the opera is extraordinary, and not until the last
act does Mozart allow dramatic tension to slip slightly,
though even here character is explored. Figaro's jealousy when
he thinks his Susanna has betrayed him adds yet another
dimension to his portrait, though Mozart adds the horns that

signify the cuckold to pile comedy on near-tragedy. Is Susanna's ravishing 'Deh vieni no tardar' in the same scene mere musical indulgence, however heartstopping? By no means, for it springs from the comedy. And at the end, the arrogance of the Count, who has had his share of arrogant music, melts; he asks for forgiveness, which is granted him – a deeply serious moment in this matchless musical comedy before the joyous finale.

The next masterpiece, *Don Giovanni* (1787), was first given in Prague where it had been commissioned, and again the city went wild over Mozart's music, and again the Viennese were to take their time before surrendering fully to the composer, who was now the Imperial and Royal Court composer in place of Gluck who had recently died. The Emperor admired the work but claimed that 'such music is not meat for the teeth of my Viennese!' Mozart replied: 'Give them time to devour it.' Time was to make it the most praised of all operas.

It is also one of the most argued-over. The nineteenth century, influenced by the Romantic in art, stressed its tragic side and would end it with the Don's descent into Hell. Yet da Ponte called it a *dramma giocoso* (a gay – in the traditional sense – drama). By no means as 'perfect' either musically or dramatically as *Figaro*, it ranges further, with the composer mingling comedy and tragedy with superb success so that da Ponte's comedy becomes sublime, and in the last act – when the statue comes to claim his supper guest – powerful as even Mozart had never been before. As for the characters, opera-goers argue happily over them, so memorably and three-dimensionally are most of them drawn (the exception perhaps being the melodious Don Ottavio).

After this tragi-comedy of Shakespearian quality, Mozart wrote, again with da Ponte, *Così fan Tutte* (1790), which means 'Thus do they all', 'they' referring to women. Both cynical and sensuous, it was too much for the Victorians and, indeed, only in modern times has it come into its own. Allegedly, the farcical plot – of the two lovers who appear to go away, then return disguised as Albanians to test their ladies' fidelity – is a true one. This does not make it da Ponte's masterpiece, neat as the story is with its two pairs of lovers and pair of sophisticated cynics, Don Alfonso, the man-of-the-world, and the delicious Despina. Yet for many, this is Mozart's most ravishing score, not least for the way he gradually suffuses it with passion, as the ladies, Fiordiligi and Dorabella, succumb to temptation. Naturally, all the characters are musically different, though basically Ferrando and Fiordiligi are more serious than Guglielmo and Dorabella. For all the farce trappings, funny enough, but, with the wrong director, liable to be ruined by arch acting, it is a deeply serious, even disturbing work, even though the basic mood is one of enchantment.

The last of the unchallenged masterpieces is *Die Zauberflöte* (The Magic Flute, 1791), which Mozart just lived to see as a resounding success. There are few more delightful yet poignant operatic stories than Mozart's own account of how he slipped behind the scenes one night, having decided to play the glockenspiel for Papageno's aria. Just where Papageno, played by Schikaneder (the librettist, actor, manager and fellow-Mason of Mozart), had a pause, Mozart played an arpeggio. Somewhat startled, the 'player' looked in the wings and saw Mozart; when the next pause came, but no arpeggio sounded, Schikaneder stopped and refused to go on, so Mozart played another chord. Schikaneder promptly struck the stage instrument and said, 'Shut up!' at which everyone laughed. 'I think,' wrote Mozart to his wife, 'that the joke showed many of the audience that Papageno does not play his instrument himself', then went on to tell her how charming the music sounded when heard from a box close to the orchestra – 'it sounds much better than from the gallery.' Less than two months later, the practical joker and incomparable composer was dead.

Die Zauberflöte may be a fantastical fairy-tale, but it has always been greatly loved, and some of its popularity must be due to the versatile Emmanuel Schikaneder (1751–1812). Is it a simple, silly show redeemed by Mozart's music? Hardly, for Mozart was commenting on humanity's and his own religious and spiritual hopes and on the search for truth. Wagner was later to comment on this many-tiered work with – as usual – a wonderful range of characters: 'Before it German opera scarcely existed: this was the moment of its creation.'

In the same year (1791) *La Clemenza di Tito*, an *opera seria*, was given in Prague. It is surely not as total a success as *Idomeneo*, yet its musical riches are awe-inspiring. Given the right cast, it can strike fire and even seem a masterpiece. Such has been the experience of opera-goers at Covent Garden in the 1970s, who heard a cast that included Janet Baker, Yvonne Minton, Anne Howells and Teresa Cahill, conducted (at first) by Colin Davis and produced by Anthony Besch with John Stoddart's monumental designs. As often happens, in the presence of greatness on stage an underrated opera suddenly flowered majestically and the textbooks were proved once again to be wrong.

What other operas Mozart might have written had he lived even to middle-age will always be opera's greatest 'if'. Yet the heritage of glory that he left is astonishingly large.

3

From Beethoven to Bayreuth

The Romantic Movement

Opera is so romantic an art form – though its visual side sometimes manages to obscure the fact – that the term Romantic
Movement is even less satisfactory a description of part of its
history than it is when applied to the other arts. The Romantic
artist – in literature, painting, sculpture and music – was more
concerned with giving expression to his feelings and passions
than with form, however pleasing. From the mid-eighteenth
century, and in music from the early nineteenth century, the
new cult blossomed, given that much more intensity by the
fevers unleashed by the French Revolution in and outside
France.

Romanticism at its peak is the passionate and exotic painting
of Delacroix, it is Berlioz in life and art, it is the volcanic actor,
Edmund Kean, who could rouse his audiences to frenzy, reduce
them to sobs, make them faint and who once sent Lord Byron,
an arch-Romantic, into a convulsion by the power of his
acting.

Romanticism is Schiller, Goethe and Heine, Keats, Words-
worth and Shelley, William Blake, Victor Hugo, the singers
Maria Malibran and Scröder-Devrient, the dancer Taglioni. In
the 1960s, a BBC TV serial of the *Count of Monte Cristo* by
chance or design managed to sum up the entire movement at
its most exuberant with Alan Badel as the Count – actor,
creation and author all Romantics – and with incidental music
by Berlioz. You cannot get more Romantic than that.

But, and it is a big 'but', especially applied to opera, there was plenty of Romance in advance of the Romantic Movement, even in the formalism of *opera seria*. Romanticism, however useful a word, is as inexact and therefore as suspect, as its opposite, Classicism. These are useful words, but essentially they refer to feelings and ideas more than concrete facts. The listener who finds no Romance in that classical masterpiece, *Don Giovanni* or even in the less musico-dramatic operas of Handel, is simply not using his ears.

The Romantic Movement in opera branched off from Paris, where more than anywhere else it began. There were two main tributaries, the German and the Italian, and both produced a titanic figure in, respectively, Wagner and Verdi. We shall be dealing with these two great schools of opera first before returning to Paris, where Italians like Cherubini, Spontini and Rossini, and the German Jew Meyerbeer, added their notable talents (and in Rossini's case, genius) to the Frenchmen who helped make the city the operatic headquarters of the world.

For Ludwig van Beethoven (1770–1827) operas like *Don Giovanni* and even *The Marriage of Figaro* were 'repugnant', 'too frivolous for me!' *The Magic Flute* was more to his taste and, indeed, he was commissioned to write an opera by Schikaneder, though *Fidelio* was finally given by the first Papageno's successor at the Theater an der Wien in Vienna, Baron von Braun.

Inevitably, Beethoven, who was as endlessly painstaking and slow at composition as Mozart was quicksilver-fast, took his time over his one opera and never got around to other projects, including one on the Faust theme. We are told that the story – of a wife who dresses in male clothes to rescue her political prisoner husband – is based on fact. It is a good-ish tale, melodramatic enough for any reputable composer to have written a suitably rousing score around it. But Beethoven rightly saw that the story had true ethical power, and with a hero and heroine who were actually married, it was moral enough to satisfy his high ideals. The themes of the opera are high ones –

justice and injustice, freedom and imprisonment, darkness (exemplified by the villainous Pizarro, governor of the prison where the husband Florestan lies in chains) and light (the noble Don Fernando, who arrives in the nick of time, just as Leonore, the wife, has revealed herself and is holding the murderous Pizarro at pistol-point). The off-stage trumpet announcing his coming is the most famous such moment in all opera.

'Fidelio' is the symbolic name that Leonore takes for her disguised role and the full title of the opera is *Fidelio, or Married Love*. The libretto was by Josef Sonnleithner after one by J. N. Bouilly, and the first performance was in Vienna in 1805. The final revision came in Vienna in 1814. As is generally known, there are four overtures, the last – and lightest – being the one that is usually used, while *prima donna* conductors, some of extreme eminence and artistic integrity, perpetrate *Leonore* No 3 between the two scenes of Act 2, their vanity thus threatening the dramatic perfection of the work.

Some may claim that 'perfection' is too strong a claim, even though *Fidelio*'s supreme nobility – of theme and music – is allowed even by its detractors. But perfection may be claimed, for though it begins as a *singspiel* with the spoken dialogue of *opéra comique*, it is in theory an *opera semi-seria*, and in fact, thanks to Beethoven, ends as a sublime music-drama. The emotion intensifies from the quartet in the first scene, 'Mir ist so wunderbar', reaching its emotional peak in the act with the Prisoners' Chorus. The first scene of the second act reveals Florestan in his dungeon and culminates, as has been indicated, in high drama, after which we are in the courtyard and all is joy. The reunited couple, who have sung a duet of such rapture in the dungeon that a lesser composer might not have been able to top it in the final scene, have another ecstatic moment when Leonore unlocks her husband's chains. Then a great chorus of joy erupts.

Ultimately, the status of *Fidelio* in the operatic cannon depends on the listener's feelings for its composer, which means that to some it is merely worthy, while others consider it the greatest of all operas and will not hear of any constructional flaws. By any standards it has an appeal unique in the annals of opera, though not until Schröder-Devrient, an actress-singer whose performance as Leonore was to have a decisive effect on the young Richard Wagner, sang the title role in 1823 for the first time, did its success become finally assured. Beethoven, stone deaf by now, was present to watch her and at least see the effect on the audience of his paean of praise to the nobility and dignity of Man.

Beethoven, the musical revolutionary who was Classic and Romantic rolled into one, did not trigger off a school of German opera. This was the achievement of Carl Maria von Weber (1786–1826), a lesser figure, but operatically more influential than the genius that he so often misunderstood.

Before virtually creating a national opera with *Der Freischütz* (1821), Weber had written several operas including *Peter Schmoll* (1803) and *Abu Hassan* (1811), a jolly one-act operetta. Five years later, reviewing Hoffmann's *Undine*, he wrote significantly of what 'all Germans want', namely, 'a self-contained work of art' in which all the arts would collaborate, disappearing, then re-emerging to create a new world.

The longed-for event was his own masterpiece, *Der Freischütz*, which means 'the free-shooter' – one who shoots magic bullets. It did not, in fact, represent a new departure, and some non-Germans tend to be faintly patronising about this charming, tuneful work because it is not a seminal part of their musical heritage. But no one could now catch the excitement that ran through a Germany which – it should be remembered – did not physically exist as a united nation for another half-century. *Der Freischütz* united Germans as Verdi was to unite Italians before their unity was achieved. The first performance took place in Berlin on June 18, 1821, amid scenes of frantic enthusiasm. To be given a national opera overnight was joy enough, but even at first hearing, tune after tune proved irresistible. Here was Romantic art to fit exactly the mood of Germans everywhere.

Some of the tunes are simple folk-songs, like the huntsmen's chorus and the bridesmaids' song, others are superb arias –

like Agathe's 'Leise, leise, fromme Weise' (Softly sighing, day is dying). All are touched with enchantment. The most famous scene is the one set in the haunted Wolf's Glen, where Kaspar, who has sold his soul to the evil spirit Samiel, forges magic bullets for the hero Max. It is fashionable to claim that the scene is naïve and simply very enjoyable, and, indeed, even if magnificently staged and performed – which usually it is not – it is hardly likely to thrill modern audiences as it thrilled earlier ones. But it is a fine piece of musical scene-painting and honest melodrama. The very first notes of the famous overture, setting the atmosphere of the forest that Wagner was to explore so fully, made history, and the work remains one of the great landmarks of opera.

It was helped by the libretto of Friedrich Kind, which is naïve, but effective, more than can be said for the text of *Euryanthe* (1825) by Helmine von Chézy, which has fatally held back the opera's chances of popularity despite some early success and a veritable flood of wonderful music. Its music is continuous – *Der Freischütz* has some dialogue – and there are some dramatic recitatives. Though it was to influence Wagner in *Tannhauser* and *Lohengrin*, operatically it does not live.

Weber was now in poor health and beset with money worries. But in 1824, Charles Kemble, brother of the immortal Mrs Siddons, had asked him to write an opera for Covent Garden. This was to be *Oberon*, with a libretto by J. R. Planché, and the result was a fairy tale, rich in romantic music, but full of spoken dialogue, always a handicap for singers, and needing a most lavish production to do it justice. Only the overture is very well known.

The composer conducted the première, but died soon afterwards, collapsing after conducting a concert. Not until 1844 was his body brought back to Germany, to be reburied in Dresden. One of the mourners was Richard Wagner.

Minor masters

For the first half of our century, many who prided themselves on their musical taste – in Anglo-Saxon countries at least – only acknowledged German opera, while German music's reputation was much greater. No-one, even a listener allergic to, say, Beethoven and Brahms, could sensibly underrate the German achievement in symphonic music, but the curious thing about the cult of German opera was that it was based on so few works. As we shall see, the nineteenth century produced its share of German composers of the second rank, but the standard repertoire – the hard core of works that keep opera houses open – in much of the non-Germanic operatic world contains, and has contained for many years, the following nineteenth-century examples of German art: *Fidelio*, Wagner, perhaps, Humperdinck's *Hansel and Gretel*, and *Martha* by Flotow.

The main reason for this is that many major German composers either avoided opera, except as listeners or conductors – Brahms, Bruckner, Mahler – or simply failed at it. Weber did not fail, but even *Der Freischütz* is not an essential part of the repertoire outside central Europe, though it ought to be.

However, there are some fine works by second-rank composers that can give enormous pleasure to those lucky enough to hear them, works that are constantly played in Germany, and not simply because there are (in both Germanys) some hundred opera houses in action.

It is hard to believe that Franz Schubert (1797–1828) would not have finally achieved a successful opera if he had lived longer. As it is, none of his works is considered stageworthy – ten operas, six of them uncompleted and one lost, and five operettas – with the possible exception of *Die Verschworenen* (The Conspirators, 1823). This Lysistrata comedy was renamed *Der Häusliche Krieg* (The Domestic War). *Alfonso und Estella*, Schubert's only all-sung work, was given at Weimar in 1854 and is sometimes broadcast. He longed to succeed in opera and with such a lyric gift it is a tragedy that he did not.

Felix Mendelssohn (1809–47) wrote three forgotten early operas and left *Loreley* uncompleted, while Robert Schumann (1810–56) wrote one, *Genoveva* (1850) to his own bad libretto from Hebbel's drama. Despite some fine music, it is dramatically unsound and far less effective than many of the Italian works he so despised.

Happily, lesser composers than these left finer works. Ludwig Spohr (1784–1859), once so famous that even the almost tone-deaf W. S. Gilbert could link him in comic verse with Beethoven, wrote a *Faust* (1816) which many consider the first true Romantic opera, the even more popular *Zemire und Azor* (1819) and, amongst others, the most successful of all his works, *Jessonda* (1823), which, according to Gerhart von Westerman's *Opera Guide*, has tunes that are too sugary and straightforward for modern tastes. (This sort of comment makes the average Anglo-American opera-lover, who knows nothing of the piece, long to sample its cloying riches.) Spohr was an early champion of Wagner, producing *Der Fliegende Holländer* in 1842 at Kassel soon after its Dresden première. He was the first major musician to hail Wagner.

Heinrich Marschner (1795–1861) was another leader of the Romantic Movement in German opera and is a link between Weber and Wagner. *Der Vampyr* (1828) should appeal to opera-goers who enjoy horror films and is given in Germany in Hans Pfitzner's re-edition. His masterpiece is *Hans Heiling*, unlike the grisly vampire work, a tragedy in which a girl is courted by a gnome king.

Better known outside Germany is Albert Lortzing (1801–51). Only collectors of rarities manage to find performances of *Zar und Zimmermann* (Tsar and Carpenter, 1837) and *Der Wildschütz* (The Poacher, 1842), but at least their names are familiar. And in Germany Lortzing is much loved. He was an actor, singer and librettist, also a conductor, director and orchestral player. The copyright laws or rather, the lack of them in his time, never allowed him to concentrate solely on composing, so his versatility was financially important as well as fitting him ideally for his main trade. A likeable, generous family man, his operas reflect his sound bourgeois background; this, plus a genuine Romantic feeling resulted in a popularity which has never waned in Germany.

Zar und Zimmermann is a comic opera about Peter the Great

in Holland working as a carpenter and the situations that ensue when another carpenter is mistaken for the Tsar. Its tunes and delightful atmosphere and humour made it a hit from the start, though today *Der Waffenschmied* (The Armourer, 1846), is equally loved. *Der Wildschütz* is more sophisticated musically and is Lortzing's masterpiece, though it has never been as popular. Other works include *Undine* (1845), a not altogether successful attempt at a grand romantic opera. Lortzing died in poverty in Berlin where he was conductor of a small theatre – a job he was about to lose – while his operas were the rage of Germany.

Friedrich von Flotow (1812–1883) lives on through a single 'singers' opera' which tends to bring out the worst in certain critics, who will not admit the validity of second-rate works of great melodic appeal. We shall be looking at this phenomenon again. The opera is *Martha* (1847), a romantic comedy set in the England of Queen Anne, in which two ladies disguise themselves as servants and are hired by two farmers. Flotow was a lesser composer than Lortzing, but there is more to *Martha* than the brilliant use of the old Irish tune, 'The Last Rose of Summer'. 'Ach, so fromm' (Like a dream), better known as 'M'appari' – with which Caruso set the international seal on the opera's success – is a magnificent aria, and so is 'Mag der Himmel Euch vergeben' (Heaven alone may grant you pardon). There are other jolly, romantic and serious moments in this delightful minor work, which shows the influence of the composer's time in Paris. The best of his other operas is *Alessandro Stradella* (1844).

Otto Nicolai (1810–1849) held major Court appointments in Vienna and Berlin. Only one of his operas remains famous, *Die lustigen Weiber von Windsor* (The Merry Wives of Windsor, 1849). Though Verdi's *Falstaff* was later to match, even excel, Shakespeare, and make any other version seem inadequate, Nicolai's remains a delight, even though only its overture is well-known outside Germany. The composer had earlier been influenced by Mozart, Weber, and Italian music, but his masterpiece, though it has Italian features, is Romantic

German at its best. It has rightly remained very popular in Germany and its occasional forays abroad are always enjoyed.

There were a handful of other successful German composers of opera, more or less influenced by Wagner and his ideas, who will be considered later, for now the time has come to meet Richard Wagner (1813–83). He is the most extraordinary figure in the history of opera, a statement even his enemies – and there are remarkably few of them about in the 1970s – could hardly challenge.

Richard Wagner

Wagner was a genius and a born survivor. His ambitions were artistically boundless and he achieved them – which did not make him an admirable character in the conventional sense. However, a man who, amongst other operatic Everests, created the most colossal work of art in musical, dramatic or literary history, *Der Ring des Nibelungen*, deserves to be judged differently from other men, even other great artists, whatever some of his contemporaries legitimately thought of him as a man.

Few artists' lives are fascinating, except to those already engrossed in their art, but Wagner's is the exception, as Ernest Newman's four-volume *Life* convincingly shows.

Wagner aimed to produce a *Gesamtkunstwerk*, unifying all the arts into his own version of a music-drama. He did not invent music-drama which, if the words have any meaning, dates back to Monteverdi, but the phrase became widely used in his day because of him and referred to the unity of musical and dramatic elements in a work and the curtailing of other considerations, notably chances for singers to become overpowerful or even predominant. Verdi was to achieve his own form of music-drama, but, as we shall see, even in his final masterpieces, he remained true to the Italian love of the voice.

Visually, Wagner was never to meet his own ferocious demands. That he was an inspired director of acting is certain;

that it is possible to find (occasionally) an entire Wagnerian cast who look their parts is certainly so now, and must have sometimes happened in his own day. Where he failed – in the view of those who followed him – was that his designs were so poor; this was not entirely his fault, for he lived at a time when German scenic art was at a very low ebb. However, it is wrong to state, as many have, that his demands for stage effects were too ambitious – dragons, mounted lady warriors, etc. Exciting 'horse races', train crashes and floods were being staged in the 'straight' theatre at that time in Britain and elsewhere, while in Venetian opera, as has been noted, virtually anything was possible in the way of scenic effect.

Reaction against the 'look' of Bayreuth, Wagner's own festival theatre, which opened with the complete *Ring* in 1876, was most strongly led by the Swiss scenic artist, Adolphe Appia (1862–1928), who saw Bayreuth as it was after Wagner's death, still exactly as before, but without the Master's presence. It was not until the 1950s that Wagner's grandsons, especially Wieland, finally solved the problem by using brilliant lighting and symbolic scenery rather than the wrong kind of realism. (A totally realistic *Ring*, following all Wagner's stage directions would be both viable and popular, if staged by a master like Franco Zeffirelli.) The new Bayreuth tradition, despite occasional failures, has been a triumph and, ironically, has saved a fortune – no bad thing in inflationary times.

Wagner, however, lives by his music and awe-inspiring genius for musical characterisation. He also lives by his stories, which are strong enough in their own right to assist in his remarkable feat of writing hugely popular operas most of which are also the longest ever composed.

Wagner struck his contemporaries as a revolutionary, which was true enough in many respects, not least in the deep seriousness which he brought to opera, but he was not an iconoclast and his reforms sprang directly from that part of the immediate past that he respected. We have noted his praise of *The Magic Flute* and reverence for Weber; but Beethoven was a far more decisive influence, especially the choral finale of the Ninth

Symphony. For him this was a stepping-stone to his own music-dramas.

Always a man of the theatre, another key influence on Wagner was the performance of *Fidelio* that he saw with Wilhelmine Schröder-Devrient (1804–60) as Leonore. The effect this great actress-singer had on Wagner was both crucial and electrifying, for he saw just what could be achieved when a performer of genius was interpreting a masterpiece musically *and* dramatically. His own ideas of music-drama were directly affected by 'The Queen of Tears', as she was known, and, though through poor training and over-singing her technique was imperfect and her top notes vanished early in her career, Wagner still chose her as the original Adriano in *Rienzi*, and as Senta and Venus. This demonstrates that opera composers have always longed for singers who can act, unlike many opera fans who are only concerned with musical perfection and are tolerant even of very poor acting.

The *leitmotiv*, with which Wagner is so closely associated, was not his invention, though he was to use 'leading motives' more brilliantly, subtly, melodically, organically and sublimely than any of his ardent followers or his predecessors. The word *leitmotiv* was coined by a Weber scholar, F. W. Jahns, to describe a short musical phrase with which a composer identifies a character, an idea or a thing. No-one has definitely established how early these occur in opera, but they are there in Weber. Wagner used them more and more intricately until, by *Götterdämmerung* they had become uniquely potent and expressive.

For Wagner they were just part of his musical equipment, not an all-important end in themselves. It was his followers who sometimes became totally obsessed with them and laid the whole concept of the *leitmotiv* open to criticism and disrepute as a mere 'musical signpost'. Wagner never labelled his *leitmotivs*, indeed never used the word at all, and there is no reason why the operas should not be enjoyed without any knowledge of them, except, perhaps, the most famous, like the Sword motif and a dozen others. His disciples did the labelling, including identifying some 90 *leitmotivs* for the *Ring*, and they are very well worth studying, for all that the composer did not identify them himself. Wagner's librettos are also worth studying closely. Wagner was never under the delusion that all that matters is the music, and, as was stressed in Chapter 1, few opera composers repay homework more than he.

Few Wagnerites are born and few listeners get much from their first experiences of Wagner except a considerable level of boredom, relieved on occasion by highlights like the Magic Fire Music and Siegfried's Funeral March. Yet such are the rewards of perseverance – and the advent of the long-playing record has made the journey to Valhalla that much easier – that, for many, a time comes when the long, long operas seem positively short. (Wagner's incomparable endings help enormously in this process, as in *Die Meistersinger*, where after a long evening and very long penultimate scene, albeit of great beauty, we are taken out into the open air for the singing contest and the salute to Hans Sachs, a radiant, romantic, stirringly melodic feast, guaranteed – unless the performance is abysmal – to send an audience out into the night in a state of euphoria.)

Wagner's training was somewhat spasmodic, but he was reasonably educated. At first his ambition seemed centred on the theatre, indeed his actor-stepfather may have been his actual father. In 1828 he started studying composition seriously, by which time his god Beethoven and goddess Schröder-Devrient had inspired him. He studied at Leipzig in 1831, becoming chorus-master of the Würzburg Opera in 1833.

This minor company gave him invaluable experience of the rough-and-tumble world of a small German opera house – invaluable because it was practical. His first opera, not produced until 1888, was written there – *Die Feen* (The Fairies), based on a Gozzi story. Beethoven and Weber influenced the piece, which showed not the slightest sign of Wagner's future greatness. Neither did the Italian-influenced *Das Liebesverbot* (Love's Denial) based on *Measure for Measure*, which was not helped by its première at Magdeburg (where Wagner had moved as a conductor) in 1836. The first night was a cruel fiasco due to hopeless under-rehearsal, the second night found the leading lady's husband and lover fighting it out backstage, a fight which soon became a free-for-all. The performance, which should have been a benefit night for the composer, was abandoned, and the theatre itself soon went bankrupt.

Wagner married Minna Planer in 1836, who proved an unfortunate wife, quite wrong for the part and all it entailed. Yet Wagner at this time, before the iron entered into his soul – the iron that enabled him to survive titanic buffets from fortune – was a pleasant enough man-about-the-theatre, if not a fitting husband for the conventional Minna. It was she who got him his next post, at Königsberg, from which they went to Riga. There he wrote his first remembered opera, the grandiose *Rienzi*, based on Bulwer Lytton's novel, and composed in the Meyerbeerian vein currently all the rage in Paris: a vast dramatic spectacle in five acts, it ends with the Roman Capitol in flames. It was a fine achievement for a man of 25, technically competent and with plenty of fine melody, as the splendid and ever-popular overture suggests.

Meanwhile, Wagner and Minna were on the run from Königsberg to avoid their creditors. On the sea voyage to London the weather – happily for posterity – was bad enough to inspire the seas that surge through *Der Fliegende Holländer*, but for the moment Wagner's objective was Paris, which he reached in 1840. Two dismal years followed, during which he was reduced to arranging operas and operettas for piano and cornet solos. But he also completed *Rienzi*, started writing the text for the *Dutchman*, and, significantly, came across the legends of Tannhäuser and Lohengrin.

The first major turning point in his fortunes came in 1842 with an appointment to the Dresden Court Opera, where he had already agreed to stage *Rienzi*. The resulting performance in 1842 was a triumph, which might have made a lesser man sit back and produce successors in the same vein. But now his mind was on the *Dutchman*, given its première in Dresden in 1843.

It is an opera that even non-Wagnerians can relish, yet for

all its conventional moments – which include most of Daland's role – the authentic Wagner is heard, along with the virility and passionate power of his musical vision. The echoes of Weber are naturally there, but the Dutchman's music, Senta's tremendous ballad, the sailors' choruses, the duet between Senta and the Dutchman, are only some of the signs of growing authority. And that most Wagnerian of themes, Redemption through Love, ends the opera. The idea was not, of course, Wagner's. Indeed it was a standby of the Romantics, but no artist in any field has been so obsessed by it.

The seeds sown in Paris as he studied German medieval poetry and legends, came to fruition for the first time with *Tannhäuser* (1845), whose full title includes *und der Sängerkrieg auf Wartburg* (and the Song Contest on the Wartburg); and, indeed, such a contest actually took place in 1210, just as the historical Tannhäuser was a thirteenth-century minstrel. But here we are in a world of legend, with the hero tormented by the conflict between lust for Venus and spiritual love for Elisabeth. Redemption being so potent a theme for Wagner, he twisted the traditional legend of Tannhäuser, who returned to the Venusberg, and made him opt for Christian love instead. Characterisation in the opera is less notable than in *The Flying Dutchman*, but *Tannhäuser* shows Wagner's growing mastery in achieving his ends and a notable advance musically – the score is full of riches.

The first Tannhäuser was Joseph Tichatschek, a favourite singer of Wagner, who had also created *Rienzi*. The Dresden public preferred the latter and did not respond to the *Dutchman*. In 1861 came the notorious fiasco at the Opéra in Paris when the revised *Tannhäuser* was given, with the extended scene on the Venusberg, written after *Tristan*. The riot at the Opéra was mainly due to the fact that the ballet took place in the first scene instead of later in the opera, the custom in Paris being for dancing to be given at a time when the fashionable members of the Jockey Club had managed to get themselves to their seats. Yet the majority of the audience seem to have been on Wagner's side, even though boos and cat-calls gave a different impression. There was also resentment that a mere foreigner had been allowed 163 rehearsals spread over six months, and the wretched composer was also crippled by a vain, disloyal star (Niemann) and a poor conductor (Dietsch). In fact, the earlier version of the opera is usually considered more satisfactory because it is an artistic whole.

Wagner's politics at this period were what would be called Left-ish today, and in 1848, without actually fighting, he was sufficiently involved in Dresden's revolution in the Year of Revolutions to be forced to flee to Switzerland with a warrant out for his arrest. He settled in Zürich, but his exile – which was to last until 1861 – saw his real fame begin, helped especially by a new champion, Liszt.

It was Liszt, a magnificent patron of talent, who gave *Lohengrin* its première at Weimar in 1850. This was Wagner's final singers' opera (for *Die Meistersinger* is music-drama despite its prodigious singing roles), and for the first time he had achieved a totally unified work of art. It is not all as masterly as *Tannhäuser*, especially its not very effective first act, but this legend of a swan knight, blended with the Holy Grail myth, inspired Wagner to create the first of his unique worlds from the first famous moments of the opera, the great prelude, built entirely on the Grail motif.

Hardly surprisingly, *Lohengrin* baffled most of its first audiences; most but not all, for already Wagner's music and ideals were attracting a minority of fervent disciples. The opera, along with *Tannhäuser*, was destined to become enormously popular, and the staple fare even of touring companies. Today, despite the tremendous resurgence in mass enthusiasm for Wagner, *Lohengrin* and *Tannhäuser* have never recaptured that sort of love, but, given fine performances (the number of processions add to a director's problems), they can both thrill and inspire and also deeply move their audiences.

By 1852, Wagner had written the major part of the text of *Der Ring des Nibelungen* (The Nibelung's Ring, the single Nibelung being Alberich). Four years earlier, in 1848, he had finished a libretto for an opera, *The Death of Siegfried*, from which was to stem the final *Ring* – 'a theatre festival play for three days and a preliminary evening': *Das Rheingold* (The Rhinegold) *Die Walküre* (The Valkyrie), *Siegfried*, and *Gotterdämmerung* (The Twilight of the Gods).

His financial difficulties continued and he exploited friends and acquaintances ruthlessly. His varied life included conducting his music in front of an interested Queen Victoria and having an affair with Frau Wesendonck that was to help inspire him in the ultimate operatic hymn to sexual passion, *Tristan und Isolde* (1865). Death relieved him of his unfortunate and uncomprehending Minna in 1860, by which time he had begun his artistically and emotionally satisfying relationship with Liszt's illegitimate daughter Cosima. She was married to the conductor Hans von Bülow, whose devotion to Wagner's music survived the misery the composer caused him.

In 1864, when Wagner's fortunes seemed at their lowest, he had the astounding, miraculous luck to meet that most fanatical of Wagnerites, the sad, lonely King Ludwig of Bavaria. In fact, the King was not so much devoted to music, even that of his idolised Wagner, as to the composer's vision and his choice of operatic subjects. But the result was the same. For the moment Wagner had no more money worries and Ludwig enabled him to achieve all his wildest hopes.

First came *Tristan*, produced in Munich with Ludwig and Malvina Schnorr von Carolsfeld in the title roles. This was a magnificent performance given before mainly uncomprehending critics and listeners, though Ludwig was ecstatic. It is the first and the most intense of Wagner's mature music-dramas, the *leitmotivs* now totally expressive; music and libretto totally welded together; Wagner's 'endless melody' reaching perfection; and a symphonic texture worlds away from older opera, even though the work may be regarded as the culmination of German Romanticism. Longing and renunciation are the twin themes of a score which ends with a *Liebestod* (Love-death) unmatched in drama, musical or otherwise, except in the last act of Shakespeare's *Antony and Cleopatra*.

There has been more explicit love-music in opera since,

notably the opening of *Der Rosenkavalier*, but nothing has ever equalled what may weakly be called the Love Duet in Act 2 of *Tristan*, the most erotic, tempestuous and tender love-scene in music, with Isolde's *confidante* Brangäne singing warnings to the lovers from a watch tower that add a dimension of unmatched beauty to their ecstasy.

Despite its legendary setting, *Tristan*, a psychological masterpiece, does not outwardly depend on magic or superhuman powers, for even the famous love potion does not promote love, as in the original legend. The love, frustrated and yearning, has been there between the two very human beings from the start of the prelude, with its famous opening bars and historic, trailblazing first chord.

After *Tristan*, Wagner's luck deserted him, for his hold over the King, his usual extravagance and dabbling in politics made him so unpopular with ministers that he was forced to return to Switzerland. In 1870 his marriage to Cosima ruptured his close friendship with Ludwig, who yet remained his artistic champion. His six years of exile were productive beyond measure, for he was able almost to complete the *Ring* and to finish *Die Meistersinger von Nürnberg*, which was first given in Munich in 1868.

This warmest of comedies, the most approachable of Wagner's later works, found the composer creating a human and bourgeois world, the only hostile character being the town-clerk Beckmesser, a direct and unfriendly comment on the critic Eduard Hanslick. This conservative, yet fine and informed writer, happened to be an ardent anti-Wagnerian. Indeed Beckmesser began life in the first libretto as Hans Lick! Naturally Wagner saw himself as Walter, the hero, an apostle of the New in music, who finds a champion in Hans Sachs, the genial, wise cobbler-poet (and a historical character). Wagner, an ardent polemicist against Jews and anyone who stood in his way, created in *Mastersingers* an opera of extreme charm about the goodness of ordinary people. With truly Shakespearean bounty, he fills the stage with many characters, even allowing some of the smallest parts to excel, as the night watchman does at the end of Act 2 after the tumult of the riot. There are a number of set-pieces in the work apart from the famous Prize Song, and its enormous popularity is surely due to its melodic appeal, warmth, characterisation, exuberance and unaffected portrayal of virtue.

There followed *The Ring*, *The Rheingold* being given in Munich in 1869, *The Valkyrie* in 1870, while *Siegfried* and *The Twilight of the Gods* were first performed along with the other two at the original Bayreuth Festival in August, 1876. Without the loyalty of Ludwig the enterprise could never have succeeded.

Though it was created over a period of more than twenty years, the *Ring* is a total entity, from the seminal low *E* flat that begins the great epic on the bottom of the Rhine to the final destruction of Valhalla and the return of the *Ring* to its guardians, the Rhinemaidens, as the river overflows its banks. And at the end there is once again Redemption through Love.

Other composers, dramatists and poets, and even a film-maker, have tried to make gold from the Nibelungen sagas, which stem from an epic poem in German and the Volsunga Saga in Scandinavian prose. Wagner adapted them to his needs and his Nibelungs (a race of dwarfs), his flawed gods led by Wotan, and his men and giants have seized the imagination of millions. In fact, these characters and their story are all Mankind, and so rich is Wagner's vision, so deeply etched his huge cast, that the *Ring* can be interpreted in a remarkable number of ways. Significantly, it has appealed both to Bernard Shaw, who saw it as a Marxist tract, and to the Nazis, for whom it meant the opposite end of the spectrum. Others have found meanings in it that make it all things to all men. It is safe to generalise that it is about the conflict between love and power; but it is also about people, characters who haunt the imagination and can be argued over in the same way as those of Shakespeare. Every human virtue and vice is on display, and the final Redemption through Love is not simply Brünnhilde's reunion with Siegfried in death, but the redemption of Mankind from the follies displayed throughout the long saga.

For all the unity of purpose and design, each part of the *Ring* has its own flavour, and not simply because of the various changes of cast. *Rheingold* is not simply the shortest; the action is by far the fastest, and though in this prelude to the tragedy, the tension and emotion is less than in the later works, it truly lays the foundations for what is to come. Swift and fascinating in story and characterisation, and with a score that is not beyond a not-too-experienced ear at first hearing, it makes a perfect introduction for newcomers to the *Ring*. This was not fully realised, at least in Britain, until the Sadler's Wells English National Opera production in English, which riveted the attention of all and enabled even those who knew the *Ring* well to enjoy it more than they ever had before.

The Valkyrie leads us to tragedy in heroic mould, and to a first act that is the most lyrical of the entire *Ring*. Human passions are now added in a scene of shining beauty between Siegmund and Sieglinde which culminates in the great Sword Motif, first heard in *Rheingold*, as Siegmund draws the sword from the tree. Space forbids even a superficial examination of these unique works, but one may surely claim that Brünnhilde, whom we meet in Act 2, is the most attractive, womanly and human of all Wagner's heroines, just as Wotan, her father and the ruler of the gods, is the most majestic and striking. Perhaps it is the last scene of this music-drama, where Wotan's anger with his daughter subsides and he leaves her in the magic fire awaiting a hero to awaken her from her slumber, that has made this the most beloved opera of the *Ring*.

Because he laid it aside for other projects, Wagner took fifteen years to complete *Siegfried*, a point of interest rather than significance, for this is a shaft of light between two monumental tragedies. Wagner's youthful hero, except for those who regard him as a precursor of the Nazi bully-boys, brings what Gerhart von Westerman has called 'thrilling and rhythmic impetus' to the *Ring*, and not until the final act do we leave the wonderful forest idyll and return with Siegfried to the rock where Brünnhilde lies sleeping. She awakens to music of great beauty and a scene of glory is unleashed as she greets her return to the world – 'Heil dir, Sonne. Heil dir, Licht!' (I hail you, Sun. Light I hail you).

The Twilight of the Gods begins ominously and quietly with the Norns prophesying the fall of the gods; then we are back with Brünnhilde and Siegfried, both ecstatically happy for the last time. The count-down to the final catastrophe now begins, with Wagner producing *coup* after *coup*, not least when he introduces a chorus for the only time in the *Ring* for both the double wedding ceremony and Siegfried's death. This last occurs in a final act of unique power, especially for those who have experienced the whole cycle. Wagner begins it lightly in a delightful scene between his hero and the Rhinemaidens, who urge him to return the *Ring*. He dies at the hands of Hagen and his Funeral March sounds out like the very ending of the world, the death of all Mankind. Yet after Brünnhilde's epic last scene and the annihilation of the kingdom of the gods, the great melody first heard in Act 3 of *The Valkyrie* surges out. Once more we are redeemed by love in music equalled in *Tristan*, but never surpassed.

It is only fair to those who have not yet experienced the *Ring*, or had an unhappy brief encounter with some of it, to stress again that no composer more repays 'homework' than Wagner. Fortunately, as has been pointed out earlier, the age of long-playing records has made this much easier. However the *Ring* has a special problem, which is Wagner's habit of recapitulating events for a character on stage when the audience know the facts already. These scenes – for example, Wotan's narration to Brünnhilde in Act 2 of *The Valkyrie* – make long operas longer. It is all very well for Wagnerians (like the present writer) to claim that the operas seem not a moment too long and to extol the musical fascination of such recapitulations, but Kobbé states emphatically that they did more to hold back the popular recognition of Wagner's genius than did hostile critics and musicians. It is better to admit that Wagner, for all his theatrical genius, could not bear to leave anything out. Lesser composers would have done some judicious cutting. Fortunately, most doubting potential Wagnerians will reach the stage when the recapitulations are no longer a strain but a pleasure, unless the listener is physically below par. Wagner wrote for ideal festival conditions, not for an audience rushing from work to make the first act. And – a final word on recapitulations – some need no apology at all, most notably Siegfried's story of his life just before he is murdered. There are few more poignant, haunting, musically inspired moments than these, where the impending tragedy hangs heavily over the scene. In the last resort, Wagner needs no apologies. The *Ring* is there, a world which gives to those that love it a continual enrichment that is like nothing else in their lives in or out of the opera house.

After the *Ring* came *Parsifal* (1882), a 'stage dedication festival play'. This was not officially staged away from Bayreuth until the copyright expired in 1914, though New York, Boston, Amsterdam and other cities had jumped the gun soon after the turn of the century. Wagner had not wanted this solemn work, steeped in religion – as well as sexuality – to become part of the repertory of ordinary theatres, though there is a nice story proving that the old Adam was still in the ageing genius. *Parsifal*, until recently performed without applause, was once interrupted by the most vigorous clapping, shocking the audience considerably. And who was the offender? Wagner himself, who remained a true man of the theatre to the end. It should be noted that the original Bayreuth programme told the audience *when* to applaud.

The opera is short of the high spots that have enabled so many to advance to the blessed state summed up by Bernard Shaw in the title of his book, *The Perfect Wagnerite*, and it remains for most the least accessible of his masterpieces. Yet for some it is Wagner's supreme achievement, even though it has never – except in those heady nights of 1914 – been as popular as the *Ring*, *Tristan* or *Mastersingers*. The hero is a 'simpleton without guile', the Percival of Malory's *Morte d'Arthur*. Once it created a furore because a virtual Holy Communion is enacted on stage, and, indeed, its religious atmosphere upset both Christians, who knew Wagner himself to be a less-than-perfect human being, and non-Christians, who found that the stifling atmosphere which borders on the religiose, was too much for them. Naturally, some of the objections are to what is part of the work's extraordinary fascination, not least the character of Kundry, both Virgin and Venus. Parsifal was referred to by Lohengrin as his father, and the heart of the story is the Christian legend of the Grail. There are few *leitmotivs* in the opera and though it is the most harmonically advanced of Wagner's scores, the music is clarity itself. Nowadays it is judged solely as a work of art by most listeners, and for the lucky ones it is a sublime one.

Wagner's influence was immense and the sheer weight of hostility to him was proof of his power to create controversy and excitement. The battles for and against him in his lifetime, and in the years that followed his death, were followed by a peak of popularity in the first half of the century, despite still violent opposition to his methods, and there followed a period when it seemed he might become a passionate minority interest. Today his time has come once again. But now – except in Israel where he is banned because of the anti-Semitism which endeared him to the Nazis – his ideas and philosophies of life are no longer the passionate concern of music-lovers, except where they are ingrained in his art. Now he is judged as a musician and to some extent as a poet.

His theatrical reforms were made easier for him because Bayreuth was *his* theatre. There he could lower houselights before a prelude at a time when everywhere else in Europe operas and plays were given with the lights in the auditorium full up. He could force his audience to judge his works seriously, not as mere entertainment. He would not allow admission after a performance had started, even to a box, which has only become common – though by no means standard – practice in some opera houses in the last few decades. He was able to enforce a high standard of acting, not least because he was an excellent actor and a born director himself. That his methods of staging took place, as has been mentioned, in a poor period of German scenic art, does not mean that his productions were not thought out to the last detail.

He died in Venice in 1882, and his wife Cosima ran his theatre until her own death in 1930 though their son, Siegfried, was officially in charge from 1903. They allowed it to become theatrically fossilised just as he left it, the very last thing, one is entitled to feel, that such a theatrical genius would have wanted. It is warming to think that his grandsons Wieland and Wolfgang were able to bring about a theatrical revolution so masterful that it helped decisively to put the old magician-genius to the centre of the operatic stage once more, as part of the supreme trinity of Mozart, Verdi and Wagner, the triple justifications of opera as an art form.

Disciples and deviants

As a postscript to the story of Wagner, some of his immediate successors must be mentioned. Greater composers than any of them were to accept or reject parts of Wagner's ideas, but the successors were true disciples, copying his methods as best they could.

Hugo Wolf (1860–1903) ranks as a disciple. Though best known for his Lieder, his *Der Corregidor* (The Magistrate, 1896), charming but undramatic, has characteristic lyrical vocal music with linking passages of declamation that show the direct influence of Wagner. It has the same story as de Falla's *Three-Cornered Hat*.

Another composer, Wilhelm Kienzel (1857–1941), began as a Wagnerian, then in his popular *Der Evangelimann* (The Evangelist, 1895), added Italian *verismo* with entertaining and dramatic results; but it was left to Engelbert Humperdinck (1854–1921) to write the only masterpiece which can definitely be described as Wagnerian, an opera complete with richly orchestrated, simple nursery-tunes, *Hansel und Gretel* (1893). Humperdinck had assisted Wagner at Bayreuth in 1880–81, when *Parsifal* was being prepared. His opera can only fail with grown-ups and children if it is inadequately done. Try as he would, he could never repeat the success of this delightful opera, his best-known attempt being *Königskinder* (The Royal

Children, 1910). At the time of writing, *Hansel and Gretel* has
been out of the British repertoire for some years.

Wagner's son Siegfried (1869–1930) also composed but was
crippled with the impossible artistic burden of being his father's
heir. He was happiest in Humperdinck land, the land of
romantic German fairy-tale opera, as his *Der Bärenhäuter* (The
Sluggard, 1899) showed, but he had no real success. Meanwhile,
the Wagner-Liszt genius is being transmitted down the genera-
tions, with the great-grandchildren turning successfully to
composition and operatic production. It is a development that
would surely delight their ancestor.

A brief note must be made of some deviants. The Austro-
Hungarian Karl Goldmark (1830–1915) was not a successor of
Wagner, his most popular work *Die Königin von Saba* (The
Queen of Sheba, 1875) being in the French, not Wagnerian
tradition. Peter Cornelius (1824–74) was influenced, though
his most popular opera, *Der Barbier von Bagdad* (1858), an
entertaining, lyric piece, is by no means Wagnerian, not least
because of the date at which it was written. Hermann Götz
(1840–76) remained uninfluenced by Wagner in his finest work,
the comedy *Der Widerspänstigen Zähmung* (The Taming of the
Shrew, 1874).

4

Italy: the Age of Glory

Most devout opera-lovers spend at least part of their time in a state of emotional frenzy and the great novelist Stendhal was no exception. His biography of Rossini (1824), a potent mixture of fact, fallacy, passion, happy irrelevance, social history and fun, begins with the splendid overstatement:

> Napoleon is dead; but a new conqueror has already revealed himself to the world; and from Moscow to Naples, from London to Vienna from Paris to Calcutta, his name is continually on every lip.

We may feel that citing the citizens of Calcutta was somewhat optimistic; but Rossini's fame was indeed very great, and in Italy at least, he, Bellini, Donizetti and Verdi, and the art of opera itself, were to achieve a popularity among all classes unique in the history of art. Only the drama of Elizabethan and Jacobean England and, especially, London, has ever so gripped a people.

But opera's hold lasted far longer, certainly until the death of Puccini in 1924. And we are talking of popularity such as football enjoys today, or pop music with the young, or cricket in the West Indies. Patriotism, the yearnings of a people longing for nationhood, increased the love of opera, especially because Verdi was able to give those yearnings simple, majestic, sublime voice, but the love of music, and especially vocal music, had been part of the Italian heritage for centuries. That the world of *opera seria* was essentially a sterile one operatically because it lacked dramatic impetus, did not mean that it had not been adored, and *opera buffa* had been loved still more. With Romanticism affecting all the arts, the Napoleon of opera, though not the most romantic of composers, timed his entrance perfectly.

The music of Gioacchino Rossini (1792–1868) was little played only a generation ago, save for the evergreen *I Barbieri di Seviglia*, but, beginning in Italy in the mid-1920s, and building up rapidly in the 1950s elsewhere, work after work has regained popularity. Now Stendhal's biography makes sense – indeed some Rossinians might claim it is a sober work, which it most certainly and happily is not.

Rossini was born in Pesaro to a trumpeter father and a singer mother, managing to make his entrance on February 29. He entered the Bologna Conservatory in 1806. His first opera, *Demetrio e Polibio*, was not staged until 1812, though written earlier. There followed *La Cambiale di Matrimonio* (The Marriage Contract, 1810), a one-act piece that had a modest success in Venice, two more *buffo* and one serious opera, also the charming *La Scala di Seta* (The Silken Ladder, 1812), which, surprisingly, was a failure.

His first major success came with *La Pietra del Paragone* (The Touchstone) given at La Scala in 1812, in which the first Rossini *crescendo* was heard. An astonishing six months followed, which produced four operas for Venice, one of which, *L'Italiana in Algeri* (The Italian Girl in Algiers) is as tuneful a work as he ever wrote, and another, *Tancredi*, that made him famous outside Italy.

Tancredi has an aria, 'Di tanti palpiti' (Of so many heartbeats) which became very popular in Italy, indeed in the whole of Europe, if Stendhal is to be believed. It was called the 'Rice Aria' in Venice as Rossini is alleged to have written it in four minutes one evening when waiting for his rice to boil. A serious opera – a *melodramma eroico*, as it is called – it contains some of the composer's most tender love-music, not usually the speciality of a master cook, operatic or otherwise. And a growing mastery of orchestration was evident. *L'Italiana* was written in under a month and remains for many one of the most delightful of all comic operas.

Rossini was no revolutionary, simply that much better than those who had gone before. His tunes, his stimulating rhythms, ear-tickling orchestration, exhilarating crescendos and un-buttoned high spirits led to an outbreak of Rossini-fever that really did sweep Europe. Today, especially if they are not well sung, some of his elaborate arias may seem facile, much too ornamented, and less immediately appealing than those of a lesser master like Donizetti. This is a point of view, but such reservations tend to crumble when Rossini gets the singing he deserves.

A slight reversal in fortunes followed. *Aureliana in Palmira* (1813) was not a success, though Rossini later used its overture and some other music for his *Barber*. *Il Turco in Italia* (1814) was not considered an adequate sequel to *L'Italiana*, though, if not so inspired, it is still a most entertaining work. *Sigismondo* (1814) also failed, but supplied some later *Barber* music.

A turning point occurred when Rossini was engaged by an ex-waiter turned circus-proprietor, turned impresario of the two Naples opera houses, Domenico Barbaia (1775–1841). He became the music director of the Teatro San Carlo and Teatro del Fondo, contracted to provide one or two operas each year. The reigning prima donna and mistress of Barbaia was Isabella Colbran, later to become Rossini's mistress, then his wife. She sang the title-role in *Elisabetta, Regina d'Inghilterra* (1815) an entertaining work about Elizabeth I, which also has some historical significance: in it recitatives were accompanied by strings, and ornaments were written out by the composer in full. Next – in Rome – came *Torvaldo e Dorliska*, not a title on every opera-goer's lips. Then, also in Rome, occurred total disaster.

This was the première of *Il Barbieri di Sivilglia* (1816), a catastrophe unequalled in Italy considering its later enormous popularity, until the first night of *Madama Butterfly* in 1904. Even the notorious première of *Norma* in 1831, disastrous as it was, cannot be compared to it.

Part of the trouble was that a previous *Barber of Seville* by Giovanni Paisiello (1740–1816) was rightly not forgotten, for if Rossini's opera is champagne, the earlier work is at least a pleasant sparkling wine. Paisiello, a former Maestro di Capella at Naples, answered a letter from Rossini politely, saying he had no objection to another *Barber*, but, not surprisingly, he is said to have assumed that it would be a failure.

The Teatro Argentina was full of 'hot-headed enemies' of Rossini, according to Giorgi-Righetti, the first Rosina, besides which the morale of the composer's friends was low owing to the failure of *Torvaldo e Dorliska*. In addition the Spanish tenor Manuel Garcia, father of two of the greatest singers in operatic history, Maria Malibran and Pauline Viardot, but now 'creating' Count Almaviva, persuaded Rossini to let him sing a Spanish melody instead of one of the composer's, under Rosina's balcony in the opening scene. Alas, the guitar on which Garcia was to accompany himself had not been tuned and whilst doing this on stage, he broke a string. The appearance of Figaro with another guitar after Garcia had mended his own was too much for the already derisive and hostile audience, and apart from something of an ovation for Giorgi-Righetti's 'Una voce poco fa', little of the rest of the opera was heard, for, as the writer-composer François Castil-Blaze later wrote: 'All the whistlers in Italy seem to have made a *rendez-vous* for this performance'.

Rossini stayed in bed for the second performance instead of conducting it, but he missed a triumph. His name was constantly called after it, and when he failed to appear, many of the audience descended on his house and cheered him to the echo.

The fact that *Aureliano in Palmira* and *Elisabetta* had already been preceded by the same overture as the *Barber* had been another factor against it, though the composer can be excused, as he only had 13 days to compose his masterpiece. Kobbé rightly points out that the admittedly splendid piece has nothing to do with 'the ever-ready Figaro, the coquettish Rosina, or the sentimental Almaviva', and raises an eyebrow at those who claim that it does. Iconoclastically, one could hope it will be abandoned now so that audiences could get directly to the exhilarating heart of the matter.

In the same year *Otello* was given at Naples, an excellent work which was doomed later to become a collector's item when Verdi made the story so convincingly his own. Rossini provided a happy ending for Rome audiences after the authentic one had upset the Neapolitans.

Rossini's output remained extraordinary. The year 1817 saw four operas from him: *La Cenerentola* (Cinderella), *La Gazza Ladra* (The Thieving Magpie), *Armida* and *Adelaide di Borgogna*. *Cenerentola*, like *L'Italiana in Algeri*, has a coloratura contralto or mezzo heroine, as did, and sometimes does, the *Barber*. *Armida* has much striking music, but *Adelaide* was a failure. As for *The Thieving Magpie*, it is a delightful comedy-drama. *Mosè in Egitto* (later *Moise* in Paris) followed in 1818 and is something of a revelation for those who do not know the serious Rossini, a worthy predecessor of Verdi. Other operas written for Italy include *La Donna del Lago* (The Lady of the Lake, 1819), *Maometto II*, better known as *The Siege of Corinth* (1820), revived for Beverly Sills in 1969 and *Semiramide* (1823), forgotten apart from its overture until Joan Sutherland starred in revivals of this impressively monumental work in the 1960s. Rossini had written 25 operas since *Tancredi* ten years before. No wonder Stendhal exalted him, for his hero was the most popular composer in the world: 'The glory of the man is only limited by the limits of civilisation itself.'

Rossini now visited Vienna, where Beethoven urged him to give the world more *Barbers*, and England, where he sang duets with King George IV; then he settled in Paris, first as the director of the Théatre Italien. *Il Viaggio a Reims*, remembered for its overture, was not an opera but a 3-hour long stage cantata complete with a ballet, staged for Charles X's coronation (1825), but two operas date from this period, both of them masterpieces. *Le Comte Ory* (1828) has been restored to popularity since the 1950s, thanks initially to performances at Florence (under Vittorio Gui) and at Glyndebourne, and has been revealed as an irresistible comic opera. It was Rossini's most sophisticated score for a comedy, and in it there is a trio, 'A la faveur de cette nuit obscure', in which Rossini matched his idolised Mozart at his best. The opera contains music from *The Journey to Rheims* and was first given at the Opéra. The libretto is in French. But Italian opera and the art of *bel canto* has been well served generally by Rossini's spell at the Théatre Italien.

Although he was to live 38 years more, his operatic career ended in 1829 with his finest work, *Guillaume Tell*. Millions who have never entered an opera house know its brilliant overture, indeed its 'hurry music' has been a cinema stock-in-trade, cartoons included, since the birth of films. But precious little was known of this great, melodic, but sombre work except for its ballet music. It was never totally discarded like so much of Rossini, but respectfully revived from time to time, a situation, sadly, that obtains to this day.

Its length has not helped. 'I heard your *William Tell* at the Opéra last night,' said someone to Rossini, who asked: 'What? *All* of it?' Even at first there were cuts, which prompted the composer's rueful reply, but it had a tremendous success, and appeals today to anyone with a love of early nineteenth-century Italian opera. It should have led to four more contracted works for the Opéra, but the Revolution of 1830 put an end to this plan.

Instead, Rossini became a Parisian Institution, composing minor delights, some entertaining religious music, becoming famed as a gourmet, and generally enjoying life. He might not be composing operas, but he never lost his interest. He met the young Wagner, publicly pronounced that in *Rigoletto* 'I at last recognise Verdi's genius', and hailed Offenbach unforgettably as 'the Mozart of the Champs-Elysées'. Half a dozen reasons have been put forward for his extended 'rest' which was to last till he died, but no one really knows. If he wanted a rest, no one deserved it more. He was buried in the Paris he loved, but in 1887 the body was taken back to Italy, where he was re-buried in Florence. Huge crowds mourned, no, celebrated, the event and 300 sang the magnificent Prayer from his *Moses*.

They did it so well that those in front of the church insisted on an encore.

Rossini was unique among the Italian composers of the age of glory in that he did not specialise in the human heart. That certainly could not be said of his first major successor, Vincenzo Bellini (1801–35), born in Sicily, and a true nineteenth-century Romantic in the Italian style. He composed some of the longest melodies in all opera, some of them as languorous as a Sicilian afternoon, and he was a marvellous writer of tunes. He was so un-British, in his frankly sybaritic, sensuous melodies that for much of this century his operas, except for his masterpiece, *Norma* (1831), were regarded with suspicion by many British musicians and critics, steeped in the German tradition. For much of this century they were not even known except by name, for Bellini, far more than Rossini and Donizetti, was unknown ground outside Italy, where he has never been out of fashion. Changing times, plus the ardent, inspired advocacy of Maria Callas, transformed the situation in the 1950s and it is impossible to believe that Bellini will ever again go out of fashion, unless opera itself vanishes, or singing standards deteriorate beyond redemption.

For Bellini needs singers who can sing, who can sustain his mighty lines. He once wished that he could write an opera at which his listeners would die with singing – an admirable sentiment that is misunderstood by some of his detractors, who still consider him a mere 'canary-fancier's' delight. In fact, when helped by the skill of his best librettist, Felice Romani (1788–1865), he could muster considerable dramatic power and, crucially, he was one of the great masters of dramatic recitative. To hear Callas singing a Bellini recitative is at once an education and a feast.

He was born in Catania and studied in Naples, and his first opera, *Adelson e Salvina* (1825), already showed his lyric gift and natural genius for flowing tunes. Barbaia, whom we have met in Rossini's Naples, heard this opera – he was now head of La Scala as well as of the San Carlo – and commissioned an opera from the handsome, rather languid-looking young man for the Naples theatre. The result was *Bianca e Fernando* (1826) and then – for La Scala – Bellini's first major success, *Il Pirata*, with a libretto by Romani and a cast that included the incomparable tenor, Rubini, in a title-role specially composed for him. It was a definite break away from the florid style needed for Rossini, while the heroine, Imogène, sung by Meric-Lalande, was given a magnificent mad scene at the end, which was to electrify audiences when Callas sang and acted it in 1958. Less successful were *La Staniera* (The Stranger, 1829) and *Zaira* (1829). Then came a Romeo and Juliet opera of extreme beauty, *I Capuletti ed i Montecchi* (1830), first given in Venice.

The year 1831 was artistically the greatest year of Bellini's short life. *La Sonnambula* is a simple, idyllic drama set in Switzerland and the sleepwalker of the title, Amina, is the first of the composer's great parts for a soprano. It is too gentle for some tastes. The lowering rock-like figure of the conductor Klemperer was seen walking out of it in mid-performance, though he admitted later to admiring *Norma*, yet the opera is far more than naïvely charming and is full of ravishing melodies. Wagner admired it, libretto included, observing how closely words and music are blended in it. Even those without Italian can grasp this given the right cast, as opposed to undramatic vocalisers. The first Amina and Elvino – he suspects her of betraying him, little knowing she has been sleep-walking – were Giuditta Pasta (who also created *Norma* and *Anna Bolena*) and Rubini. Bellini later heard Maria Malibran singing the role at Drury Lane, London, in a performance in English, and went nearly mad with delight at the most exciting of all the actress-singers of her day. She was to die a year to the day after him, aged only 28, mourned by the musicians, artists, writers and poets of the Romantic Age as no singer has ever been mourned before or since.

Norma, like *Sonnambula*, was first given in Milan in 1831, with Pasta, Grisi and Donzelli. The age of *bel canto* joined hands with great music-drama in this work, one of the grandest and noblest in the repertoire and with a title-role that has been described as more taxing than Brünnhilde. It begins with an

aria which if he had written nothing else would have proclaimed Bellini a master – 'Casta diva' (Chaste goddess). Like
almost all of Bellini's master-strokes it is simply scored, for
Bellini was concerned even more than most Italians with the
voice. His orchestrations were ideal for their purpose, being far
more than the giant banjo accompaniment of legend. There are
many moments in the opera where marvellous tunes are predominant – the duet, 'Mira, O Norma' is such a moment – but
the drama never flags, again helped by Romani's libretto.
Norma herself, the high-priestess of the Druids who has loved
a Roman, Pollione, born his children, been betrayed by him and
is almost driven to killing her children, is a part for a major
actress as well as a great singer. Which is why the royal line of
Normas from Pasta to Callas contains few names. The final
scene of *Norma* is worthy of Verdi, a sombre, sublime climax
that has Norma and a repentant Pollione walking together into
the sacrificial flames. Here the orchestration rises far beyond
mere effective accompaniment.

Beatrice di Tenda (1833), revived with Sutherland at La
Scala in 1961, showed anticipation of Verdi, and seriously
portrayed fifteenth-century Italian history on the stage. It was
not a success in 1833 and was Romani's last collaboration with
Bellini. *I Puritani* (1835) was handicapped by his absence,
Count Carlo Pepoli's libretto being barely adequate. It was
first given in Paris with a cast to make the historically-minded
gasp: Grisi, Rubini, Tamburini and the giant bass Lablache,
who was later to give the opera-loving Queen Victoria singing
lessons. Bellini hoped to adapt the part of the heroine Elvira –
the plot is set in Civil War England – for Malibran, a mezzo
contralto with a soprano's range, but he died before he could
do it. (Though set in England, the opera is allegedly concerned
with the Puritans of Scotland; Italian librettos were always
suspect geographically: Donizetti's *Emilia di Liverpool* has
mountains beside the town.)

I Puritani lives through melodies that even Bellini never surpassed, and, fortunately, the story is just enough to keep the
action going. Callas and Sutherland are the most famous Elviras

of our time, and a production at Chicago in 1955 had a cast of which legends were instantly made: Callas, Giuseppe di Stefano, Bastianini and Rossi-Lemini.

In 1835 at the Théatre Italien, the stirring duet, 'Suoni la tromba' roused the audience to a frenzy, with ladies waving handkerchiefs, and men their hats. Bellini was forced to take a call then instead of waiting to the end. As for the mad scene, beginning 'Qui la voce', it reduced the audience to audible tears, and this astoundingly beautiful scene, culminating in vocal fireworks, remains with 'Casta diva' as a pinnacle of Bellini's art.

Bellini had been over-working and his already poor health was weakened still more by dysentery. He died in Paris, his body being removed to Catania in 1871. Now that his music is both loved and understood by so many, it becomes clearer that his early death was a tragedy, for his steady progression must have resulted in other masterpieces to set beside *Norma*. And many consider *I Puritani* a masterpiece as well. Like Malibran and the great actor, Edmund Kean, who died of drink in 1833, he was a darling of the Romantics, and he was served by a galaxy of great singers whose names are not forgotten to this day. Musically he had a disciple in Chopin.

Gaetano Donizetti (1797–1848) was a rival rather than a disciple. His output was prodigious, for he composed some 75 works for the theatre, many of which have now been resurrected, few of them offering nothing in the way of melodic plunder. He rarely rose above the honourable trade of the master craftsman, but he knew how to serve the needs of great singers and public alike. Except in Italy and at the Metropolitan Opera in New York, his works had almost disappeared from the repertoire by the 1940s, only his masterpiece, *Don Pasquale* (1843), being reasonably well known. Now, thanks to a change in public taste and the advocacy of Callas at just the right moment in the early 1950s, the situation is transformed.

He was born and trained in Bergamo, then moved on to Bologna. His parents objected to his plans for a life in music, so he joined the Austrian army, but continued to study and compose. The result was his first success, *Enrico di Borgogna*

(1818), given in Venice, while *Zoraide di Granata* (1822) was a big enough triumph to get him excused any further military service. The next eight years saw him produce a flood of operas, almost 30 of them, many of them sub-Rossinian, but Bellini's successes led him to achieve his first major work, *Anna Bolena* (1830), with Pasta and Rubini in the original Milan cast.

This is a fine work, powerful enough for modern audiences, some of whom, however, cannot forgive Donizetti for not being Verdi. Romani's libretto as usual contributed to the success, and the final scene is a total triumph. Its modern fame dates from the Callas performances at La Scala in 1957 in Visconti's production, and with Italy's leading Donizetti scholar, Gianandrea Gavazzeni, conducting in the pit.

After this opera made Donizetti a European name, a steady flow of works that are still remembered appeared. *L'Elisir d'Amore* (The Elixir of Love, 1832) is again a popular favourite after many years of neglect, except in Italy and America. Elsewhere, only Nemorino's aria, 'Una furtiva lagrima' was well known. This enchanting, tuneful work was given by the La Scala Company at Covent Garden in 1950 and provoked most British critics to write what seemed even then to ordinary opera-lovers blush-making paroxysms of highbrow outrage. *Lucrezia Borgia* (1833) is a melodic feast, while *Maria Stuarda* (1835), with its unhistorical confrontation between Mary and Elizabeth I (after Schiller), is an effective piece which – depending on opinion – either ranks with *Anna Bolena* or does not quite match it. *Marino Faliero* (1835) has a good reputation, while *Lucia di Lammermoor* (1835), appealed to the imaginations of so many in the Romantic Age that it has never completely vanished from the international repertoire. Though its reputation was not helped by undramatic coloratura sopranos, it came into its own again in the 1950s. Typically, an Italian company visiting London in 1957, with Virginia Zeani as Lucia, had to repeat the Sextet. There had been Callas revivals before this, plus a long-playing record, which had swung public opinion behind the opera, so that when Joan Sutherland triumphed at Covent Garden in 1959, and then elsewhere, the *zeitgeist* was completely with her. Her mad scene at that first performance remains a legend. And the opera in the 1970s? If well done it remains hugely enjoyable and often very moving.

There followed several more major works and some that are not forgotten, including *Roberto Devereux* (1836); *Poliuto* (1839), another Callas revival (1960); *La Fille du Régiment* (1840) with a French text, and full of simple delights and opportunities for fine singing, as Sutherland and Pavarotti, amongst others, have shown; *La Favorite* (1840), a fine French grand opera; *Linda di Chamounix* (1842) and *Don Pasquale* (1843).

This last had a stellar cast at its first performance – Grisi, Mario, Tamburini and Lablache – and is a flawless romantic comedy of extreme melodic charm. All the four main parts are good ones and the opera works well with an ordinary cast, as long as reasonable standards of singing and acting are on display. With a major cast the proceedings become joyous and intoxicating, as happened at Covent Garden in 1974 when Ileana Cortrubas, Ugo Benelli, Sesto Brustcantini and Geraint Evans were, respectively, Norina, Ernesto, Dr. Malatesta and Don Pasquale. Donizetti was to die insane of syphilis a few years after producing this masterpiece.

Like Bellini, Donizetti wrote primarily for singers in an age of great singing, and the sheer size of his output makes his operas vary considerably in quality. He was always a brilliant tunesmith and he knew how to draw appealing characters even if many of them were one- or two-dimensional. And naturally his orchestration was variable, too. A certain jauntiness will keep breaking in at serious moments; he cannot always keep up and sustain greatness, as shown by the second half of Lucia's mad scene from 'Spargi d'amaro pianto', where he introduces slightly trivial melody after holding the audience spellbound with Lucia's haunting 'Alfin son tua' (I am yours for ever). He gave delight, while occasionally slipping gracefully into the more rarified atmosphere of genius. His career encompassed Paris and Vienna – where *Linda di Chamounix* prompted the Emperor to make him Court Composer and Master of the

Imperial Chapel – but he died where he was born in Bergamo.

A brief note must be made at this point of Saverio Merca-
dente (1795–1870) some 60 of whose operas survive but are
hardly ever performed. With his *Il Giuramento* (The Oath,
1837), and influenced by Meyerbeer, he began modest reforms,
including richer orchestration and more dramatic force than
was usual in the Italy of his day, but he was not gifted enough
to achieve major works. Verdi was among those who admired
him.

The hero of Italy

Giuseppe Verdi (1813–1901) had the most Shakespearean
career of any great operatic composer, though he came of even
humbler parentage. His comparatively crude early works
blazed, like Shakespeare's, with a vitality that their respective
contemporaries rarely achieved, and in his Olympian old age it
was Shakespeare (and his librettist Boito) who inspired him to
surpass himself and reach that corner of opera's Valhalla in-
habited by Wagner and Mozart and no-one else.

Only a generation ago it would have been impossible to
write such an opening paragraph about Verdi without seeming
controversial, and earlier still it would have seemed – certainly
outside Italy – well-nigh incredible. As late as 1931 Francis
Toye's brilliant biography of the composer found the author
so much on the defensive that at times it reads like an apologia.
Had not a poet written: 'The music's only Verdi but the
melody is sweet'? Today, the only danger a chronicler of Verdi
faces – apart from stiff competition from a number of excellent
writers – is over-lavish use of superlatives. Verdi is, of course,
now understood. In the 1950s Ernest Newman, doyen of
British critics, was still roasting some of his operas, notably *La
Forza del Destino*, for not being built on Wagnerian lines. (Mr
Newman used also to criticise Mozart for use of coloratura
which to his ears lowered the dramatic tension.)

In Italy, Verdi's fame never waned, though many of his
earlier works dropped out of the regular repertory, and *Falstaff*

was respected rather than loved. This was also the case elsewhere where the name Verdi meant four works of unending popularity, *Rigoletto*, *La Traviata*, *Il Trovatore* and *Aida*. Admittedly, the *Requiem* was also popular, though Anglo-Saxons used to find it too operatic for their sensitive tastes.

It was in Germany in the 1920s that the Verdi revival began, gathering maximum momentum elsewhere after 1951, the fiftieth anniversary of his death, in which interest built up in almost forgotten works. In the 1950s and 1960s it was possible, for a Londoner at least, to enjoy practically every opera Verdi ever wrote. Even *Un Giorno di Regno* was given at St Pancras Town Hall in 1961 and proved superb entertainment instead of the total failure it had always been alleged to be.

Verdi was born in Le Roncole in the Duchy of Parma near Busseto, which was then part of Napoleon's French Empire, but soon to be under Austrian domination. A plaque added to others there in 1951 called him 'the pure expression of the soul of the Italian people', and it must always be remembered that for all the universal love of Verdi that exists today, he can never mean so much to us, or even to Italians, as he did in that long period when he was indeed the musical soul of a people struggling to be free.

The 'peasant from Parma' as he was later proudly to call himself, was lucky to survive his first year, as Russian soldiers looted the village in 1814, massacring women and children. Giuseppe and his mother hid in the belfry. It was a good beginning for a patriot musician. His first training came from the local organist and he was helped by a local music-lover, Antonio Barezzi, whose daughter he later married. He failed to get in to the Milan Conservatory, a discouraging start for anyone, let alone a genius, and returned to Busseto as organist and conductor of the town's orchestra. His first opera, *Rochester* (1836) is lost, but in 1839 *Oberto, Conte di San Bonifacio* was given at La Scala, partly through the interest of the soprano, Giuseppina Strepponi, who was to become his mistress and then his ideal wife.

For Verdi lost his first wife and their two children in the

space of a few months. He had been offered a contract by Merelli of La Scala for three more operas after the moderate success of *Oberto*, when this shattering tragedy occurred. Artistically, it surely added dimensions to his later work, for his father-daughter relationships, notably in *Rigoletto* and *Simone Boccanegra*, were to be particularly poignant even by his own usually high standards in portraying friendship and love. At this bleak time his *Un Giorno di Regno* (King for a day, 1840) was being composed and was a total failure. Yet like *Oberto* it foreshadowed later glories. His mood was of darkest despair, but Merelli believed in the young man who had lost the urge to compose and offered him the libretto of *Nabucco*, or *Nabucodonosor* as it was first known. It happened to fall open at the point where the exiled Jews long for their distant homeland, as they lament beside the waters of Babylon.

This was one of the greatest moments in the story of opera, for it inspired him to return to composition and resulted in the haunting chorus 'Va pensiero, sull ali dorate', which was to become a veritable national anthem during the fight for Italian freedom, and which still means more to Italians than it can ever do to the millions around the world who love it.

Like the operas that immediately followed it, *Nabucco* (1842) appeals simply and directly to the emotions, but unlike some of them (the products of what Verdi called his 'galley years', so fast was he having to turn them out) it is a masterpiece. Some of the sophisticated thought the new composer crude compared with Bellini and Donizetti – Robert Browning was one of them – but the ordinary opera-goer was delighted with the warmth and vitality of the score, the great swinging tunes, the unmistakable sound of a new voice who passionately cared about people, and the total commitment to the characters – despite the fact that harmonically and rhythmically the score was unpretentious. One writer called it 'agitators' music', which, given the patriotic overtones, it most certainly was.

Even when Verdi's very early operas had apparently been consigned to near-oblivion, *Nabucco* was not forgotten, unlike many of its successors. The first Abigaille, heroine of the opera, was Giuseppina Strepponi, who left the theatre to live with him seven years later, marrying him in 1859. *I Lombardi alli Prima Crociata* (Crusade) followed the next year, and the finer *Ernani* in 1843, which was even more of a melodic feast. Both are patriotic works and both were hugely successful. The latter had a libretto by Piave based on Hugo's *Hernani*. Characters in these melodramatic works tend to be two-, sometimes one-dimensional, but the vengeful Silva in *Ernani* is a major creation. Now Verdi was in great demand and became a musical slave in the galleys.

I due Foscari (1844) was significantly hailed by Donizetti. 'Frankly, this man is a genius,' he said, seeing through the still somewhat primitive sledgehammer strength and blazing melodies to the heart of the matter – that Verdi was a born opera composer. *Giovanni d'Arco* (1845), *Alzira* (1845) – the only Verdi opera the author of this book has not yet managed to 'catch' – and *Attila* (1846) are typically rich in superb arias, followed by fiery *cabalettas* and impassioned melodies, some in march tempo, some in slow waltz time, a potent trade-mark of Verdi and his contemporaries in these years. *Attila* opened in Venice where the Venetians were able to experience the birth of their city on stage in a scene of simple grandeur and power. Solera, the librettist, wrote a line that was to become a battle cry; Ezio sings: 'Avrai ti l'universo, Resti l'Italia a me' – 'You may have the universe, let Italy remain mine'.

Next came a masterpiece in *Macbeth* (1847, revised 1865). It would be foolish to claim that much of it is of Shakespearean stature (the sleepwalking scene apart), but it is Verdi's first music-drama (not a phrase he used), grandly conceived and well characterised, though perhaps marred by an excess of witches. The town-band sound of Duncan's arrival at the castle has been mocked – the Busseto town band has been detected in several early Verdi operas – but it is actually a brilliant stroke, a jaunty tune in striking contrast to the brooding atmosphere and violence to come.

Lady Macbeth is the true leading part in the opera, and how far Verdi had already advanced from the high noon of the age of *bel canto* can be judged by his requirements for his heroine: 'Mme Tadlioni sings perfectly. I would not have Lady Macbeth sing at all ... Lady Macbeth's voice should be hard, stifled and dark ... should be the voice of a devil.' In other words, Verdi wanted vocal acting of a very high order, not a stream of beautiful tone. Callas, alas, never recorded the role, but she has left two excerpts from it on disc in which she obeyed Verdi's instructions. Of course, she sings in the sense that she does not speak, but, as Verdi wanted, she characterises in a totally committed way. Verdi also wanted good physical acting, later leaping up on stage (in his 80s) to show his stiff Otello, the trumpet-toned Tamagno, what he wanted. Naturally, he had no hope of getting the acting standards that Wagner could insist on at Bayreuth. In the nineteenth century, and well into our own times, those that could act did, those who could not or would not, did not. For all today's higher standards, lack of rehearsal can still produce the same inartistic results.

I Masnaderi (The Brigands, 1847) was written for Jenny Lind, the Swedish Nightingale, and was given its première in London with Verdi conducting. It was cheered to the echo by an audience that included the Queen, the Prince Consort and the Duke of Wellington – deservedly, for it contains much fine music. Even *The Times*, no friend of Verdi's, managed praise. *Il Corsaro* (1848) is possibly Verdi's least interesting opera, but *La Battaglia di Legnano* (1849) is a stirring work and made history at its première in Rome. The whole fourth act was encored and a soldier was so enflamed by the proceedings that he flung first his accoutrements, then himself from a box. The opera helped fan revolutionary flames – a rare event in artistic history, though, as we shall see, Auber's *Masaniello* actually started a revolution.

Next came an enchanting work, *Luisa Miller* (1849), an intimate work full of warmth and humanity and pathos. It is greatly loved by those who know it, possibly more today than any other of Verdi's pre-*Rigoletto* operas. *Stiffelio* (later *Aroldo*, 1850/57) ended the 'galley years', it must be admitted less than sensationally, though it has some fine moments. But no true

Verdian will admit that any of the long line are not worth hearing.

There followed three masterpieces. Two of them instantly became enormously popular and the third, *Traviata*, soon recovered from a notorious première to make a trio that opera-goers and opera managers have been rejoicing in ever since.

Rigoletto (1851) was Verdi's first work of complete genius, as the *Concise Oxford Dictionary of Opera* neatly puts it. There had been several earlier operas that can now be claimed as masterpieces, but here there can be no dispute. Piave adapted Victor Hugo's *Le Roi S'Amuse* with conspicuous success, turning the King into the Duke of Mantua for censorship reasons, reigning monarchs not being permitted to be seen as libertines on stage. Besides, in the aftermath of the revolutions of the year 1848 an attempt to assassinate a sovereign on stage (in the last act) was frowned on by the Austrian authorities who still ruled Venice, where *Rigoletto* had its première. There were other ludicrous objections, but in the end Verdi had a mighty triumph.

Apart from its wealth of melody and fine dramatic structure, the opera's most remarkable feature, possibly its chief glory, is the character of Rigoletto himself, a flawed hunchback hero, and a startling innovation. The famous scene in which he feigns gaiety while searching for his abducted daughter, then pleads with the courtiers and finally rounds on them savagely is the greatest moment of a great role. The other parts are finely characterised, not least the Duke, whose two hugely popular arias are ideally simple, frivolous and hedonistic. The great quartet, the pinnacle of a totally successful last act, is in reality a double duet and was one of the two points in the opera that swung Victor Hugo round from hostility to admiration, the other being the sombre duet between Rigoletto and the hired killer, Sparafucile.

Il Trovatore (The Troubador, 1853) was in one sense a return to the earlier Verdi, yet it has many breathtakingly exciting and lovely tunes which make it better than anything that had gone before, except *Rigoletto*. The much-abused libretto is actually perfectly adequate, since it has strong situations and equally strong, if two-dimensional, characters. Given the white-hot fire Verdi poured into the opera, there is nothing surprising about its popularity down the years. For some critics it was a vulgar opera, but not for the people. As Joseph Wechsberg has put it, they 'sensed the integrity of Verdi's melodic passion'. Space does not permit a recital of its felicities, but it may be noted that Leonora's 'D'amor sull'ali rosee' ranks with the finest of Bellini as *bel canto* at its incomparable best. As for the Anvil Chorus and the Miserere, they are known to very many who have never been in an opera house.

La Traviata (The Woman Gone Astray, 1853) is probably now the best loved of the trio. It is based on Dumas' *La Dame aux Camélias*, a good play which does not live beside Verdi's strong but tender masterpiece. The story of the fashionable courtesan, both very moving and completely believable, has been summed up by Toscanini in a word – 'truthfulness'. The consumptive heroine Violetta (Marguerite Gautier in the novel and play, Maria Duplessis in real life) is not only one of the most glorious soprano roles, but also one of the most challenging, for she has to range from coloratura to the most passionate drama and be able to act and, happily, look right as well. Like Carmen, Violetta suffers much in the event of physical mis-casting. The opera has survived shoddy performances – visual nightmares like the soprano Tetrazzini and the tenor John McCormack in Edwardian times – and a long spell where it was played in seventeenth-century costume, the public not wishing to see what was a very contempory opera presented in a contemporary setting.

Just how much of a fiasco the legendary first performance was is open to question. The first Violetta, Fanny Salvini-Donatelli, was undeniably too fat, the tenor was in poor voice and the baritone insulted by the size of his part. But Harold Rosenthal has found that the opera was not played in the clothes of the day – an alleged reason for failure – but those of 1700, and also that Verdi was vigorously applauded at the second performance. So, if not a success, and if the composer judged it a failure, it was by no means a fiasco in the *Barber/Butterfly* class. Now it may be claimed, with little fear of contradiction, as an intimate music-drama of surpassing charm and compassion.

Les Vêpres Siciliennes (Sicilian Vespers, 1853) was written for the Paris Opéra which Verdi dubbed 'La Grande Boutique' (The great toyshop), and it remains the only one of the composer's later works to suffer neglect. It is inevitably full of riches, but Verdi disliked the text by Scribe and Duveyrier and also conditions at the Opéra, and was never able to enjoy his Parisian assignment. *Simone Boccanegra* (1857, revised 1881) is a far better work, though its sombre atmosphere and complicated story make it harder to savour than most Verdi at first hearings. He decided his first version was monotonous and cold, and today we hear a combination of two versions, the finest scene – in the council chamber, to a text of Boito's – being added for the second. It is greatly loved by most Verdians, but many perhaps simply admire it.

Meanwhile, after years of strife and disappointment, Italian unity was no longer a dream – indeed, at the special request of Cavour, Verdi was to sit, rather quietly, in the new Italian parliament from 1861–5. Cavour, no great music-lover himself, knew Verdi's symbolic value to the nation. We have seen the patriotic fervour at the heart of so many of his operas, but Verdi meant more to the Risorgimento than that. His name was a hidden rallying cry, for *VIVA VERDI*, scrawled on walls and elsewhere, meant *Viva Vittorio Emanuele, Re D'Italia*.

Before his parliamentary stint, Verdi had written *Un Ballo in Maschera* (A Masked Ball, 1859), one of his most tuneful works, and a happy blend of lightness, drama, humour and tragedy. However, it roused much opposition from the censors. Though now it is usually staged as originally written, as a story of the life and death of the historical Gustavus III of Sweden, who was murdered at a masked ball in his own opera house, the killing of a king was too much for the authorities at the time. So Verdi had to allow the action to be transformed to seventeenth-century Boston. This did not increase its realism especially for Anglo-Saxon audiences, but at least this well-characterised. beautifully orchestrated score was heard. Today it is one of Verdi's most popular works, more so, perhaps, than *La Forza del Destino* that followed it. Yet good or great performances of this sprawling, coincidence-ridden, but magnificent work tend to carry away all doubts about its stageworthiness, and for those with the gift of prophecy, Friar Melitone must have suggested that Verdi had the ability to create a major comic figure, who was to materialise 31 years later as Falstaff.

Verdi next revised *Macbeth*, then wrote a masterpiece for Paris, *Don Carlos*, a grand opera which has come into its own in the last generation after being either neglected, or misunderstood, or badly cut, and is now loved and admired by some more than any of his other operas. This has been particularly so in Britain, where the 1958 Covent Garden production, conducted by Giulini and produced by Visconti, with the crucial first act included, not only set new standards of performances of Italian opera, but buried for ever the lie that the opera was unsatisfactory. And in the 1970s, the English National Opera gave an even more complete version of the work, music previously unheard being included.

Don Carlos, usually given in Italian, to the annoyance of purists, is perhaps musically not quite on the same level as *Aida*, but its characterisation is far finer, musically and dramatically. Its text by Méry and Du Locle is based on Schiller's play. Never before had the composer presented such a totally believable teeming world; psychologically truthful, subtle, passionate, even epic, but also intensely human, it contains one scene that is often claimed as the finest in all Italian opera.

This is Act 4, Scene 1, which begins with King Philip of Spain's extraordinary, deeply-felt and melancholy 'Ella giammai m'amo' (She has no love for me), and continues with an equally extraordinary confrontation between the King and the Grand Inquisitor (both superb bass parts). Then, after other impassioned confrontations, it ends with the vehemently frantic – and musically magnificent – lament, 'O don fatale' (O fatal gift) sung by the King's mistress, Eboli. But the riches are too great to list. After this feast, and Roderigo's stirring death scene, the last act begins with an aria for the unfortunate Queen, 'Tu che le' vanita', in which she laments past joys. This aria has a particularly fine line like a great arch of melody. Then the lovers bid each other farewell. Only the ending is weak, as if to remind us that Verdi had not yet achieved total mastery at all times, though some claim the *auto-da-fé* scene also is less thrilling than it might have been. Yet this opera of personal and political tensions is surely the noblest that Verdi ever wrote.

There followed *Aida* (1871). This is Verdi's grandest opera, which was not, as is often claimed, written for the opening of the Suez Canal, but to open the Italian Theatre in Cairo. Its popularity has never wavered, with audiences, singers and managements alike, and it is one of the best introductions to opera. The characters of its principals are superbly drawn and form the main interest, once the listener is happily sated with the vocal and visual splendours, notably in the Triumph Scene. Indeed, musically the most rewarding scenes are in Act III beside the Nile, and the tremendous outburst of jealousy unleashed by Amneris in the penultimate scene. The brazen splendour is best experienced in huge houses, or the open air, especially at the Verona Arena, with 25 000 people gripped in Verdian fever, but paradoxically the greatness of *Aida* lies in its intimate scenes. Those who have claimed that the characters are slightly cardboard creations have not listened to some of Verdi's finest music.

Many years were then to pass before he returned to opera, though, as noted, he revised *Simone Boccanegra* in 1881, helped by Arrigo Boito (1842–1918), his incomparable librettist for *Otello* and *Falstaff*.

Boito was a composer in his own right and earlier, in the fashion of the younger generation, and influenced by a visit to Germany and his enthusiasm for Beethoven and Wagner, he made strongly worded attacks on contemporary Italian composers, which were personally wounding to Verdi. It was Angry Young Man material, for even then, Boito knew the magic of his future colleague. He wrote of the ravishing tenor aria, 'Quando le sere al placido' from *Luisa Miller* in a way that showed that his heart was in the right place, even when he was bemoaning the 'fact' that the honour of Italian music was being 'befouled by the filth of the brothel'.

Boito's *Mefistofele* (1868) was not a success at La Scala, but is a deeply impressive work, not least its Prologue in Heaven, an astonishing musical feat. It is based on the first part of Goethe's *Faust*, plus – less happily – some of the second part. *Nerone* (posthumously produced, 1924) aims even higher, but is a lesser work.

Verdi and his erstwhile critic gradually came together. After the trial run with the revised *Boccanegra* came *Otello* (1887) – (the *Requiem* had first been given in 1873).

Otello, it is not bold to claim, is the most perfect of tragic operas. Arguably it is marginally finer than *Othello* for two reasons. The first is that Boito's compression of the play is quite brilliant, not least by starting with the Landing at Cyprus, thus allowing Verdi to begin with what must surely be the most exciting opening in all opera. The other reason is that Verdi's characterisation of Desdemona is stronger than that of Shakespeare; it culminates in a Willow Song of divine simplicity, and with the sudden passionate, heart-rending cry of 'Ah! Emilia, Emilia, addio!' which is one of the supreme emotional *coups* in opera.

Otello himself is vividly drawn, but only a heroic tenor who can act can do the role justice. *Otello*'s opening begins with a tremendous clarion call of *Esultate!* and the entire title-role demands rare intelligence and artistry together with the necessary vocal prowess. The great Act 2 scene in which Iago enflames the jealous Otello follows Shakespeare closely, with Verdi superbly turning Iago's speech beginning 'I lay with Cassio lately' into the insinuating, deadly 'Era la notte'. Iago's famous Credo, however, which precedes the whole scene, is pure Boito-Verdi, a piece of characterisation that certainly suits one of Shakespeare's few totally evil creations.

Though infinitely more subtle and skilled than early Verdi,

melody is still sovereign, but arias and recitative are now closely linked and a phrase can carry the emotional content of an entire aria. It is a fast-moving work and, if tragedy is greater than comedy, it is Verdi's supreme masterpiece. The public, after the initial excitement had died down, respected rather than loved *Otello*, but over the last generation it has become a house-filler, and greatly adored. To match Shakespeare in one of the handful of great tragedies is a unique feat, but such was Verdi's achievement. Even the drinking song in Act 1 has an air of danger and is an expression of character, and the love duet between Otello and Desdemona at the end of Act 1 is particularly fine, ending with a phrase that is used again with moving effect just before the final curtain.

Musicians and critics often claim that *Falstaff*, not *Otello*, is Verdi's masterpiece, yet audiences have never warmed to it so much. That it is yet another musical miracle is unquestioned. Indeed, considering Verdi's advanced age when he wrote it, it could be ranked as a supreme miracle. The score is perhaps too fast for the average opera-goer, though now the opera often fills the houses. And for all the wealth of melody, there are scarcely any conventional arias. Boito used some of *Henry IV* for the opera, most notably Falstaff's 'Honour' monologue, which raises the status of the fat knight beyond the rather insulting position of butt in *The Merry Wives of Windsor* – a play which, anyway, is not generally considered one of Shakespeare's masterpieces. A full thousand words would not do justice to the felicities of the score, but two may be mentioned.

The first is Ford's impassioned outburst of jealousy in Act 2, Scene 1 when, in true Shakespearean manner, Verdi injects deep seriousness into a previously farcical situation. We even hear the horns used to signify the horns of a cuckolded husband, horns that we have heard before when Philip II lamented the fact his wife did not love him in *Don Carlos*. And Falstaff has a short paean of self-esteem, 'Va, vecchio John', that expresses the essence of the born survivor, a marvellous affirmation of the life-force and Man the unconquerable optimist. And to end his last opera the 'peasant from Parma', who failed to get into the Milan Conservatory, finishes with a choral fugue in a final outburst of volcanic exuberance.

Verdi was a more complicated and often less likeable man than sentimentalists will allow. Like Wagner, his struggles affected him, though the Italian was a far more admirable man. Frank Walker's *The Man Verdi* has revealed a flawed hero, but a hero nonetheless that the people of Italy, and now the world, rightly regard as a human being fit to be loved as well as revered. There is no operatic composer at once more melodious and more virile than he. He even 'died magnificently, like a fighter, formidable but mute', wrote Boito, who also said that 'we had all basked in the sunshine of that Olympian old age.' More than 200 000 are said to have lined the streets of Milan to say farewell to the Lion of Busseto, and they sang his chorus from *Nabucco*, as their descendants were to sing it when his greatest interpreter, Arturo Toscanini, died. The poet d'Annunzio wrote of Verdi: 'Pianse e amo per tutti,' though, as Francis Toye has written in his biography, the literal translation of those words, 'He wept and loved for all', 'gives little idea of the implication of the Italian'. But Toye was writing in 1931 before the Verdi revival was truly under way. Today, when Verdi's star is destined to shine radiantly as long as opera exists, countless thousands know instinctively what the poet expressed so simply and beautifully.

They also served

Time is cruel to the lesser composers of an age. Who remembers Petrella, Platania, Pisani, Montuoro, Pedrotti, and Marchetti now, except specialists in the nether regions of nineteenth-century Italian opera? Yet the great Czech soprano, Teresa Stolz (1834–1902), Verdi's constant companion after the death of his Giusseppina, sang in operas by all of them between February 1865 and February 1871. Apart from *Mefistofele,* only two operas between Donizetti's *Don Pasquale* (1843) and Mascagni's *Cavalleria Rusticana* (1890) are remembered: *La Gioconda* and *La Wally*. Mascagni's sensational and influential one-acter belongs to Chapter 7, but the other two works are very much of their age.

La Gioconda (The Joyful Girl, 1876) is the only one of Amilcare Ponchielli's (1834–86) nine operas to survive, and survive it does because it is a splendid vehicle for splendid singers. It has rarely been absent from the Metropolitan, New York, with its long tradition of stellar casts, and a production in Berlin in 1975 proved a sensation. It is the sort of work that audiences adore but that critics – at least in Britain – tend to sniff at. 'Musically it is full of old-fashioned clichés and is crudely scored,' proclaims the *Concise Oxford Dictionary of Opera*, an attitude that has helped confine the work in Britain to one concert performance in London in a generation.

Toscanini was one of the conductors associated with the work and for *La Wally* by Alfredo Catalani (1854–93) he had an even softer spot, even naming his daughter after the heroine. One British history of opera leaves both works out altogether. *La Gioconda* is a lurid melodrama set in seventeenth-century Venice; *La Wally* is set in the Tyrol in 1800 and has its lovers perishing in an avalanche. The only other opera of Catalani's to contain music that is sometimes heard outside Italy is *Loreley*, which is still played there. Influenced by German Romanticism, there is nobility in Catalani's finest music, although his masterpiece sounds very akin at times to the new era that dawned with *Cavalleria* and soon culminated with Puccini, of whom Catalani was to become increasingly jealous before dying of tuberculosis.

It may be that some hidden treasure from the age of Verdi has yet to emerge, but it seems highly doubtful. Only the finest pages of *Mefistofele* are in the same league as Verdi's, although one aria, Marguerite's haunting description of the drowning of her baby, 'L'altra notte in fondo al more' is one of the most tremendous moments in Italian opera. As interpreted by Maria Callas on records, it is awe-inspiring.

5

French Follies and Grandeur

It is dangerously easy today to underrate the French school of opera. Lully and Rameau, for all the praise bestowed on them, are honoured more than they are performed. Many foreign composers settled in Paris and worked there, but hardly rank as French. And the two indisputable geniuses of nineteenth-century French opera, Hector Berlioz and George Bizet, had such frustrating, often distressing careers, that the listener and reader become biased against the entire French establishment. Verdi's experiences, to say nothing of Wagner's, only reinforce the feeling.

Added to this, remarkably little French opera is heard outside France, despite a magnificently long tradition, and in our own century the fame of French singing slid dangerously low, though it is recovering. And ironically the Paris Opéra has at last re-established itself in the 1970s as a great international house, in no small part due to the good work of its current Intendant, Rolf Liebermann, a Swiss composer famous for his work at the Hamburg Opéra, and Sir Georg Solti, a Hungarian turned Briton. As for the Opéra's repertoire, it is anything but nationalist.

Having painted so pessimistic and down-beat a picture of French opera down the years, the more cheerful part of the story – along with the dismal details – must be given. And we must retrace our steps back to the dawn of the Romantic Movement in music.

Though Gluck left no obvious successor in Paris, there were native and emigrant composers of genuine talent. Étienne

Nicolas Méhul (1763–1817), a favourite of Napoleon, is remembered best today for some of his overtures, but Beethoven and Weber were among his admirers. His *Joseph* (1807) with an all-male cast, was popular in France and Germany for many years, and his dramatic truth and seriousness, even in *opéra comique*, were particularly notable.

Better remembered is the emigrant, Luigi Cherubini (1760–1842). Berliozians despise him for the deep conservatism that so upset the young Berlioz: Cherubini held the key post of Director of the Conservatoire from 1821 until he died. But the Italian was passionate enough once. He achieved a single masterpiece, *Médée* (1797), a famous vehicle for Callas in the 1950s, and had two major successes with *Lodoïska* (1791) and *Les Deux Journées* (The Two Days, 1800) which is also called The Water Carrier. This last was an early Romantic opera, a melodrama suitable for a revolutionary age. It should be noted that theatres thrived in Paris in the Revolution even at the height of the Reign of Terror.

Another Italian emigrant was Gasparo Spontini (1774–1851), who was directly responsible for raising standards at the Opéra, which had now become the Académie Impériale de Musique. *La Vestale* (1807) made him famous, a classical but passionate drama much admired by the young Richard Wagner (as *Rienzi* shows). Revived in modern times for Rosa Ponselle and Maria Callas, it was followed by two more major works along with many that have been forgotten. *Fernand Cortez* (1809) even had propaganda value, or so Napoleon thought, hoping it might help his war in Spain, though this great success was not considered by its composer to be as fine as *Olympie* (1819).

Even the critical Berlioz admired Spontini, whose insistence on fine orchestral playing and equally fine staging helped raise the general standard of French opera to notable heights. Yet this gifted man, who helped pave the way for French grand opera, was to be overtaken by the younger generation who embraced the Romantic Movement in a way he never could. This told against him in his new appointment as the head of the Berlin Court Opéra. After the epoch-making première of *Der*

Freischütz, he lost his popularity, even though he retained the support of the Court, and when he tried his hand at German opera he failed. He returned to Paris but died in Italy, a notable, most worthy link between two very different ages.

We have seen Rossini's impact on the French scene, but it would be bending the truth to consider him truly part of it musically, for all that he wrote the masterpieces, *Le Comte Ory* and *Guillaume Tell* to French texts. Yet the latter was most influential in inspiring native grand opera, developing what had been begun by Spontini. This was the time when grand opera and *opéra comique* became more clearly defined, the latter being given at its own theatre, the Opéra-Comique. Grand opera had continuous music and mostly historical, heroic plots, whereas *opéra comique* had dialogue instead of recitatives. It was a much more bourgeois art, more related to 'ordinary' people than to heroes. The home of grand opera was the mighty Opéra where not a word was spoken on stage and where by now each opera had to have the obligatory ballet at the right moment. It was the lack of this dancing at the right moment which was to help in the downfall of *Tannhäuser*.

A composer who was happy in serious and comic vein was the now absurdly neglected Daniel François Esprit Auber (1782–1871), who mainly lives today through his overtures, which even turn up in Disney cartoons and often on bandstands. Yet *Fra Diavolo* (1830), later a vehicle for Laurel and Hardy, is a total delight, one of many operas he wrote with the very successful librettist, Eugene Scribe (1791–1861). Other works include *Le Cheval de Bronze* (1835) and *Le Domino Noir*, but it is one of his serious operas that has a unique place in operatic history.

This was *La Muette de Portici*, better known as *Masaniello* (1828), the first title meaning 'The Dumb Girl of Portici'. Playwrights and, more especially, their most ardent champions, like to believe that on occasion they can influence events, but scarcely any have. They may have helped to alter the climate of opinion on occasion (like John Osborne's *Look Back in Anger*) but opera, which some of them despise, has in two cases, really changed or at least stimulated events. The first, Verdi's *La Battiglia di Legnano*, has already been mentioned, but the second, Auber's opera, had a far more decisive effect. Based on historical events in Naples in 1647, when the Neapolitans rose up against the Spaniards, it was played in Brussels in 1830, two years after it was written, and it set off the Belgian Revolution against the Dutch.

The audience on August 25, 1830, were so inspired by a story in which the people and their hopes and fears were treated heroically in opera for the first time, that they ran into the street, fired the populace with their enthusiasm, and directly set off the events that were to lead to independence. As it happens, the music of the opera, unlike Verdi's, ranks as the composer's supreme achievement. The work rapidly conquered Europe and Richard Wagner was among its admirers.

There were three other French composers of the day who are remembered still. Adrien Boïeldieu (1775–1834) is best known for the overture to his *Le Calife de Bagdad* (1800) and *La Dame Blanche* (1825), a very fine *opéra comique*; Ferdinand Hérold (1791–1833) for his *Zampa* (1831), again best known for its overture; and Fromental Halévy, a French Jewish composer whose masterpiece was *La Juive* (1835), which was one of Caruso's operas. It is interesting to note here that Caruso's career ended while he was singing Eleazar on Christmas Eve, not, as the film *The Great Caruso* had it, Lionel in *Martha*. Halévy's brother was the dramatist Leon Halévy, whose son was Ludovic, the co-author, with Meilhac, of *Carmen* and several Offenbach operetta masterpieces.

Better known than any of them, though still waiting to be fully rediscovered, is Giacomo Meyerbeer (1791–1864), a German of Jewish parentage. If others paved the way for French grand opera, it was this rich, much-envied and hated man who finally made it into a famous art form. He has taken much abuse down the years from those who have never seen one of his works staged, works that in his own day were given by stars of the first magnitude, which they need to make their true effect. His art was on the shallow side, but it was impres-

sive by any reckoning. It is no credit to Wagner that he abused
Meyerbeer in print, for the older man helped him – and others
– by persuading Berlin to produce both *Rienzi* and *The Flying
Dutchman*. Why should his reputation as a musician be further
compromised by the fact that he softened up the critics with
'gifts'?

Meyerbeer had begun his operatic career in Venice, where
he wrote operas in the Italian style; then he gravitated to Paris,
very much his spiritual home. He collaborated with Scribe, a
wise choice, and he had the sense to learn all he could about his
adopted country and its culture. With Scribe he wrote *Robert
le Diable* (1831), which had a triumph at the Opéra. The
Berlin-trained composer exploited his German methods, provided Italianate melodies and displayed his newly acquired
French sense of identity, also doing his best to surpass everything that had gone before in grandeur. There were big crowd-
scenes, bigger scenic effects, and mighty ensembles, as well as
an instantly famous 'resurrection of the nuns', a striking ballet
featuring the ghosts of nuns who had taken to sex before they
died. The whole was a veritable Barnum and Bailey, Cecil B de
Mille opera, but an even bigger and better work was on its way.

This was *Les Huguenots* (1836), with Scribe providing a
striking text woven around the Massacre of St Bartholomew.
Given a stellar cast of vocal champions, and vast sums of
money, the opera is a vastly impressive affair, and was much
admired by the critic Hanslick who stated that anyone who
could not appreciate the dramatic power of the work must lack
certain elements of the critical faculty. Even Wagner managed
to praise parts of it, but Schumann, such a poor judge of
schools of opera with which he had no sympathy or, indeed,
understanding, savaged it like some knightly warrior in a holy
war, the while praising Mendelssohn's blameless oratorio, *St
Paul*. The opera needs at least six stars, preferably seven, hence
the legendary *les nuits de sept étoiles* at the Metropolitan, which
included Melba, Jean and Édouard de Rezske, Nordica,
Plançon, Maurel and – less well known to operatic history
buffs today – the wide-ranging mezzo, Sofia Scalchi. This

amazing line-up performed on December 26, 1894, a night when prices were first raised to $7!

In 1842, Meyerbeer became musical director to the King of Prussia and two years later wrote *Ein Feldlager* for Jenny Lind, then at the start of her meteoric rise to immortality. *L'Étoile du Nord* (1854) was staged in Paris, as was *Le Pardon de Ploermel*, better remembered as *Dinorah* (1859) of 'Shadow Song' fame. These were basically French *opéras comiques*, but *L'Africaine*, produced posthumously in 1865, was a return to his grand manner, indeed it originally ran for more than six hours. It is considered his masterpiece, though today only one aria from it is well known, the radiantly beautiful 'O Paradis,' better known by its Italian title, *O Paradiso*. Though La Scala gave *Les Huguenots* in the 1960s with an impressive cast, inflation must surely have finally put paid to any present-day chance of a real attempt to start a Meyerbeer revival, although he needs no more outlay of money than Wagner and Verdi at his grandest.

The Outsider

By the time that Meyerbeer died, Hector Berlioz (1803–69) had not long to live. Opinions are divided as to whether he was the greatest operatic genius his nation can claim or a flawed master, and the individual opera-goer must make up his own mind. The choice of the word opera-goer is significant, for at least nowadays it is possible to hear his works in the opera house from time to time, most notably *Les Troyens*. That he remains controversial to a degree is extraordinary to his champions (among whom, it is only fair to state, is the author of this book).

His frustrating operatic career – tragic would be an even more apt description – began in the 1830s. As we have just seen, Meyerbeer's star was in the ascendant and Auber was in his prime. In 1836, Charles Adolphe Adam (1803–56), best remembered for his *Giselle* music, produced the delightful comic opera, *Le Postillon de Longjumeau*. And into this world of entertainment came a composer who refused to conform to the tidy pattern of Parisian opera and was rejected as firmly as his contemporary Meyerbeer was welcomed and adored, though he was to win some recognition ouside the opera house.

Berlioz's first opera, *Benvenuto Cellini* (1838) had originally been aimed at the Opéra-Comique, but finally appeared at the Opéra, the only one of his operas to be staged complete in his lifetime. This exuberant, youthful work, based on the historical Cellini, and centred round the casting of the statue of Perseus for the Pope, is full of melody, fire, high spirits, drama and enchantment, though its plot is not always an ideal blend of comedy, seriousness and the heroic. Yet Berlioz and his librettists, de Wailly and Barbier, created a unique world in which the most famous scene is the Roman Carnival. Characterisation is at least adequate and musical riches abound, though despite Covent Garden's advocacy in the 1960s and 1970s, performances have been few.

The first performance was a failure, partly because this was a work that had originated as an *opéra comique* and did not conform to the pattern of the day at the Opéra, which was for well-constructed librettos by Eugene Scribe and others. There was also much personal hostility to Berlioz, whose career was already a controversial one. Yet intellectuals admired the opera, along with a significant minority of the audiences at the three performances that took place. The final one was acclaimed by a full house. But the great tenor Duprez left the cast and, despite very encouraging signs of real appreciation in some papers – 'Berlioz opens out to us a new continent . . . *Benvenuto* is a masterpiece' – the opera vanished. It received one further performance in 1839 and was not seen again in Paris until 1913. Liszt gave it at Weimar in 1852 and Covent Garden in 1853 – in a single performance in front of Queen Victoria. It was a disgraceful fiasco, for the opera, with Berlioz in the pit, was deliberately wrecked by 'a gang of Italians', so the composer wrote, who 'virtually drove *Benvenuto Cellini* from the Covent Garden stage by hissing, booing and shouting from beginning to end.'

Yet it was the cutting, emending and diluting during the

first Parisian rehearsals that had so upset Berlioz, and which did such an injustice to his conception. For many years all that was known of the opera were the two brilliant overtures, *Benvenuto Cellini* and *Le Carnival Romain*.

Next came a 'dramatic legend' in four parts for the concert stage: *Le Damnation de Faust* (1846), which was first staged in 1893 at Monte Carlo with Jean de Reszke as Faust. Whatever purists may say, the work, if properly, that is, very imaginatively, staged, makes a superb opera, but it was not written as such. As a result we have the pathetic spectacle of one of the most dramatic composers produced by France or anywhere else, forced to cut himself off from the art form that best suited him. *Roméo et Juliette* is even further from the opera house in its structure, yet it contains some of the most ravishing and exhilarating music Berlioz ever wrote and love-music that is both worthy of the play and uniquely Berliozian in melody and atmosphere. Meanwhile, the French contented themselves with talent, not genius.

It was hardly surprising therefore that *Les Troyens* (composed 1856-8), his most ambitious and, for many, his greatest work, was to result in heartbreak for Berlioz. He had vain hopes that Napoleon III might prove its salvation, but the Emperor was no Ludwig of Bavaria.

Les Troyens, like its composer, remains controversial, but less so than it was because it is now reasonably well known and has been recorded. The reader should be warned that although the present author considers it a total masterpiece, many consider it a flawed one. It is long, but so are some of Meyerbeer's operas and many of Wagner's. A mutilated version of Part 2, *Les Troyens à Carthage*, was given at the Théatre-Lyrique in 1863, but not until 1890 was the whole work, including Part 1, *La Prise de Troie* (The Capture of Troy), given over two nights at Karlsruhe.

The great breakthrough came in 1957 when it was performed, not quite complete, but over one now legendary evening at Covent Garden, with Rafael Kubelik as conductor, Sir John Gielgud as director, and with Jon Vickers as the most ardent Aeneas, vocally and dramatically, that anyone could wish for. Paris meanwhile had occasionally staged heavily cut versions, and a Glasgow performance in 1935 under Eric Chisholm had led Sir Donald Tovey to propound unerringly that the work was 'one of the most gigantic and convincing masterpieces of music-drama', a bold statement then, which would be disputed by some even now.

Since those days it has been heard in Italy, New York, Boston under the redoubtable Sarah Caldwell, and elsewhere, but the crucial performances have been again in Britain. For in 1969, the centenary of Berlioz's death, first Scottish Opera (conductor, Alexander Gibson, with Janet Baker a majestic, tragic and radiant Dido) gave the entire opera for the first time, then Covent Garden too, under the leading Berliozian of the day, Colin Davis. This last was the first complete performance in French.

The structure of the work has been criticised. Berlioz had first had the idea of an epic Virgilian opera around 1851, but he had been passionately devoted to the *Aeneid* since his childhood. Berlioz provided his own libretto and it is hard for those who admire the work to understand the criticism levelled at it. Perhaps the listener who thrills to the very word 'Troy' gains an extra dimension, but the story line is good and full of theatrical moments. Hector Berlioz thought big and could construct dramatic effects even without music. He could also create characters, major and minor. In the latter category is Hylas, a young Trojan sailor, whose song in which he yearns for home has the seashore of the Mediterranean stealing through its accompaniment, while in Part 1 a mute Andromache, Hector's widow, and her son, make a brief, anguished entrance to music that takes the mind and heart back to Gluck's 'Dance of the Blessed Spirits'.

For Part 1 of this monumental opera, warm and passionate as it is, is of Gluckian nobility and spirit, classical, grand and profound. The most striking character in it is Cassandra, who knows what is to befall Troy and her lover, Choroebus. There are great set scenes and choruses, and the Trojan Horse makes its obligatory appearance. The very last scene of The Fall of Troy is perhaps the only dangerous moment, when the women of Troy, like the Jewish heroes of Masada, decide to commit mass-suicide rather than become slaves of the Greeks; but the danger here is one of performance and production, and the scene is a flaw in the conception of the composer-librettist.

In Part 2 the atmosphere is instantly revealed in the music as warm, romantic and potentially passionate, a passion that rises to the ecstasy of a love-duet between Dido and Aeneas which even Berlioz never equalled elsewhere. This duet is in Act 4 of the opera as a whole, the second act of Part 2, and it ends ominously with Mercury intoning 'Italy'. For Berlioz never lets us forget his Virgilian theme. In the next act, Aeneas at his most urgent and heroic summons his men to sea leaving us to the abandoned Dido and her cries first for vengeance, then of farewell to her beloved city. The boy Berlioz wept at Dido's fate and her noble, tragic suicide; the man invested the scene with majesty and pathos. She foresees the coming of Hannibal who will avenge Carthage, but she also sees the glory of Rome. The Trojan March may blaze out defiance, proof of the wars to come, but she has lost her love and her city's future to Rome.

After this greatest of French operas had been written, Berlioz turned to Shakespeare's *Much Ado about Nothing* as a rest, so he said. The result was *Béatrice et Bénédict*, which was produced at Baden-Baden in 1862 and – by Liszt – at Weimar the following year. Indeed, his German successes made him vainly believe that his *Trojans* had an immediate future, but not, he prayed at the inadequate Théatre-Lyrique where it would suffer 'a fresh assassination'.

Berlioz cut the whole of the Don John plot against Hero and Claudio from *Béatrice et Bénédict*, while introducing a non-Shakespearean character, Somarona, an orchestral conductor. Berlioz loved Shakespeare with an unending passion and musically his opera has many pages worthy of the original. Act 1 ends with a Nocturne, a duet between Hero and Ursula, a 'marvel of indescribable lyrical beauty', in W. J. Turner's and many others' opinion. (On the whole it is best for writers to eschew the word 'indescribable', but the peculiar quality and fragrance of Berlioz's romantic music is, indeed, particularly hard to describe.) Again, a trio for Hero, Beatrice and Ursula in Act 2 is lyrically ravishing, while the opera ends with a notable duet for Béatrice and Bénédict, sparkling as no other Shakespeare-inspired operatic music does except *Falstaff*. There is a weakness in the work in that the sheer amount of spoken dialogue, which is always so difficult for the average singer to encompass, does not make it easy to perform and therefore makes *opéra comique* that much harder to put across. Consequently, concert performances of this opera often feature two pairs of hero and heroine, one pair singers and the other actors.

Melody-makers and a masterpiece

Charles Gounod (1818–93) is out of fashion in sophisticated music circles now, although the public flocks to his *Faust* (1859) when it is allowed to hear it. Once, *Faust* was the most popular opera in the world, even more adored than *Carmen* or *Trovatore*, *Aida*, *Bohème* or *Butterfly*. In Germany it is known as *Margarethe*, rightly, for it does not pretend to inhabit the same lofty world as Goethe's *Faust*, but the Germans have always loved it.

The success of *Faust* turned Gounod away from his rightful path as a delightful writer of lyrical music and a portrayer of the emotions of ordinary people and domestic virtues, although *Faust* contains such moments. But he was seduced into believing himself the master of the grand manner, and grandeur could too easily turn to the grandiose and, worse, religiose, though *that* – it must be admitted – was popular enough in Victorian times.

His first opera was *Sapho* (1851), and later works included the amusing *Le Medicin Malgré Lui* (The Doctor Despite Himself, 1858) and *Philémon et Baucis*. *Faust* came between the two and it is interesting that it was started as an *opéra comique*,

Fig. 1 Monteverdi's *The Coronation of Poppea*. Richard Lewis as Nero and Saramae Endich as Poppea, Glyndebourne, 1964. *Credit: Guy Gravett*

Fig. 2 Mozart's *The Marriage of Figaro. Left to right:* Geraint Evans as Figaro, Robert Kerns as the Count, David Lennox as Don Curzio, Covent Garden, 1972. *Credit: Donald Southern*

Fig. 3 Bellini's *I Puritani*. Joan Sutherland as Elvira and Joseph Rouleau as Sir George Walton, Covent Garden, 1964. *Credit: Donald Southern*

Fig. 4 Donizetti's *Don Pasquale*. A poster and print of the first London production. *Left to right:* Grisi as Norina, Mario as Ernesto, Lablache as Pasquale, Fornasari as Malatesta. *Credit: Illustrated London News*

Fig. 5 *Above:* Meyerbeer's *Les Huguenots* 'The Massacre of St. Bartholomew's Day'. Her Majesty's Theatre, London, 1858. *Credit: Robin May Collection*
Below: Gounod's *Faust*. First London production at Her Majesty's Theatre 1863, with Gassier as Méphistophélès and Santley as Valentine. *Credit: Robin May Collection*

Fig. 6 Berlioz's *Benvenuto Cellini*. Nicolai Gedda (sitting in profile) in the title role of the Covent Garden production, 1966. *Credit: Houston Rogers*

Fig. 7 Bizet's *Carmen. Left to right:* Teresa Cahill as Frasquita, Francis Egerton as Remendado, Shirley Verrett as Carmen, John Dobson as Dancairo, Anne Pashley as Mercédès, Covent Garden, 1973. *Credit: Reg Wilson*

Fig. 8 Verdi's *La Traviata*. Maria Callas as Violetta and Cesare Valletti as Alfredo, Covent Garden, 1958. *Credit: Houston Rogers*

Fig. 9 Mussorgsky's *Boris Godunov*. Boris Christoff as Boris and Anne Pashley as Feodor, Covent Garden, 1974. *Credit: Donald Southern*

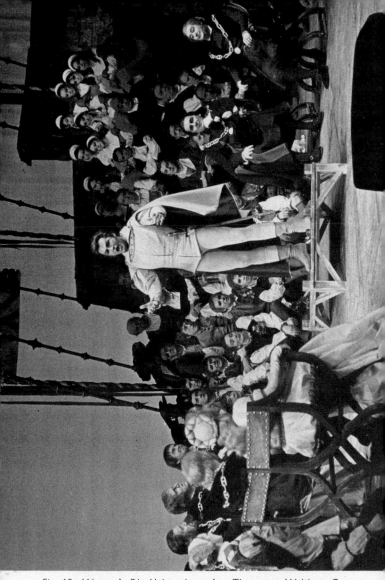

Fig. 10   Wagner's *Die Meistersinger*. Jess Thomas as Walther, Covent
Garden, 1969. *Credit: Donald Southern*

Fig. 11   Verdi's *Falstaff*. Geraint Evans as Falstaff and Robert Bowman as
Bardolph, Covent Garden, 1961. *Credit: Zoe Dominic*

Fig. 12 Puccini's *La Bohème*. *Left to right:* Wendy Fine as Musetta,
Gwynne Howell as Colline, Thomas Allen as Schaunard, Peter Glossop as
Marcello, Katia Ricciarelli as Mimi, Placido Domingo as Rodolfo, Covent
Garden, 1974. *Credit: Donald Southern*

Fig. 13   Richard Strauss's *Salome*. Josephine Barstow as Salome, English National Opera, 1975. *Credit: John Garner*

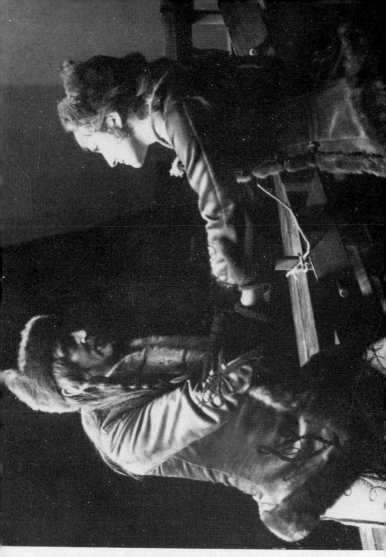

Fig. 14 Janacek's *The Cunning Little Vixen*. Robert Hoyem as the Fox and Norma Burrowes as the Vixen, Glyndebourne, 1975. *Credit: Guy Gravett*

Fig. 15 Schoenberg's *Moses and Aaron*. Covent Garden, 1965. *Credit: Houston Rogers*

Britten's *Peter Grimes*. Geraint Evans as Captain Balstrode and ...rs as Peter Grimes, Covent Garden, 1975. *Credit: Donald Southern*

but gradually turned into a lyrical opera with grand effects: the scene in which Marguerite prays in church shows a stage complete with a full organ, but it is not as fine as the beautiful and very accomplished Garden Scene. But everything conspires to make *Faust* splendid entertainment: the Soldiers' Chorus, the entire role of Méphistophélès, the dance music in 3/4 time, the Jewel Song (ditto), Faust's 'Salut! demeure chaste et pure', Valentine's Prayer, added by Gounod for Sir Charles Santley, the notable English baritone, and the no-holds-barred, emotional final scene.

Nothing Gounod later wrote matched this feast, and, oddly, nothing in the entire work is as near the world of Goethe as the opening bars of the introduction before 'Even bravest Heart' is heard in orchestral form. The entire proceedings are musical melodrama of the most entertaining and skilled class.

La Reine de Saba (1862) has not stood the test of time, but *Roméo et Juliette* (1867), though never as successful as *Faust*, was regularly given for many years, and remained in the repertoire of French opera houses until recently, occasionally being given elsewhere, especially in America. Indeed, the only productions listed in *Opera* magazine's 1975 index were in Miami, Philadelphia and at the Metropolitan, New York.

In 1876, Gounod began concentrating on religious compositions, and his later operas are as forgotten as Sir Arthur Sullivan's serious works. The last opera in which he demonstrated his old charm was *Mireille* (1864), which could be heard in Paris fairly regularly until the 1960s and, occasionally, elsewhere. (The closure of the Opéra Comique in Paris did not help French opera, which has been steadily declining for half a century now, with the exception of a handful of works. In 1976, happily, it reopened.)

Until the early 1960s, visitors to Paris could hope to catch *Mignon* (1866) by Ambroise Thomas (1811–96). This sentimental piece, after Goethe's novel, *Wilhelm Meisters Lehrjahre* (Wilhelm Meister's Apprenticeship) is an enjoyable affair with several notable moments, particularly the coloratura showstopper 'Je suis Titania'. A school of wholesome, appealing bourgeois opera was now in full flow, but the first Mignon, the legendary Galli-Marié, was soon to find herself involved in an opera that was a little too daring for the staid middle-classes who patronised the Opéra-Comique, where *Mignon* had had its première. The opera was *Carmen*.

Georges Bizet (1838–75) did not begin his career as if about to produce a masterpiece, and, tragically, he died young. To judge by Berlioz's experiences in the squabbling, corrupt, and all too often second-rate world that was musical Paris in the mid-nineteenth century, Bizet might easily have been defeated by the atmosphere in a similar way. Yet he was not such an outsider as Berlioz, and, besides, the Parisian scene gradually improved a little. And with the triumph of *Carmen* outside Paris after his death, the world would have been open to him. His was surely the most disastrous death in operatic history.

Most of his operas written before *Carmen* had poor to bad texts, though all are lit by his gift for melody, orchestral colour, and musical delight. *Docteur Miracle* (composed 1856 or 1857) is a promising one-act operetta, and was followed by *Don Procopio* (composed 1858–9). Both show the influence of Donizetti and Rossini, but both, like the youthful Symphony in C, have moments of originality. Parts of *Ivan IV* composed 1862–3), a forgotten work, were to be used in later compositions. Then came *Les Pêcheurs des Perles* (The Pearl Fishers, 1863).

This is the only one of Bizet's operas apart from *Carmen* that can be seen fairly regularly in the theatre today. The librettists Cormon and Carré set it in ancient Ceylon and provided not the most probable of tales; but the opera is most enjoyable, and there are two inspired passages, the tenor's 'Je crois entendre' (I hear as in a dream) and the tenor-baritone duet, 'Au fond du temple saint' (In the depths of the temple), which is quite simply one of the most glorious, melodious and totally satisfying duets in opera. Perhaps its 'friendship' theme is brought back a shade too often, without the variety which enabled Verdi to make each reprise of his own 'friendship' theme in *Don Carlos* a new-minted experience.

There followed a notably finer opera, *La Jolie Fille de Perth* (1867), occasionally given as a whole, while its beguiling Serenade is often heard, *La Coupe du Roi de Thule* (The Fall of the King of Thule, 1868), only some of which survives, and – amongst others – *Djamileh* (1872). Many of these operas show some signs of future glory, but none match the splendour of Bizet's incidental music to Daudet's *L'Arlésienne* which, if we did not possess *Carmen*, would be his masterpiece.

Carmen (1875), with at long last an excellent libretto (by Henri Meilhac and Ludovic Halévy), is generally regarded as a perfect opera. It is the apotheosis of the *opéra comique*, though, ironically, the fact that it has spoken dialogue is often a handicap in performance because, as has been mentioned earlier, so many singers cannot speak lines convincingly. This is not Bizet's fault, and the recitatives by Guiraud added for the production in Vienna six months after the Parisian première, are artistically wrong even if they solve the problem. (At Covent Garden, where villainous French is often heard now, there was even a time when English versions of this and other operas included American, Canadian, Welsh, Scottish accents, and every shade of English accent, plus occasional European variants. The Sadler's Wells/English National Opera's 'sound' has been better, at least to tolerant opera-lovers.)

Carmen's perfection is the result of the following assets: a wealth of instantly enjoyable tunes which never seem to stale, except by the sort of over-hearing that can dull the effect of any melody; a most moving and genuinely dramatic story, constructed by composer and librettist with the utmost flair; a diamond-sharp score which is brilliantly orchestrated, powerful, passionate and humorous, and at times suitably 'local' in colour, a colour which, whatever Spaniards say, is stunningly effective in the theatre; and, as important as the rest, the opera is brilliantly characterised.

It is all the more startling to those who know little of the Parisian operatic scene that an opera so endowed with everything needed to make it popular could have failed so lamentably at its first performance, but that is what happened. The omens were unfavourable from the start. Adolphe de Leuven, co-director of the Opéra-Comique, started to get cold feet about the subject matter soon after Bizet began composing, for the theatre was essentially a 'family' one. No opera had ever ended with a violent death on stage, the death that overtakes Carmen, and, to make matters worse for the gently nurtured, so respectable patrons, the heroine's friends were not quite the sort of people one would invite to one's house. De Leuven sold his share in the theatre to his fellow-director, Camille du Locle.

Now a financial crisis hit the theatre, which was also suffering casting problems, for Marie Roze, chosen for the title-role, turned it down because it was too 'scabrous'. Fortunately, Celestine Galli-Marié, though she found the role less than moral, was a true artist and accepted it. At rehearsals Bizet tried without success as noted earlier, to turn the ladies of the Opéra-Comique's chorus into convincing cigarette girls, and the shortage of cash led to the first night being postponed. It finally took place in front of an audience that included Offenbach, Thomas, Gounod, Massenet, Vincent d'Indy. Dumas the younger, Daudet and Delibes on March 3, 1875.

The night was not the disaster that legend has made it. It was in no way comparable to the fiascos of the first *Barber* and *Butterfly*. The first act was excellently received, after which the audience grew colder, until the last act received next to no applause, the main reason being that most of the audience had left. The critics proceeded to disgrace their calling, lambasting both music and text as undramatic, unmusical, un-French and un-Spanish, and also as Wagnerian.

This last was particularly ironic in view of Friedrich Nietzsche's attitude to it, for he considered it a healthy antidote to Wagner's exaggerations. Indeed, Nietzsche noted the thrilling moment in the overture when the strikingly sombre theme breaks out over a string tremolo suggesting Don José's fatal obsession with Carmen. It has been dubbed 'an epigram of passion' and gave the philosopher a fine chance to contrast its concision with the vast, slow apparatus of the *leitmotiv*. Of course, both are perfect in their way, but there is nobody more vindictive than a lapsed disciple, which Nietzsche was.

Carmen was kept in the repertoire until the winter and was given 46 performances, not a bad score for a failure. But audiences steadily dwindled, and in June Bizet had died, not knowing that his opera was soon to be the rage of Europe and America from its triumph in Vienna onwards. His cast, particularly Galli-Marie, had not betrayed him, for Pierre Berton, who saw the second performance spoke of them as equal to their tasks and admirable. And it was Berton who was to describe the moment when the opera finally returned to Paris in 1883 as a 'brilliant reparation'.

Such, in short, is the story of Bizet and his masterpiece, which has been filling theatres ever since, despite the rarity of a perfect performance and the shortage of actress-singers with true Carmen allure and vocal quality. It is totally unsinkable, ultimately because of its melodies and story, surviving brilliantly a transformation on stage and screen into *Carmen Jones*, and also the worst that bad companies can do with it. That Bizet died disconsolate, is not only one of the most wretched stories in the history of opera, but a reminder that, as with Berlioz, the French preferred talent to genius.

Camille Saint-Saëns (1835–1921) showed undoubted operatic talent in the only one of his twelve operas to have staying power. This was *Samson et Dalila* (1877), once considered Wagnerian, which led to a first performance at Weimar and not in Paris. Damned by some as a near-oratorio, and certainly a stately rather than an impassioned affair, it invariably entertains an audience if done well, and its two protagonists are well-drawn. There is more to Dalila's part than 'Mon coeur s'ouvre à ta voix', the ever-popular 'Softly awakes my heart'. Indeed some would claim that her earlier aria, 'Printemps qui commence' is even more bewitching, while Samson's scene in which, blind and in chains, he turns the mill in Gaza, is stirring and effective. If the subject was not the ideal choice for the composer, he still turned it into a genuine opera of the second rank. That

Samsons have included Tamagno and Caruso is a sure sign that it is a singers' opera.

Jules Massenet (1842–1912) lives more securely in the international repertoire than Saint-Saëns, yet, considering his melodic charm, considerable craftsmanship and sensibility, his operas are unjustly neglected. For more than a decade he has seemed to some one of the composers most in need of a reappraisal, or certainly more of a hearing. But despite recordings of rare works and the championship of Joan Sutherland and Richard Bonynge, this has not yet happened. His was not the most robust of talents, however, and poor performances can damage his operas more than, say, Puccini's, which are seaworthy enough to survive everything but total artistic shipwreck.

Massenet's first success was *Le Roi de Lahore* (1877), and in all he wrote 27 operas. If only *Manon* (1884) can be said to be (fairly) firmly in the repertoire – as befits a minor masterpiece – *Hérodiade* (1881), *Werther* (1892), *Thais* (1894), *Le Jongleur de Notre-Dame* (Our Lady's Juggler, 1902) and *Don Quichotte* (1910) are reasonably well known outside France. His works were especially popular in the 1920s in Chicago, where Mary Garden, the Aberdonian who created Debussy's Mélisande, championed him, not least because his roles suited her so well. Vincent d'Indy commented devastatingly on Massenet's 'discreet and semi-religious eroticism', which made him a favourite of Parisians in a way that a Berlioz or a Bizet could never be in their own day. Indeed he was once dubbed 'the daughter of Gounod'. Yet if his melodies are exquisite and sometimes effeminate, they have always appealed to singers and many are sheer delight.

Manon shows his gift for 'scented, voluptuous melody' (Stephen Williams) at its best, and perhaps nothing illustrates this better than the magical moment in the Cour-la-Reine scene when Manon, now the *belle* of fashionable Paris, sings two songs, the second being the rightly famous Gavotte, as sensuously exquisite as it is lighthearted and haunting. And Massenet could rise to passion, as in Des Grieux's 'Ah! fuyez, douce image' (Ah! depart, fair image), as he desperately implores the image of his beloved to leave him so that he can give imself to God.

Comparisons between *Manon* and Puccini's *Manon Lescaut* are interesting rather than conclusive. Puccini's youthful opera is an unrestrained melodic feast with one great dramatic scene on the quay at Le Havre and as his heroine goes to America with her lover, while Massenet's expires before reaching the port. Massenet's opera is more perfect a work of art, but Puccinians find it less compelling than *Manon Lescaut*. Some, with the authority of Constant Lambert, may be heard shouting: 'The wrong *Manon*' when Massenet's is performed, but it is possible to love both.

The operas Massenet wrote in this century are forgotten except for the two mentioned above. It was as if he had become the slave of his own mannerisms, yet gradually more and more of his music is being heard and proves delightful if not 'important', like his Cinderella opera, *Cendrillon* (1899). *La Navarraise* (1894) has been shown to have fine music in it, as records reveal, while those who have enjoyed *Werther* are amazed at the rarity of performances. The heroine Charlotte, something of a priggish cipher in the first two acts, has a letter scene in the third which almost rivals Tatiana's in *Eugene Onegin*. And anyone listening to Maria Callas on disc singing 'Pleurez, mes yeux' from *Le Cid* (1885) may well wonder what other treasures lurk in Massenet after this remarkable display of power.

Meanwhile, before ending this account of nineteenth-century opera – and Massenet is essentially of that century even if he lingered on into our own – mention must be made of two other composers of opera and one of operetta. Operetta is not strictly the subject of this book, but Offenbach was a greater composer than most of his more serious contemporaries in France.

The first of the two operatic composers was Léo Delibes (1836–91), best remembered for his ballet music and for the Bell Song from *Lakmé*, a charming work and a linear descendant of *The Pearl Fishers* in setting, though in this case we have moved north to British India. The Bell Song, which has attracted so many famous coloratura sopranos, including the oversized Tetrazzini and the *petite* Pons, deserves its fame, and another delight is the hero Gerald's aria 'Fantaisie aux divins mensonges' (Fantasy to divine lies). The closure of the Opéra-Comique as a public opera house virtually banished *Lakmé* from the world's stages, though Wexford happily revived it in 1970.

Less well known is Édouard Lalo's *Le Roi d'Ys* (1888), best known for the tenor's famous 'Aubade' but with a striking aria for the heroine, 'Lorsque je t'ai vu soudain'.

The reader may be surprised to find how few of the operas in this chapter are to be heard, even though reasons have been given. Small-scale festivals might so easily allow some of them to be staged in preference to very minor Italian works. Massenet at least treated his singers with consummate skill even though he wanted parts to be cast perfectly, both physically and vocally. His *Manon* appears to need a soprano able to do justice to its remarkable vocal lines, but, as Philip Hope-Wallace noted in his *A Picture History of Opera*, it is 'in fact well within the reach of quite a slender talent', although the Manon 'seemingly makes a great effect of soaring to heights of passion and vocal grandeur.'

The Wexford Festival has been the chief patron of nineteenth century French opera abroad, having given, since 1961, *Mireille*, *Don Quichotte*, *Fra Diavolo*, *La Jollie Fille de Perth*, *Lakmé* and *Les Pêcheurs de Perles*. As, notoriously, this is the most intoxicating of all festivals (no pun intended), there is a lesson to be drawn that a great reservoir of pleasure is waiting to be tapped. But for total pleasure of an even higher class than most of the composers listed above, Berlioz and Bizet always excepted, we must turn to operetta.

The Mozart of the Champs-Élysées'

Fortunately there is no room in this book to cover operetta adequately, 'fortunately' because the word is so blurred that discussion of the genre can be carried forward to *My Fair Lady* and *A Little Night Music*, thus straying too far from the subject. For operetta/operette is a wide-ranging word to describe a play containing overture, songs, dances and interludes. This definition could also describe some comic operas, musical comedy and that most useful of terms, the musical.

The phrase 'classical operetta' is helpful in the sense that classical can mean 'first class', which the best operettas of Jacques Offenbach (1819–80) most certainly are. Some claim his one opera, *Les Contes d'Hoffmann* (The Tales of Hoffman, 1881) as his masterpiece, others hold that a handful of his lighter masterpieces, which strive less, achieve more. Comparisons are odorous, as Dogberry said, but it is hard not to compare Offenbach and Johann Strauss, the Strauss of *Die Fledermaus*. Yet it is a useless exercise, for both were masters and the choice is a matter of taste.

Offenbach was born Jakob Eberst in Cologne, going to Paris as a youth. He became a noted 'cellist and a conductor, then the manager of the Théatre des Champs-Élysées in 1855. Here he had his first successes, but it was in the tiny Théatre Comte, whose name he changed to Les Bouffes-Parisiens, that he became immortal.

Orphée aux Enfers (Orpheus in the Underworld, 1858), arguably his masterpiece, marks the birth of operetta, though the social satire and operatic parody had an ancestor, as has been noted, in *The Beggar's Opera*, and though, clearly, the work has its links with *opéra comique*. Today we can appreciate Offenbach's music as much as its first hearers, but much of his mockery is lost, for his devastating satires on the Second Empire, its personalities and its frenzied pursuit of pleasure, were totally topical. We can enjoy his characters, but not identify them unless we are Second Empire experts. And how can we recapture the flavour of the first night of *La Grande Duchesse de Gérolstein* (1867) when Bismarck sat in the audience watching a parody of himself on stage – and knowing that one day he would topple the whole pack of cards of the Emperor Napoleon III's pleasure-mad capital?

The other supreme operettas are *La Belle Hélène* (1864), *La*

Vie Parisienne (1866) and *La Périchole* (1868). It was Rossini who called Offenbach 'The Mozart of the Champs-Élysées', a marvellous tribute from a master who judged his words with care. His music is successively exhilarating, tender, happy, cynical, sexy and funny, while his orchestration deserves always to be played by a full orchestra conducted by a sympathetic interpreter. Yet the man whose *Can-Can* is known to millions who have never seen any of his works cannot be sunk by even the most unlikely of combinations, so good are his best tunes. If his high spirits are unequalled in operetta, so are his finest sweetly sensual melodies, like the Hymn to Bacchus from *Orphée* and the Letter Song from *La Périchole*.

It is hardly surprising that the arbiter of musical fashion of the Second Empire suffered something of an eclipse after its fall. He wrote some 90 operettas, and the success of revivals of *Robinson Crusoe* suggests that many of them deserve inspection. It is hard to believe that there is another *Orphée* waiting to be resurrected, complete with 'honeyed melodies and irresistible rhythms' (Gerhart von Westermann), but the musical riches must be there.

Wagner with reason attacked him after Offenbach wrote a sketch about the fiasco of *Tannhauser* in 1861, a sketch in which Mozart, Gluck, Weber and Grétry attack the unfortunate composer, who demands that they listen to his *Symphony of the Future* (supplied, of course, by Offenbach himself). But Wagner later understood Offenbach's genius as well as Rossini had, saying: 'Il savait faire comme le divin Mozart', which may be translated as 'he had the know-how of the divine Mozart'. With such tributes from two masters, it is hardly daring to claim the works of this naturalised German Jew, the outrageous joker cousin of Berlioz and Bizet, as one of the three pinnacles of nineteenth-century French lyric art.

And *Les Contes d'Hoffmann* (The Tales of Hoffmann)? The only opera of Offenbach that remains hugely popular – he tried several times to write a success, but failed – was produced on February 10, 1881, but the composer had died the previous October. 'Make haste to mount my piece', he had implored

Carvalho of the Opéra Comique, 'I am in a hurry and have only one desire in the world – to see the première of this work'. It was a cruel jest of the gods to play on a master joker.

The opera is a giant box of tricks and romantic extravaganza combined, and regularly fills the house even when – as often happens – it is inadequately done. The libretto by Barbier and Carré is taken from stories by E. T. A. Hoffmann (1776–1822) himself an opera composer of some ten romantic pieces, as well as a popular novelist. In its peculiar blend of the fantastic and realistic, it has no counterpart in operatic history, as Arthur Jacobs and Stanley Sadie have pointed out in their *Opera Guide*. They are among those who hail it as an outright masterpiece, but for some it fails to move, and is not quite so rich in melody as some of Offenbach's lighter works.

Yet is is magnificent entertainment and the score is nicely varied, from being dazzling in the Olympia act to emotional in the Antonia episode and, finally, magical and languorous in the Giulietta episode in Venice. Offenbach wanted the acts played in this order, but more often than not the Antonia scene ends the opera. The opera begins with a prologue in which Hoffmann sings the legend of the dwarf Kleinzach, surely not one of his better inventions. Much better are the processional march in the Olympia scene, Olympia's delectable coloratura aria (in which she has to be wound up – being a doll), most of the music in the Antonia scene, and, in its right setting, the over-familiar Barcarolle in the Venetian act.

As Offenbach died before completing *The Tales of Hoffmann*, Ernest Guiraud, who had added recitatives to *Carmen*, orchestrated the opera and also added recitatives, which Offenbach had not wanted. Today his wishes are often followed. The four villainous roles – Lindorf, Coppelius, Dr Miracle and Dapertutto – are sung by the same baritone, but the heroines, all of them reincarnations of Hoffmann's loves, are normally sung by three different singers.

Offenbach easily transcended national boundaries in his own day, though in Britain at least he was neglected in modern times – *Hoffmann* always excepted – until the Sadler's Wells productions of several of his masterpieces in the 1960s startled delighted music-lovers into realising what they had been missing for so long. Austere critics rail against the un-French nature of the productions – which began with Wendy Toye's fizzingly inventive *Orpheus in the Underworld* in 1960 – but the enormous audiences delight in the modern gags, which would surely not have worried such a man of the theatre as Offenbach, and revel in some of the most entrancing music ever written for the stage.

6

Operatic Advances

Nationalism

In opera, the word 'nationalism' is even more suspect than 'Romanticism'. This is because opera-goers, like concert-goers, detect nationalist sounds because they are led to expect them, a notorious concert-hall example being the famous slow-movement melody of Dvořák's New World Symphony, which has nothing to do with America but is a Czech tune expressing the composer's homesickness. Yet it is totally established as an 'American' melody, even more completely, according to Ralph Hill in *The Symphony*, thanks to 'some wrong-headed person who arranged it as a Negro-spiritual to the words *Goin' Home*'. Of course, there are some turns of musical phrase and dance-rhythms that act as fingerprints and proclaim Spain, Poland, or wherever, but these are secondary features of a score, even in *Carmen* where Bizet so deliberately and superbly added 'Spanish' colour to the delight of everyone except actual Spanish purists. 'Ah!' sighs the music-lover hearing an arrangement of an English folk tune by Vaughan Williams. 'How English it sounds!' But would a well-travelled deaf person, suddenly restored to hearing recognise it as representing the England he knows?

Even dances that proclaim their nationality do not necessarily do so. The Polonaise is a Polish dance. Do we listen to the splendid Polonaise from *Eugene Onegin* and detect that it is Russian, not Polish? And which is more Spanish, Verdi's very Italian score for *Don Carlos* or his 'Spanish' Veil Song in the opera? What matters, of course, is that the Italian-born Verdi, using a condensed version of a German play, and his sublime imagination and skill, recreated Philip II's Spain.

This does not mean that each nation does not have at certain periods its own distinct 'sound', whether Russian, Italian, or French, etc. This was very much in evidence in the late nineteenth century, but again it can be exaggerated. So when nationalist composers are discussed in the following pages, it should be understood that they were essentially musical patriots, like the Russians who deliberately founded their own school and attacked Western influences like Verdi. And Verdi, of course, was a supreme nationalist, musically and patriotically, not least because even in his final masterpieces the voice never lost its supremacy, for all the marvels of the late Verdian orchestra.

The Russian nationalists who staged a hostile demonstration against *La Forza del Destino* just after its première in St Petersburg in 1862 may appear to have chosen a strange target, for no composer more truly reflected his countrymen's longing for an end to foreign domination than Verdi. But the demonstration in this case was against the musical domination of Russia by foreigners in general and Italy in particular; and the fact that Verdi had been paid 22 000 roubles for his work against the going rate for a Russian of 500 roubles, hardly lowered the temperature of the demonstrators.

This fierce nationalism was to result in the most conspicuous of all the nationalist schools of the nineteenth century. Italian opera had reached Russia in the 1730s and its dominance was almost total. Several eminent composers made the long journey from Italy to work there, including Galuppi, Paisiello and Cimarosa, and many of the finest singers appeared at the Imperial Opera in St Petersburg. In 1764, French *opéra comique* reached Russia and by the turn of the century – with French the language of the aristocracy – it, too, had gained a hold, though the events of 1812 changed things. And meanwhile, Russian composers had produced operas in the Italian manner beginning with Berezovsky's *Demofoonte* (1773), the first opera written by a Russian. Catherine the Great was soon providing propaganda librettos for her composers, one aimed at Gustavus III of Sweden, while German fairy-tale opera set off local composers along that cosy path. Then *Der Freischütz* reached Russia, to indicate just how nationalist flavour could be achieved, while *opéra comique* had set local composers working on a form of Russian *Singspiel* using sentimentalised folk songs sung by equally sentimentalised peasantry.

None of this had fathered a school of Russian opera, but at least the ground had been prepared for the right man to start one. The man was Mikhail Glinka (1804–57).

He had a now forgotten trailblazer in Alexis Vertovsky (1799–1862), whose admiration for *Freischütz* led him to use Russian folklore as the basis for his operas, but though his *Askold's Tomb* (1835) and other works were popular, they do not make him a rival for Glinka's position as the father of Russian opera. Martin Cooper has called *Askold's Tomb* an 'ill-assorted romantic hotch-potch'.

Glinka was not a conscious reformer in the sense that he set out to write 'reform' operas, but he wanted, patriotically, to write genuinely Russian operas. His first was *A Life for the Tsar* (1836), now known as *Ivan Susanin*. The choral music is the finest and most Russian feature of a score that is often, as in the lovers' music, Donizettian, while the second act, set in the Polish headquarters – the story is set in 1613 with a war raging between Russia and Poland – contains Polish national tunes. A Frenchman proclaimed that the work was more than an opera, that it was a national epic, and its success was colossal. Glinka followed it with *Russlan and Ludmilla* (1842), which is even more Russian, a colourful fairy-tale opera which showed that Glinka still had not achieved a truly personal style, but which proclaimed that, like the early work, a truly Russian school of opera had been founded.

Glinka's immediate successor was Alexander Dargomizhsky (1813–69), who used the legend of the water nymph in his *Russalka* (1856), a legend also used by Dvořák. This was very popular and he also wrote *The Stone Guest*, produced in 1872, its orchestration completed by Rimsky-Korsakov. It has the same story as *Don Giovanni* and is historically important, despite the composer's lack of major talent, because in it he tried to create an opera based on the inflections of the Russian tongue.

But more important are 'The Five' – 'The Mighty Handful' who inherited Glinka's legacy: Balakirev, Cui, Borodin, Rimsky-Korsakov, and, greatest by far, Mussorgsky. These five were the leaders in the fight to purge Russian music of Western influences which, in opera, meant the Italian influence. Like other reformers they had strong views on how music should be relevant to the drama and the text, indeed shared some of Wagner's views which were then almost unknown in the East. Modest Mussorgsky (1839–81) was by far the most powerful of the five and one of the most original figures in operatic history. An ex-guards officer, his life makes bleak reading, for he became an alcoholic and died of epilepsy. Yet this was the man who created the greatest masterpiece in Russian music, a work fit to be mentioned in the same breath as Shakespeare, yet which still divides opinion as to how it should be performed – *Boris Godunov* (1874).

It has two heroes, the guilty Tsar who has killed to get the throne, and the Russian people. This *Macbeth*-like drama of a ruler, with the teeming world of Russia unloosed on the stage in song and action, was given a wonderfully free sound by the composer, totally linked to the Russian language, which was his answer to the endless melody created by Wagner. It also has great choral moments and the effect is monumental, passionate, tender and moving.

Mussorgsky's own orchestration is the only one that purists will accept, but its stark strength held its popularity back, and it was Rimsky-Korsakov's re-scored and revised version that finally made the opera world famous, especially after the supreme actor-singer Feodor Chaliapin (1873–1938) made the role of Boris his own. Rimsky added colour to the score, or rather altered the sombre character of the original.

Yet whichever version is given, whichever way round some

of the scenes are played, whatever the cuts, the mighty work never fails to make a deep impression. The most notable question mark is whether to end the opera with the death of Boris or, more correctly, with the Russian people in the forest, and with the Idiot singing his pitiful lament for Russia at the end. The high points in the opera are too numerous to begin to list, but from the moment Boris guiltily recalls how 'I have attained the highest power', through the tremendous scene with Prince Shuisky, to the staggering scene of the chiming clock when he sees the ghost of the child he has murdered, we are in the presence of naked genius unequalled in Russian opera and unsurpassed anywhere else. And, strangely, Boris, the co-hero of the work, has the shortest part – great in the narrowest sense of the word – in the entire repertoire, a mere 60 pages out of 300 in the Rimsky version. Yet a Boris who can sing, act and look the part can haunt the minds and hearts of a whole generation, as Chaliapin did and Boris Christoff does.

Apart from an earlier work, *Salambô*, *Boris* was the only opera actually completed by the composer. His *Khovanshchina* was left unfinished and completed by Rimsky-Korsakov and given its première in 1886. The plot, based on late seventeenth-century Russian history, is a complex one, being about the Khovansky conspiracy. The music, without the supreme moments of *Boris*, is endlessly fascinating and of the utmost grandeur at times, while its haunting quality is apparent from its wonderfully evocative prelude as dawn breaks over Moscow.

Mussorgsky's other famous opera is the comedy *Sorochinsky Fair* from a Gogol story. It was completed and orchestrated by a pupil of Rimsky-Korsakov's, Nikolai Tcherepnin, and is rich in Russian songs and rhythms.

Rimsky-Korsakov (1844–1908) left a long line of operas in his own right behind him, but for all his brilliant orchestration and use of the exotic, they mostly lack drama and, indeed, emotion. The finest of them make magnificent and spectacular entertainment, but ordinary human feelings only obtrude in the historical *The Maid of Pskov* (1873) about Ivan the

Terrible, and *The Tsar's Bride* (1899), the bride being given a mad scene. His strong feeling for ballet has always made his works popular in Russia, but better stories and characterisation would have made them more universally popular. However, *The Snow Maiden* (1882), given its lack of 'heart', is entertaining, and *The Golden Cockerel* (1910), for all its fantastical story (which was once topical and satirical) is even more so. But the fact that most opera-goers can view its seizure by ballet companies with equanimity is hardly a good sign. These operas are regularly given in Russia, as is the spectacular *Sadko* with its Hindu Song and Song of the Viking Guest, the latter being stirring enough to make the listener sigh for what might have been.

Rimsky-Korsakov also had a hand in *Prince Igor* by Alexander Borodin (1833–87), for it was completed by himself and Glazunov and given its première three years after the composer's death. Nothing is as fine as the Polovtsian Dances in the score, but the opera is a splendid one, full of lyrical music and with a true epic feeling. Two acts are Polovtsian and are suitably and effectively oriental in atmosphere, while the Russian scenes are stately, with an abundance of fine choral music. But Borodin handicapped himself by writing a not very dramatic libretto and a mainly static last act.

Pyotr Ilich Tchaikovsky (1804–93) was as true a Russian as any of the composers we have been considering, but he did not abandon the West. Indeed, though he could recognise Mussorgsky's genius, the latter's steely realism was far away from his own beautiful and elegant world. He is best remembered theatrically for his ballet music, yet opera never ceased to fascinate him.

The first of his operas that actually pleased him was *Vakula the Smith* (1876), which was to be revised as *Cherevichki* (The Little Shoes, 1886) and which once appeared in film form as *Magic Slippers* – and once was known in Europe as *Oxana's Caprice*. This welter of names is an unfair burden for a delightful and professional folk-opera, which was to be followed by the second Russian masterpiece, *Eugene Onegin* (1879). This greatly loved work is from Pushkin, like so many Russian operas, and is accurately described as 'Lyrical or Elegiac Scenes' in three acts. Admittedly the three scenes of the first act follow hard on each other, as do the two scenes of each of the other acts, but the dramatic construction is still somewhat loose. The opera lives by its heroine Tatiana, of whom its composer became greatly enamoured, and whose celebrated Letter Scene became a wonderful outpouring of emotion. The name-part, the Byronic Onegin, who at the end is turned down by Tatiana – once, as a simple young girl, turned down by him – is less memorably drawn. Among many felicities, the two famous dances can be cited as proof of the composer's mastery; the waltz played at Tatiana's birthday party is marvellously right for country gentlefolk, just as the equally famous Polonaise in the last act is the essence of aristocracy. The whole of Act 2 is splendidly dramatic, and the second scene culminates in the death of Lensky, shot in a duel by his friend Onegin. We are close to the world of Turgenev in this charming, often captivating work, which is liable to elude newcomers, but rarely fails to ensnare those who hear it more than once.

The Maid of Orleans (1881), from a Schiller play, is far less true to Tchaikovsky's nature, being an almost Meyerbeerian work, though Joan herself has some fine music. With *Mazeppa* (1884) Tchaikovsky returned to a Russian theme with some success, but *The Sorceress* (1887) is an empty melodrama. *The Queen of Spades* (1890) has some melodramatic moments, particularly in the famous scene where the hero Herman tries to extract from the aged Countess the secret of the three cards, but here the melodrama is superb theatre. The work is an excellent example of a 'night at the opera': splendid entertainment, if not lyrically in the same class as *Eugene Onegin*. Yet Lisa's aria before she commits suicide by plunging into the River Niva is as fine as any he wrote, and the score as a whole is notably exciting. There is even an eighteenth-century pastiche of great skill and charm. The role of the Countess, who holds the fatal secret of the cards, but falls dead with shock as

Herman threatens her, is a magnificent one for an actress-singer.

Tchaikovsky only wrote one more opera, the one-act *Iolanthe*. Considering the number he had written, he cannot be considered one of the great composers of opera, but the two of his that live are rarely out of the repertoire completely, and are naturally greatly cherished in Russia.

European endeavours

Czechoslovakia is one of the most operatic of countries, yet, strangely, its operas have not exported well. We shall come to Janáček later in this book, but Smetana and Dvořák belong here, and their outputs are usually represented in the world outside by a single opera, the former's *The Bartered Bride* (1866). Bedřich Smetana (1824–84) lived at a time when Czech nationalism was particularly strong after the yoke of Austrian oppression had been partly lifted from his country, and although he is a lesser figure he ranks as the Verdi of his nation. *The Branenburgers in Bohemia* (1866) was a frankly patriotic work, but it was the lighthearted *The Bartered Bride* that the Czechs were to make the musical symbol of their country. In it village life is portrayed in a cheerful, romantic way, with plenty of humour, rhythmic exuberance and happy orchestration. *Dalibor* (1868) is a vaster, almost Wagnerian opera of heroic rescue, while *The Two Widows* (1874) is a pleasant French comedy transferred to Smetana's own country. Also charming are two dramas, *The Kiss* (1876) and *The Secret* (1878), but most of these works, *The Bartered Bride* apart, tend to be done by small companies for two night stands, or not at all, unless a Czech company takes them abroad. Yet as radio audiences know, there is delightful music in nearly all of them.

Antonin Dvořák (1841–1904), so popular in the concert hall, wrote ten operas, none of which have established themselves outside his native land. *Russalka* (1901) is sometimes exported and contains a tune, 'O Silver Moon', which is a popular favourite. It is by far the composer's best-known opera. Others that are given in Czechoslovakia are *The Jacobin* (1889), the *Pig-headed Peasants* (1874, produced in 1881), a 'folksy' piece as its name suggests, and *The Peasant a Rogue* (1878). His *Dimitrij* is about Boris Godunov's usurper.

Spain, which had been dominated by Italian opera, found a handful of native composers with an authentic Spanish voice in the late eighteenth century, notably Rodriguez de Hita, and the *tonadillas* of the day were not unlike Neapolitan *intermezzi*. But it is the *zarzuela* that best expresses Spanish identity. Though some are serious, they are usually Spanish *opera buffa*, wide-ranging in subject, and satiric as well as amusing. They sometimes allow for improvisation and contact between cast and audience is close. Each region has its own examples, and the form was exported to parts of South America by the Spaniards. It dates back several centuries, though the Teatro del Zarzuela in Madrid only dates from 1856. Spain's nationalist opera composers belong to the twentieth century, and to another chapter.

Poland's one famous national opera is *Halka* (1848) by Stanislaw Moniuszko (1819–72), which is somewhat Polish in flavour without being a folk-opera, but is basically an Italian opera with native colour added; in fact, it is a typically Romantic work of its period, and none the worse for that. Karol Szymanowski (1882–1937), a fine Romantic, wrote *Hagith* (1922) and *Kuis Roger* (1926).

Other countries dominated by Italy, but showing signs of independence in the nineteenth century, included Sweden, whose national composer was Ivar Hallström (1826–1901), Hallström used folk-song in his once popular *The Enchanted Cat* (1869) and *The Bewitched One* (1874), while in Hungary, Ferenc Erkel (1810–93) was a genuine nationalist whose *Bánk Bán* (1844–52, produced in 1861) became and remains *the* national opera and had a reception in its day similar to Verdi's blazingly patriotic pieces.

Meanwhile, Britain had far more opera than it was to have between the two World Wars, but precious little major creative talent. Italian opera was in demand at Covent Garden, then called the Royal Italian Opera House, the language serving German and French operas too until towards the end of the century. Opera was to be heard from time to time all over Britain: Madeleine Smith heard Donizetti's *Lucrezia Borgia* in Glasgow in 1857 the night before she (almost certainly) murdered her lover, though opera-goers cannot honestly claim that the plot of the opera inspired her to do the deed.

But where was a school of English or British opera? Plenty of composers tried to establish one, for in his *The Rise of English Opera*, Eric Walter White tracked down around 200 premières during the nineteenth century, no bad record for a land allegedly without music, let alone opera. But unless there are some hidden masterpieces waiting to be exhumed, one can only summarise the situation as one of pleasant but minor talent and much effort, but no genius. And genius would have been needed to end an Italian domination as complete musically as the Romans had exercised politically nearly 2 000 years before.

Until some 40 years ago, three operas survived, Italian rather than English but giving the pleasant feeling of being locally inspired. They were *The Bohemian Girl* (1843) by Michael Balfe (1808–70), *Maritana* by Vincent Wallace (1812–65) and *The Lily of Killarney* (1862) by Sir Julius Benedict (1804–85). They recalled, too, the ballad operas of the previous century and all three are tuneful. But otherwise only *Ivanhoe* (1891) by Sir Arthur Sullivan (1842–1900) is remembered, mainly by name. This was the opera that was meant to start a National Opera at what is now London's Palace Theatre.

Before returning to Sullivan and his difficult but inspired colleague, W. S. Gilbert (1836–1911), the hostility of the English musical establishment to opera should be noted. Prepared to swallow oratorios, however banal, because they were 'serious' art, many musicians and critics looked on opera, and Italian opera, with hostility. Music meant German music and the true seriousness of Wagner at least compelled respect late in the century. But the most confirmed enemies of opera wrote the entire art form off as bastard. Sir Hubert Parry (1848–1914) actually hated opera, though apparently he once wrote one. Besides, opera was theatre, and the theatre was not respectable: how great were the rejoicings when Jenny Lind abandoned opera for oratorio and religious music generally.

Queen Victoria was an exception, for throughout her life she followed the latest trends, eagerly listening to Wagner, and with Prince Albert she enjoyed excerpts from *Lohengrin* and *Tannhäuser* in the 1850s and demanded a Command Performance of *Cavalleria Rusticana* as soon as it reached London in the 1890s. She also persuaded Sullivan to write a grand opera (he did not, in fact, need much persuasion) for neither she nor he could know that his true genius lay in the Savoy Operas (which the Queen also enjoyed).

Gilbert and Sullivan are so British, in particular so English (for all Sullivan's Irish ancestry) that their comic operas are nationalist in the true sense of the word.

With respect to the hallowed D'Oyly Carte Company, Sullivan's reputation, and, indeed, the reputation of the Savoy Operas generally, has been raised since the end of the copyright on his music, and on the librettos. Played by a symphony orchestra, Sullivan has been heard to be a master to rank with Offenbach, Strauss, and Lehár, as was known by many all along. There is one essential difference between him and Offenbach, however. Sex, as opposed to romance, was never allowed to creep into his music any more than into Gilbert's chaste texts: it was, after all, the Victorian Age. Sullivan's style developed, though it never lost its fresh individuality, and only opera-lovers and music-lovers fully appreciate his affectionate parodies of Handel, Verdi, Mendelssohn and others. The partnership began in 1871 and ended in 1896, the famous – and worst – quarrel taking place during the run of *The Gondoliers* (1889),

Only their first success, *Trial by Jury* (1875) has no spoken dialogue, and is much liked by opera-goers because it is so full of parodies of the Italian opera of a generation before. Space does not admit a complete survey of the operas, but the most popular is probably *The Mikado* (1885), and – arguably – the most ravishing musically is *Iolanthe* (1882). Rupert D'Oyly Carte's managerial genius should be noted and so should *The Yeoman of the Guard*, the nearest Sullivan came to grand opera in his lighter works.

Sullivan's serious longings never left him, so his career is an ironic one, yet another example of an artist who does not know where his true skill lies. His tetchy partner was a lyricist of genius, despite the fact that some of his wit has not worn well, while Sullivan, however frustrating he found his subsidiary role, never ceased to be charmingly inventive, and often amusing in his own right.

The Savoy Operas, so called after the London theatre where so many of them had their premières, and to which Carte had moved in 1881, are likely to be immortal even though Anglo-Americans are their chief admirers.

The Americans welcomed Gilbert and Sullivan from the start. There can be no place in this chapter for American nationalists of the nineteenth century, for there were then few American composers of opera. However, operatic activity was intense enough long before the Metropolitan Opera House opened in 1883; indeed ballad operas were given in New York before the Revolution. But the real beginning of opera in the city came in 1825 when the Garcia Family gave *The Barber of Seville*, with the 16-year-old Maria Garcia, soon to be Maria Malibran (her husband's name) as Rosina. Malibran, the incomparable, ranks as America's first *prima donna*.

Opera spread rapidly. Typically, San Francisco, a village in 1848 when gold was discovered in California, but soon a boom town, had flourishing Italian opera from 1852. But native opera was to be a twentieth-century phenomenon, and the chief contribution of the USA has been singers rather than composers.

Meanwhile, South America was able to supply some native talent, even though, as almost everywhere, it was Italian Opera that reigned supreme. Brazil, with opera houses from the eighteenth century, was more influenced than most by German music, while local composers did not make much use of their own folk-tunes, preferring the Italians as inspiration. Argentina, whose first regular company appeared in the 1820s, produced little nationalist music until the twentieth century, but in Mexico the importation of *zarzuelas* from Spain (see p. 125) in the last century led to genuine local works. The first Mexican opera based on the nation's history was Aniceto's *Guatimotzin* (1871).

Viennese confectionery

Viennese operetta may be included here, for in its days of glory it was a truly native art. Offenbach had a colossal success with his operettas in Vienna and this, plus the tradition of the *singspiel*, made it natural that the local impresarios should hope to found a lucrative school of their own.

Fortunately, Johann Strauss the Younger (1825–99) was already a world-renowned composer of waltzes and though his first operetta, *Indigo und die Vierzig Räuber* (Indigo and the Forty Thieves, 1871) was more of a local sensation than a great success, that success was not long in coming. (The libretto had been much to blame and, given a new one in 1906, and retitled *The Thousand and One Nights*, it was and remains popular.)

The breakthrough for Strauss came with *Die Fledermaus* (The Bat, 1874) which is generally regarded as the perfect operetta. Melodies, orchestration, charm, champagne and exhilaration are in it in abundance, and its wonderful second-act finale, was to be very influential on future Viennese composers. A less happy precedent perhaps was the last act, which is less inspired than the rest and which needs a fine comedian to put across the role of Frosch, the comic jailer. Later operettas were to make the last act the point where the comic could give his all.

The operetta is so superb that it is almost unsinkable, and only an abysmal cast could wreck it totally. But it needs some singing. Act 2 alone contains the strange, but captivating song of Prince Orlofsky (a mezzo role), 'Chacun à son goût' (Everyone to his own taste), Adèle's delicious waltz song, 'Mein Herr Marquis', and also the tremendous *csardas* (Hungarian dance) sung by the disguised Rosalinde. Surely Offenbach must have admired the toast to King Champagne, for it was he who first directed Strauss's steps to operetta.

Strauss was to write two more great successes, *Der Zigeuner-baron* (The Gypsy Baron, 1885) and *Eine Nacht in Venedig* (A Night in Venice, 1883). Like the immortal *Fledermaus*, they are regularly given in opera houses, operetta theatres, and often in ordinary theatres, and are also staged by amateurs; but neither match the eternally youthful 'Bat'.

A lesser master of operetta, but a genuine one, was Franz von Suppé (1819–95), best known abroad for some stirring overtures. He was influenced by his training in Italy, but soon fell into the Viennese style. His best-known work is *Boccaccio* (1879), about the author of the *Decameron*, the role being assigned to a mezzo, but the earlier *Die Schöne Galathee* (Beautiful Galatea, 1865) is finer, and fascinating because it resembles Offenbach in its parody of mythology.

Other Viennese operettas include *Der Bettelstudent* (The Beggar Student, 1882) by Karl Millöcker, who also wrote a 'horror-operetta', *Gasparone* (1884). With Strauss and Suppé, Millöcker makes up the trio of major Viennese operetta composers. Lesser lights were Richard Genée (1823–95) who with Karl Haffner had provided the text for *Fledermaus* before writing a number of operettas, including *Der Seekadett* (The Naval Cadet, 1876), also Karl Zeller, two of whose works, *Der Vogelhändler* (The Bird-seller, 1891) and *Der Obersteiger* (The Master-miner, 1895) travelled far beyond Vienna. The former is still widely played in Germany and Austria for this folk-opera is well-made and very tuneful.

This is a good place to end this wide-ranging chapter, for an even more famous composer of operetta, Franz Lehàr, belongs to the twentieth century for all his nineteenth-century charm; he revived single-handed what appeared to be the dead world of Viennese operetta with a triumph such as none but Offenbach and Johann Strauss have ever enjoyed.

7

Italy: a Slice of Life

Realism

Realism on stage and screen is not to be confused with 'the real thing'. An extreme example is the war film, some examples of which are dubbed 'realistic' and claimed as showing the truth about war. Yet no film has shown a body disintegrate, a head blown from a pair of shoulders. Suggestion is all. In the theatre great art can contain even less realism, and yet be more harrowing and illuminating than prosaic fact.

'Realism' therefore is a word, like 'Romanticism' and 'Nationalism', both discussed earlier, which needs to be treated with some suspicion when applied to opera. This has to be stressed, for we have now reached the Italian *verismo* school, beginning with Mascagni and culminating with Puccini. Some authorities who should know better claim that *verismo* can be equated with the depiction of the seamy side of life, which is simply not so. Many *verismo* operas, Puccini's *Il Tabarro* for instance, could be so described but wrongly; the word 'seamy' has snobbish connotations. The violence in some *verismo* operas is just violence, whatever its 'class' setting. *Verismo* is the Italian for Realism – or Naturalism, which is an even more loaded word.

With a salute to *Carmen*, which can be described as the first *verismo* opera, our story begins with Pietro Mascagni (1863–1945), who studied under Ponchielli, and then, to escape from the discipline of the Milan Conservatory, abandoned his course to learn the hard way as a conductor with one of the many companies that toured Italy in the late nineteenth century.

Realism had become very much a part of European literature by this time – Émile Zola's writings are only one example – and it was perhaps inevitable that a realistic school of opera would arise in contrast to the romanticism and heroism of Verdi and Wagner. Not that Verdi had not attempted realism and succeeded triumphantly, for *La Traviata*, that most romantic of works, is also operatically speaking realistic, which was one of the reasons it failed at first. But Mascagni's *Cavalleria Rusticana* (1890), with which he won a competition organised by the publisher Sanzogno, was the real father of *verismo* opera.

He had already written two operas, *Guglielmo Ratcliff* and *Pinotta*, when he wrote his one ever-popular and stirringly lurid melodic melodrama. The title means 'rustic chivalry', even though there is precious little chivalry on display in it. It was taken by the librettists, Giuseppe Targioni-Tozzetti and Guido Menasci, from Giovanni Verga's hugely popular one-act play of the same name in which Eleonora Duse made such a success.

Its music is eminently singable and adored by all audiences except the austere, for all that it is almost primitively direct, a series of vastly enjoyable hammer-blows to the senses and emotions. Its conquest of Europe followed rapidly and this steamy Sicilian piece will remain popular as long as opera itself, a superb example of the first-class second-rate. Musically it does not aspire as high as its 'terrible twin' *Pagliacci* and only a minority of Anglo-American critics dare revel in it in print; but if anything, it is even more popular.

Mascagni never managed to repeat this colossal success, though the charming *L'Amico Fritz* (1891) is still given, especially in Italy, and its dramatic intermezzo deserves to be as popular as that of *Cavalleria*, which regularly appears in lists of the world's ten most-loved 'classical' pieces. The opera-lover probably most enjoys the gut-impact of the confrontation in *Cavalleria* between Santuzza and Turiddu.

Iris (1898) is occasionally revived, though *Il Piccolo Marat* (1921) is said to contain some of Mascagni's finest music. The composer, who ended his life under a cloud for having become

Mussolini's musical spokesman, had a unique operatic débâcle in 1901. His *Le Maschere* (The Masks), inspired by the *commedia dell'arte* tradition, was given its first performance in six towns simultaneously, being halted in one, hissed in four more and only completely unscathed in Rome, where the composer was also the conductor.

Ruggiero Leoncavallo (1858–1919) is remembered also for a single work, his two-act *Pagliacci* (Clowns, 1892). The plot is based on an actual event that took place when the composer was young in which his father, a judge, had to try a jealous actor who had killed his wife after a performance. The operatic version is splendidly dramatic from the superb Prologue sung by Tonio in front of the curtain to the famous ending – 'La commedia e finito' (The comedy is ended).

Pagliacci and *Cavalleria* do not simply provide magnificent, undemanding entertainment, but also make an excellent introduction for newcomers to opera. It is significant that though double or triple bills are rarely very successful at the box office in the theatre and the opera house (though popular in ballet), there has never been any questioning the appeal of this immortal pair.

Like Mascagni, Leoncavallo tried to repeat his success, but failed. He hoped to achieve a trilogy about Renaissance Italy beginning with *Chatterton* (1886), but *I Medici* (1893) flopped and he gave up. His *La Bohème* (1897) had the misfortune to coincide with Puccini's masterpiece, yet it is a highly effective and fascinating opera, which stresses Marcello and Musetta rather than Mimi and Rodolfo. *Zazà* (1900) can be heard by 'collectors' occasionally, but not *Roland von Berlin* (1904) or his ambitious *Edipo Re* (1920), nor a number of operettas. Indeed, he remains even more of a one-opera-composer than Mascagni. Yet the latter never rivalled one unique achievement. That potent show-stopper, *Vesti la giubba* (On with the motley), as sung incomparably by Caruso, was the very first record to achieve the magic million sales (though we are told that the million includes several different recordings by the great man).

Umberto Giordano (1867–1948) wrote ten operas, none of

them now universally popular in the *Cavalleria* and *Pagliacci*
sense, but one of which, *Andrea Chénier* (1896) is greatly loved
still in Italy and fairly regularly revived elsewhere. With the
right cast, this stirring *verismo* opera, set in the French Revolution, and loosely based on the life of the poet Chénier, makes
a striking effect, and is very popular with audiences, though less
so with the more puritanical critics who, as has been noted, will
often not recognise the value of good operas of the second or,
some might say, the third rank. This is the refrain for much of
this chapter, Puccini apart, and even he is still patronised in
some quarters and occasionally abused. It must be admitted,
however, that not all of *Chénier* lives up to its finest pages;
indeed Giordano's inspiration sometimes burns low. But the
hero's *Improvisso* is a glorious outburst of revolutionary fervour,
fit to rank with anything in Italian opera in its visionary intensity. The last act contains the beautiful 'Come un bel di
Maggio' in which the poet describes his emotions in the face of
death, and a duet between Chénier and Madeleine as they
await their last journey to the guillotine which shows the composer's passionate lyricism at its finest. Of his other works only
Fedora (1898), based on a once-famous play by Sardou about
Tsarist Russia, has survived, in Italy at least. The listener who
does not rejoice in the hero Loris's short 'Amor ti vieta', the best-
known piece in the opera, will probably never comprehend the
vice-like grip that Italian opera has on its happy prisoners.

Francesco Cilea (1866–1950) wrote his successful *Gina* while
he was still a student in Naples, though like his equally successful *La Tilda* (1892) it is now forgotten. *L'Arlesiana* (The Girl
from Arles, 1897) was less popular, though the gentle lyric
quality of 'Lamento di Federico' has made it a favourite with
tenors, despite the fact that it is far removed from many
verismo arias. Cilea lives, however, through a single opera,
Adriana Lecouvreur (1902), taken from the play by Scribe and
Legouvé about the great French actress of that name of the
eighteenth century and her love affair with the Marshal de
Saxe. The work remains immensely popular in Italy and is
occasionally given elsewhere. By no means a great score, it is

very effective theatrically and some of the music is fine, notably the heroine's 'Io son l'umile ancella' in which she modestly claims that she is only the handmaid of the arts. It speaks well for the operatic health of Italy that works like this and *Chénier* were appearing, but the reaction of most of the London critics to a performance of the former at the Camden Festival in 1972 tells a different story. The burden of their reports was outrage at having been subjected to such a work.

In the past some critics have been outraged by Puccini. At least one otherwise admirable writer, Edward J. Dent, teacher and librettist, the author of one of the best short histories of opera, could actually embarrass his admirers with the phrase 'slobbering erotics' and accuse the composer of manufacturing his arias to fit on records. Others, while admitting a certain theatrical skill (as if that was not of some moment in opera), could scarcely conceal their contempt. Meanwhile, the vast majority of the operatic public fell in love with Puccini's operas and have been in love with them ever since. Sir Thomas Beecham, one of a number of brilliant Puccinian conductors, went so far as to say that to the average man Puccini means opera, and though, since he noted this, the Verdi revival has been so tremendous that 'Puccini and Verdi' would be more in order, his point was a sound one.

Giacomo Puccini (1858–1924), the most famous of a line of musicians, was born in Lucca and studied under Ponchielli in Milan. He was to come into his own comparatively late and become the only opera composer since Verdi and Wagner 'to make a large and effective contribution to the regular international repertoire'. Those soberly judged words by Desmond Shawe-Taylor are beyond dispute, yet even now one occasionally hears those long soaring melodies dubbed cheap or empty, and in *Famous Puccini Operas* Spike Hughes noted that Puccini's music was considered sickly; added to these criticisms was much sheer jealousy of his success.

Except, perhaps, in *Il Tabarro*, Puccini was never as complete a *verismo* composer as Mascagni. His Bohemians in *La Bohème* are seen through a more romantic glow than an outright realist would have allowed. He was Verdi's true and only successor, though he sensibly knew his place and did not try – in his maturity – to match Verdi's grand themes of heroism, patriotism, epic love, friendship, and honour. Puccini could have brilliantly handled a *Traviata* theme, even *Falstaff*, witness *Gianni Schicchi*, but not the surging world of *Rigoletto*, *Simone Boccanegra* and *Otello*. Yet as soon as one has doubted him, the grandeur of *Turandot* comes to mind, though at once one remembers the most vivid character in that black fairy-tale masterpiece, the last of Puccini's 'little women', Liu.

So it was that the composer lived mainly in a more limited world than his mighty predecessor, a world that suited his lesser, but still extraordinary, talent. His gift for melody – lyrical, sensuously stirring, striking and insinuating – was supported by his masterly orchestration and by a theatrical flair never surpassed in opera and rarely equalled in consistency. He had a keen ear for the music of his contemporaries and he was quite prepared to use their ideas, fortunately without blurring his own fingerprints. There are Debussyian harmonies that cannot be missed even at first hearing of his *La Fanciulla del West*, and, in *Gianni Schicchi*, a passage of neo-Stravinsky. Verdi naturally influenced him, but so did Wagner, not least in his use of the *leitmotiv*. And the magnificent opening act of *Turandot* has choral music of such power and ambition that as Puccini's biographer, Mosco Carner, has noted, it calls to mind the dramatic crowd scenes of *Boris Godunov*. Yet like all the masters of opera, Puccini remains unique, the creator of his own world. Others have been inspired by him, including Lehàr and innumerable composers of film scores (who have also learnt from Tchaikovsky, Richard Strauss and others) but, alas for opera, he has had no successor and now – such is the change in the language of music since his day – he cannot have. It is our loss. And it is the loss of many who claim to be devoted followers of this self-confessed hunter of wildfowl, libretti and women, that they rarely get to know all his major operas, simply concentrating on *La Bohème*, *Tosca*, *Madame Butterfly* and, some of them, on *Turandot*.

His first opera was *Le Villi* (The Witches, 1883), the *Villi* being better known as the *Wilis* from their role in the ballet *Giselle*. The opera is in one act and it is interesting to know that Verdi, while approving of it, was worried about the young composer's evident symphonic tendencies: it has a middle section which except for a few bars of choral writing, is given over to dance, mime and speech and music. It was a success, but one can imagine old Verdi, always true to the Italian belief in the prime importance of the voice even in his matchless late masterpieces, worrying about what the younger generation were getting up to. Performances today are few, but the full recording, released by RCA in 1974, proved *Le Villi* to contain a number of exciting anticipations of later triumphs, even though the story was decidedly un-Puccinian.

Edgar (1889) was much less successful. It was bad in its own right and bad for Puccini, who had no idea as yet where his true future lay (and let us remember that it appeared before *Cavalleria Rusticana* changed history). Fortunately, the House of Ricordi, which had played so notable a part in the career of Verdi, had immense faith in the young composer, a faith not damaged by the failure of *Edgar*. Their reward came with *Manon Lescaut* (1893). Having made a fortune from the works of Verdi, the famous music publishers now began to make another from Puccini, who was to become immensely rich himself.

Manon Lescaut does not supplant Massenet's *Manon*, but is another variation on this potent theme. As has been noted, it is for the listener to decide which he prefers: the lucky ones can love both. Just as Mozart flooded the score of his youthful *Seraglio* with an endless succession of fresh, often intoxicating melodies, so the young Puccini (young in career, rather than in years) unleashed a veritable torrent of tunes. As Stephen Williams noted in his *Come to the Opera*, these are not very subtle, but 'big passionate tunes sailing along the lines [of the score] like ships across the horizon'. If only the third act – on the quay at Le Havre – shows genius, the rest is far beyond mere talent. The last act, set in 'a vast plain on the borders of

New Orleans', is only an anti-climax if the singers are inadequate, and Manon's aria 'Sola, perduta abbandonata' (Alone, lost and abandoned), sung when Des Grieux has gone to look for help and she is overwhelmed by her terror of death, rises beyond pathos to tragic grandeur.

The libretto by Giuseppe Giacosa, Luigi Illica, Giulio Ricordi, M. Prago and D. Oliva, after the Abbé Prevost's novel, is not, perhaps as one might expect, as good as later ones. Amongst other things, we are uncertain how the lovers come to be on that vast plain, for Manon's explanation that her beauty has brought new misfortunes is unsatisfactory, and by later standards the musical characterisation of the lovers is not quite adequate. But generally it is an effective opera.

Manon had a première in Turin more totally triumphant than any of his later masterpieces were to enjoy. It took place eight days before the first *Falstaff* and the opera rapidly went round the world. When it reached London, the young Bernard Shaw, a much better opera critic than most of his contemporaries, hailed Puccini as 'more like the heir of Verdi than any other of his rivals'.

La Bohème (1896) is not so much the most popular of Puccini's operas as the one that unites Puccinians and non-Puccinians alike in praise. With this work, which has a libretto by Giacosa and Illica after Henri Murger's novel of Paris, *Scènes de la Vie de Bohème*, Puccini reached maturity and total mastery. Episodic, and varying between fast action and radiant lyrical passages, between sentiment, pathos and comedy, its craftsmanship is as astonishing as its freshness. Written when Puccini himself was no longer young, it is a hymn to youth which captivates young and old alike. The attractions include the swift opening and high spirits, a first act with one of the most famous of all operatic love scenes, the kaleidoscopic excitement and melodic feast of Act 2, the surging lyricism of Act 3, and, finally, the last act in which, after a quiet opening, a scene of happy horseplay is suddenly and very dramatically chilled as Musetta enters with her tragic news. If cast and conductor cannot reduce the audience to tears at the ending – as well as along the way – they have failed.

The première, with the young Toscanini in the pit, took place at the Teatro Regio in Turin, with Puccini worrying about the acting of his male leads. Most of the critics, except for Pozza of the influential *Corriere della Sera*, made fools of themselves, possibly because Puccini had not written another *Manon Lescaut*, but a lighter piece, or possibly because their ears were still ringing with their first *Götterdämmerung*. What can one say about Bersezio's comment? '*La Bohème*, just as it leaves no great impression on the mind of the spectator, will leave no great mark on the history of our opera'.

Perhaps the realism surprised people, as it had surprised the first audiences of *Traviata* and *Carmen*. Whatever the cause, the opera had only a modest success at Turin, then, finally, in Rome, successes that seemed like failures to the sensitive composer. Then came Palermo in the following April, and soon the world was conquered. It is reckoned that *Bohème* is being played every night of the year in one or more theatres, and so it will go on as long as opera lasts.

There followed *Tosca* which Joseph Kerman, the notable but puritanical author of *Opera as Drama*, dubbed a 'shabby little shocker'. It is more *verismo* than *Bohème* and less moving. On the other hand its musical and theatrical impact is colossal. Not for nothing is one of the supreme moments in operatic history the performance given by Callas and Gobbi in Act 2 of Zeffirelli's production at Covent Garden in 1964. This was totally true to the opera, melodrama at its peak, and, indeed, a shocker. It shocked. It is based on a once-famous Sardou play and Puccini was to admit that he had coloured the drama, rather than illuminating it from within. That cannot be denied if we consider the composer's usual methods, but audiences have never ceased to respond to its melodies, strong drama and atmospheric power. The first night in Rome was not helped by rumours of an attempted political assassination to occur during the opera, and rivals of the composer were also suspected of looking for trouble. But allowing for this and the consequently nervous atmosphere, the critics' reactions were once again unfriendly, even though the libretto received the most attacks. Soon, however, *Tosca* was sweeping the world.

The fiasco of the first night of *Madama Butterfly* was in a different league, for this was on a level with *The Barber*'s appalling baptism. Puccini had seen David Belasco's play and instantly saw its operatic possibilities. The fiasco was sheer sabotage, for though the opera was to be revised and turned into a three-act piece, it was basically the *Butterfly* we know. Soon after the bestial display of jealousy by the wreckers at the première at La Scala, it triumphed at Brescia and Puccini had his third and last total success starting round the world.

Butterfly is a true tragedy, as any major actress-singer always reveals. Its detractors claim that only the star role lifts it to tragic heights, but tragedy is there throughout. Only the lesser artist descends to sentiment and sentimentality. The heroine is the ultimate 'little girl/woman' so loved by Puccini, who invests her and the rest with a guilt that leads to death. A most expressive and subtle score is enlivened by some *leitmotive* based on authentic Japanese tunes, and the oriental atmosphere is always convincing. Butterfly herself develops as a woman in each act, which in itself makes the soprano's task harder, and her final scene reaches heights of grandeur that Puccini rarely attempted. Belasco's play is forgotten, so is the story by John Luther Long that led to it, but the opera is literally adored by millions. It takes a horrible performance to rob it of all its impact.

This masterpiece was followed by *La Fanciulla del West* (The Girl of the Golden West, 1910), which was taken from a Belasco melodrama about the Californian Gold Rush. Short of the expected arias, this haunting and masterly score is heard less often than it should be, though its Wild Western setting makes it hard for some to swallow. Oddly, the sentimentality of the miners and their respect for a fine woman is true to its historical setting. It must be admitted that by Puccinian standards the characterisation is a little thin, though the angelic Minnie, who is yet quite willing to cheat at cards to save her man from the villainous Jack Rance is certainly an exception. The opera has a happy ending and given a good performance and a brilliant Minnie the entire proceedings are excellent entertainment.

La Rondine (1917) is not highly regarded, a 'poor man's *Traviata*' being a standard jibe. Yet there is plenty of Puccinian charm, and the crowd-scenes are striking. It may lie uneasily between opera and operetta, but there is much pleasure to be had from it.

There is far more to be had from *Trittico* (1918), three one-act operas that are sometimes deprived of their central sister, *Suor Angelica*, to the fury of most opera-goers. The three are not linked, but perfectly complement each other in their contrasting moods. *Il Tabarro* (The Cloak) is a melodrama set on a barge in the Seine and is perhaps the finest work of the entire *verismo* school (to which otherwise Puccini only half-belonged, as we have noted). Atmospherically the score is a triumph, and the characterisation is very fine, especially that of the betrayed husband and skipper of the barge, Michele. He is by turns sinister, then sympathetic as he tried to regain his wife's love, and finally homicidal as he kills her lover, hides him under his cloak, then reveals the body to his wife. It is a most passionate opera – not simply sexually – for all its Grand Guignol qualities.

Suor Angelica has a charming convent atmosphere, a marvellous central confrontation between the heroine and her ice-cold aunt, and an ending complete with a miracle that is too much for many Catholics to take and sheer banality for many non-Catholics. Yet the nuns in Puccini's sister's convent loved the piece when he played it to them, and it is barbarous to remove it from the trilogy, not least because the heroine is a tragic creation and a gift for a fine actress-singer.

Gianni Schicchi is the musicians' and critics' pet, and, happily, has vast audience-appeal as well. It is genuinely funny orchestrated scintillatingly and has several superb tunes, including 'O mio babbino caro' (O my beloved daddy), which is not a solemn religious prayer, but a heady bit of teasing in which Puccini satirises himself in a totally ravishing manner.

Finally came *Turandot* (1926), given its first performance under Toscanini at La Scala two years after the composer had died. Franco Alfano (1876–1954) did a workmanlike job of completing the third act, but the task would have taxed even Puccini, especially the thawing of the icy and unsympathetic Princess into passionate womanhood and the portrayal of her lover, Calaf, who has given away friends and risked his life for love. The 'little woman' here is Liu, some of whose music is as touching as anything the composer wrote. We have mentioned the grand choruses inspired by the example of *Boris*, and this black fairy-tale is Puccini's grandest score. Adami, who wrote the libretto, based on a play of Gozzi, did a fine professional job, as he had with *Tabarro*, but it should always be remembered that, like Giacosa and Illica and the rest, he had to prove his case to the composer, whose ideas on libretti were usually as sound as his ideas on everything else to do with the theatre he so enriched. *Turandot* is now widely popular, especially when the right cast is available. It is the last opera in the international repertory that is loved by a majority of opera-goers. This is a careful way of stating the truth, which is that opera as a totally popular form of people's art died with Puccini, who understood the human heart so well.

A handful of non-Italian composers tried their hand at *verismo*. Very few German ones did, but the naturalistic *Tiefland* (1903) by Eugen d'Albert, who began as a Wagnerian, was very popular and is still given in Germany. A famous pianist, the only other of his twenty operas to be heard occasionally is *Die Abreise* (The Departure, 1898), a pleasant comedy he wrote before turning to *verismo*.

There is one notable French *verismo* opera (unless one includes *Carmen*). This is *Louise* by Gustave Charpentier (1860–1956), a most charming work, once widely heard, but now rarely given outside France. One aria from it is a soprano favourite, 'Depuis le jour' and part of the opera's charm is that the heroine has a rival, the city of Paris, which is painted atmospherically with considerable skill.

8

Richard Strauss: End of a Line

In 1945 Strauss' street was liberated by American troops, but how could he identify himself to these foreigners? Tall, but stooping, the old man met the officer in command of the detachment, put out his hand to him, and said in English: 'I am the composer of *Der Rosenkavalier*'. The Americans knew it, as well they might at least by name, for it is the most loved German opera since Mozart's day. Dedicated Straussians may prefer *Elektra*, and a growing band are hailing *Die Frau ohne Schatten* as the composer's masterpiece, but like almost all opera-goers, they love *Rosenkavalier*. Even performed in German in front of non-German audiences faced with acres of words, notably from Baron Ochs, the response of the audience is warm and loving.

The point is being emphasised for we have reached the end of the operatic line with Richard Strauss (1864–1949). *Turandot*'s popularity has been stressed in the last chapter, but in terms of adoration, *Rosenkavalier* now seems to have reached a place in the tiny handful that includes three Puccini operas, three Verdis and very few more. And when Strauss died, the last of the giants was dead. We will be covering modern opera fully enough, but not at the expense of opera as it is known in the opera house. Strauss was the last of the elect.

He was the son of a renowned horn player and he made a striking reputation as a conductor before turning to opera. *Guntram* (1894) and *Feuersnot* (Beltane Fire, 1900) were influenced inevitably by Wagner, but the closing music of the latter gives sumptuous hints of things to come.

Salome (1905), from Oscar Wilde's notorious play, made his name and caused a splendid scandal in many countries. It is revived quite frequently in most operatic countries, and still has tremendous power, much of its music being violent, with the aroma of claustrophobic sensuality being a notable feature. To some people parts of the music are sickly sweet, but that does the brooding atmosphere no harm. The opera is in one act and ultimately everything depends on the heroine. With Strauss making even greater demands on his orchestra than Wagner did, she has to try to be a convincingly nubile 16-year-old, yet with the voice of an Isolde.

Strauss passionately adored the soprano voice, but his demands on it could be taxing, especially as Salome is expected to perform her own Dance of the Seven Veils. Amazingly, a number of sopranos in each generation can convincingly portray Salome. London alone has seen three in the 70s – Grace Bumbry, Gwynneth Jones and Josephine Barstow. During a rehearsal of the first *Salome* Strauss called out: 'Louder! louder! I can still hear the singers!' which was presumably a teasing demand. Other good quotes include: 'Gentlemen, there are no difficulties or problems. The opera is a scherzo with a fatal conclusion.' And once he told an orchestra to play the score as if it were Mendelssohn's fairy music.

Elektra (1909) saw his first collaboration with the great librettist – and poet and dramatist – Hugo von Hoffmannsthal (1874–1929). It is an even fiercer score than *Salome*, but it towers over the earlier works as the ghost of the murdered Agammemnon towers over the work in one of the most powerful, yet simple, *leitmotive* in all opera. Characterisation is altogether finer, and the music-drama, again in one act, is genuinely tragic as befits its theme. Psychologically it is again an advance, most notably in the fearful scene where Elektra and Klytemnestra confront each other, after the latter has made an entrance to nightmarish music as frightening as a snake-pit. The work is scored for a huge orchestra of 115 players and it take several hearings to begin to find its secrets. Once they are solved every performance becomes a shattering experience, provided conductor and cast are worthy of this masterpiece. Only the music for the triumphant, frenzied dance of death that Elektra performs after her mother has been destroyed, along with her lover Aegisthus, has been questioned. It is up to the individual to decide whether it is on a par with the rest of this cataclysmic score, which still sounds so much more modern than much of today's 'modern' music.

There followed *Der Rosenkavalier* (The Knight of the Rose, 1911) whose unending popularity has already been noted. It was an astonishing contrast to what had gone before and rapidly triumphed far beyond Dresden where it had its première. In the aftermath of the First World War it became even more loved, a symbol of vanished beauty, for the final trio, for all its radiance, has an almost unbearable quality, an evocation of loss as well as love. The librettist played a key role in the opera's triumph, and the music – Strauss at his most human and genial – in spite of all its lusciousness, captivates the heart by its very simplicity at crucial moments, such as the presentation of the rose by Octavian to Sophie in Act 2. The waltzes that play so crucial a part in the score are nineteenth-century, for all that the story is set in mid-eighteenth-century Vienna, and the result of the composer's deliberately anachronistic approach is a total triumph.

There are an enormous number of parts, all beautifully characterised, as well as the four legendary leading roles, the Feldmarschallin, Octavian, Sophie and Baron Ochs. The first is one of the finest characterisations in opera and her appeal is such (if the singer can achieve it) that we should be left wondering if the young and inexperienced Sophie can hold Octavian, even though the Feldmarschallin has led Sophie up to him and withdrawn. Newcomers to the opera are always somewhat worried by the fact that Octavian is taken by a mezzo, though many fine mezzos have been magnificent in the part, the problem is that a tenor young enough to be right for the role would be hard to find, for Octavian is only 17. The worry is legitimate, for after the explicit love-making in the prelude, the sight of two women, however convincing the Octavian, is unexpected, as no doubt Shakespeare's boy actors would be if we saw them today. One may hope that the newcomer experiences a fine first performance which will probably dispel all doubts.

Ariadne auf Naxos (1912) followed, the first version of which preceded a performance of *Le Bourgeois Gentilhomme* with incidental music by Strauss. This sumptuous version is occasionally done, but as it requires actors as well as singers and consequently extra money to stage it, a second version was written by Strauss and Hofmannsthal. In this, the would-be gentleman, who has hired an opera troupe and *commedia dell'arte* players, orders them to their consternation to perform simultaneously so that they will be finished by fireworks time. Splendid as the first version is, this second contains one of Strauss's most glorious creations – the Composer – a soprano (in male costume). And the blend of the Ariadne story with the interjections of the *commedia* players is both expert and fascinating. The final love duet between Bacchus and Ariadne (Bacchus being a tenor, in case the suspicious are wondering) is a rich climax to the work, while the heroine of the *commedia* players, Zerbinetta, has one of the most astounding and demanding coloratura arias in opera.

Die Frau ohne Schatten (1919) has Hofmannsthal at his most ambitious aiming at a complicated allegory, almost a modern *Magic Flute*. The fact that the Empress has no shadow symbolises the fact that she is childless, and in the opera there is a chorus of unborn children. Psychologically a most ambitious piece, this long work lives by Strauss's contribution, which is prodigious. It is hard for Londoners, used to a steady diet of magnificent performances under Georg Solti to understand why the opera is regarded by so many as a failure, for even those who do not regard it – as some do – as the composer's masterpiece, still rate it highly. Strauss's characterisation of Barak the dyer, a good unselfish man, with radiantly good music to prove it, is all the more masterly because goodness is not the easiest thing for a composer to put across in musical language. One of the finest moments, some of the warmest bars in German opera since *Meistersinger*, comes when the voices of watchmen are heard singing a hymn in the street, urging couples to love one another. And as the curtain falls on Act 2, Barak, whose shrewish wife will give him no love, lies down to rest alone. The opera ends most happily.

Intermezzo (1924) is a two-act 'bourgeois comedy with symphonic interludes' and the middle-class couple are Strauss and his wife. The opera is based on a misunderstanding between them, and when it was first given at Dresden, the singers were made up to look like the originals. If it is not one of his major works, Strauss's mastery of his art was now so complete that it is enjoyable and its music is often delightful. The next opera, *Die Ägyptische Helena* (The Egyptian Helen, 1928), is a serious work, but its dramatic feebleness detracts from some superb music, including a magnificent love-scene. Next came *Arabella* (1933) in which Strauss worked with his librettist for the last time. This is surely the most successful and appealing of all the composer's later operas, and there are many who rank this second Viennese comedy almost as high as the first. Characterisations are excellent and Strauss's love affair with the soprano voice remained at its peak. It is a most charming work and the atmosphere is carefree and happy. *Arabella* is a marvellous part for a charmer with a radiant voice: the finest in modern times has been Lila della Casa. The forthright hero Mandryka is another splendid role.

Die schweigsame Frau (The Silent Woman, 1935) from Ben Jonson's play *Epicoene* is amusing, but musically below the composer's best. His librettist was Stefan Zweig, with whom Strauss was soon forbidden to work as Zweig was a Jew. He turned to Joseph Gregor for *Friedenstag* (The Day of Peace, 1938) which was a single-act historical drama. *Daphne* (1938) was also a one-act piece, described by Gregor as 'a bucolic tragedy'. *Die Liebe der Danae* (1938–40; produced 1952) is in three acts and was a return to mythology. It has some of his most beautiful music even though Gregor's libretto was by no means ideal. The 'rain of gold' in the first interlude shows that the composer had lost none of his gift for the orchestration that makes him the darling of so many orchestral players the world over.

He was to write one more opera, *Capriccio* (1942). It lasts $2\frac{1}{2}$ hours without an interval and after years of being caviare to the general, has begun to be generally admired, though it needs to be understood fully if it is to be appreciated. As the argument in the opera is a dramatisation of the relative importance of words and music in opera, it is pointless if those words cannot be understood. The heroine, the Countess, who is Opera, cannot decide at the end between her suitors who respectively represent Poetry and Music, and this musical conversation-piece ends on an indecisive note. The whole question had fascinated Strauss for many years and now he ended his wonderful career by posing it in a most delightful form. 'We must end with a question mark,' he said, but in fact a phrase of the character of the Composer is the last heard. 'It sounds, when you consider,' wrote William Mann in his *Richard Strauss*, 'like a probable answer to the concluding query.' Only in *Salome* and, especially, *Elektra*, had words been definitely at a discount, though naturally music never lost its supremacy. In successful operas it never does.

It must be admitted, Strauss has his detractors as a musician and as a man. His musical temperament is not to the taste of some, but even his most ardent admirers would not deny that his operatic reputation rests securely on *Salome*, *Elektra*, *Rosenkavalier* and *Ariadne*, though one may hope that the time will come when his *Frau ohne Schatten* is generally admitted to be a masterpiece. As for his character, his interest in making money is regularly held against him, despite the fact that it is a subject that has exercised the minds of the majority of artists, though not all. He enjoyed making it, however, especially as he found it easy, and that seems to have rankled: for some, it was unforgivable.

Master of restraint

In the days when Richard Strauss was in his operatic prime it can have occurred to no-one that opera was soon destined to lose its public, not for old works, of course, but for new ones. Consider the position. Strauss himself was clearly destined to advance the frontiers of opera still further (which in the event in his mellow old age he did not wish to do). Puccini was surely ushering in a new century of Italian glory (whereas in fact he was the final flowering of the old glory). And then there was Debussy.

Claude Debussy (1862–1918), like Strauss, advanced the frontiers of opera, but his one work, *Pelléas et Mélisande* (1902), opened and closed a particular frontier. One may write of Strauss's contemporaries, men who were influenced by him or by Wagner or both, and some will be discussed, but *Pelléas* remains a lonely masterpiece unique in the story of opera. Some claim it as part of the Romantic Movement, indeed Gerhart von Westerman boldly calls it the last independent representative of the movement. But Alfred Loewenberg sums it up as the masterpiece of modern impressionistic French music.

Its interludes are Wagnerian and carry even more of the opera's emotions than the orchestral score of the rest of the work, yet *Pelléas* is as restrained as Wagner is not. For despite his plot, taken from Maurice Maeterlinck's Symbolist play, which included murder, jealousy and passion, Debussy opts for subtlety, and understatement to the point of extreme reticence. We are in a twilight world, virtually the world of *Tristan and Isolde*; but Wagner's world is as red-blooded as Debussy's is phantom-like. Not even the founding fathers of opera were as insistent as Debussy on the importance of the dramatic situation, with recitative at once crystal-clear and following natural speech. Though the opera has a devoted band of admirers and though musically it is as superb as one would expect from a major composer, the characters are not vividly drawn and the drama is not strong, however atmospheric and lovely the score. It is probably one of the worst first operas for a newcomer, though the experienced opera-goer who never unravels its secret is to be pitied.

So it came about that Debussy, a veritable musical giant, failed to start a school of opera, though his influence as a musician can be detected in the works of later composers, including, as we have seen, Puccini in his *Girl of the Golden West*.

Though Strauss and Debussy had shown that new styles of opera could be created, the newer styles, so rapid was the change in musical language, were not to come through them or through *verismo*, but from others who, for all their virtues, were not able – because of the relentless march of that language – to capture the popular tastes in the old way. In the last half-century 'modern' opera has become a minority taste, whereas in the nineteenth century audiences thronged to hear the latest new works. As a result, when new operas are staged, they seldom get star casts, conductors or producers. Such was Benjamin Britten's prestige and – for a modern opera composer – his popularity, that he attracted very fine artists for his premières, plus good conductors, producers and designers; but in the nineteenth century the equivalent of Callas and Sutherland were often to be found associated with new works, not just very occasionally, as with Leontyne Price in Barber's *Antony and Cleopatra*.

These facts should be borne in mind when reading the next chapter which covers opera in our own century since the giants departed, and a few who were working at the same time as the giants and who are still remembered today. Because this history of opera aims to present the operatic scene as it is, the chapter will not be an over-lengthy one. For today opera houses are basically museums – which they never were in the past. There is nothing wrong with a museum. Only disgruntled composers and critics who refuse to recognise popular taste object to the museums, which are treasuries of art, just as the Royal Shakespeare Theatre at Stratford-upon-Avon is a treasury. But opera as a living art-form, embraced by the multitudes who will always flock to the works of Verdi, Wagner, Mozart and the rest, is sadly a pipe-dream. We shall see some of the reasons as the changes that have come about are related.

9

A Brave New World?

Italy

Savagery was the keynote of the attacks launched by the younger generation of musicians on Puccini and the other *verismo* composers, but especially on Puccini. Some of the attacks were nothing but jealousy, but many were idealistic. We know that Puccini's artistic integrity was admirable, but it did not seem so to the generation that followed him; and this was a battle that went further than the usual dispute between the young and the old, parents and children.

As early as 1912 the musicologist Fausto Torrefranco spearheaded the attack against not only *verismo* but Italian opera generally in his *Giacomo Puccini e l'Opera Internazionale*. In this it was claimed that the true tradition of Italian music was the instrumental music of the seventeenth and eighteenth centuries and that opera did not even represent the native genius for music. (A full account of this and later attacks may be found in Mosco Carner's definitive biography of Puccini.)

Few went so far as this, for such an attack was patently absurd; but the generation immediately after Puccini firmly believed that opera had become bourgeois and effete (despite its appeal to the masses, which the reformers carefully avoided mentioning) and that a return to the old masters was essential. Some even demanded that composers who wrote only operas should be banned.

Naturally, these extreme feelings softened with age, and young enemies of opera like Pizzetti, Malpiero and Casella gradually turned to it more and more. The tragedy was that none of them had a quarter of Puccini's flair, and so it has come about that apart from a few *avant-garde* composers, the average new Italian work over the last generation has only been accorded respect, at the most.

Before looking at this school, and at the last of the *verismo* composers, it can be demonstrated how strongly the post-*verismo* generation felt, by simply looking at the career of Carlo Maria Giulini (1914–   ), one of the greatest conductors of our times. A student between the wars, he was totally out of sympathy not only with *verismo* but with Verdi as well, and though he was later to become the greatest Verdi conductor of the day, he has never managed to love Puccini. And is it just his demand for the highest standards in the opera house and his suspicion of the vast power of the star director that has led him virtually to abandon opera? Is it not, perhaps, that unlike so many Italians, he can function without it? His total integrity and supreme ideals are unchallengeable, but if he loved opera enough, could he keep away?

Of the composers who remained within the *verismo* tradition, while benefitting, like Puccini, from musical developments elsewhere, the most notable was Riccardo Zandonai (1883–1944). His operas include *Conchita* (1911), which was a success and *Francesca da Rimini* (1914) which was a triumph. Later works included *Giuletta e Romeo* (1922) and *I Cavalieri di Ekubu* (1925) and his operas are not forgotten in Italy. Italo Montemezzi (1875–1952) was not so much a *verismo* composer as a disciple of Boito. His first opera, *Giovanni Galurese* (1905), was a triumph, but his later works, including his masterpiece, *L'Amore dei tre Re* (1913), had more luck abroad than in Italy.

Ottorino Respighi (1879–1936), best known for his magnificent orchestral scene-painting, was very much one of the anti-*verismo* school, but his nine operas, inspired more by Germanic and older Italian trends, have not remained in the repertoire. They were not sufficiently dramatic, a charge never levelled against the *verismo* composers, but they are superbly and richly scored, and several were once popular: *Belfagor* (1923), *Maria Egiziaca* (1932) and *La Fiamma* (The Flame, 1934).

Gian Francesco Malipiero (1882–) was an even more ardent champion of old music than Respighi, like him editing Monteverdi. A long line of operas includes *Giulio Cesare* (1936), and he was busy composing until well into the 1950s. His son Riccardo is a critic and composer using the twelve-note system. Better known outside Italy is Ildebrando Pizzetti (1880–1968), whose most acclaimed works are *Debora e Jaele* (1922), *La Figlia di Jorio* (1954) from a play by D'Annunzio, and *L'Assassinio nella Cattedrale* (1961), from T. S. Eliot's play *Murder in the Cathedral*.

None of these composers deserve less than our respect, but, alas, respect does not automatically guarantee immortality. The reformers' motives were high, but, as Mosco Carner has pointed out, it is Gian-Carlo Menotti (1911–) who has had real success, by going back, not to Monteverdi or Vivaldi (or forward beyond Boulez) but to Puccini. True, his musical talent is considerably less than any of the *verismo* school, but his theatrical skill is unbounded, hence the success of *The Consul* (1950), also of his one-act pieces, the atmospheric *The Medium* (1946) and the amusing *The Telephone* (1947), and the Christmas favourite *Amahl and the Night Visitors* (1951). He has been panned regularly by critics and been hurt by them, so that the Spoleto Festival which he started in 1958 has occupied much of his time, giving both delight and opportunities to young musicians. It is a Festival of Two Worlds, for Menotti is an American of Italian birth, but musically he belongs to this section.

Two half-Italian, half-German composers may be included at this point. The first of them, Ermanno Wolf-Ferrari (1876–1948), though he had one *verismo* triumph (now best remembered for its intermezzo), *I Gioielli della Madonna* (The Jewels of the Madonna, 1911), wrote two operas that are still heard from time to time, and with much pleasure. The first was *I Quatro Rusteghi* (The Four Curmudgeons, 1906), known in Britain as *The School for Fathers*, which is genuinely funny and has a musical charm part-Rossinian, part of its own day, and *Il Segretodi Susanna* (Susanna's Secret, 1909), an entertaining one-act piece (the secret being her smoking). *Il Campiello* (1936) is given regularly in Italy and his first, *La Donne Curioze* (The Inquisitive Woman, 1903) in Germany.

Ferruccio Busoni (1866–1924) was a famous pianist, whose operas are best known in Germany, to whose cultural tradition he really belonged. His *Turandot* and *Arlecchino* (Harlequin) were given as a double bill in 1917 at Zürich. Despite atmospheric merits, the former sank after Puccini's opera appeared, but the latter, a *commedia dell'arte* piece, has been successfully revived, including performances at Glyndebourne in the 1950s. His finest work, *Doktor Faust*, was given in Dresden in 1925 after his death, having been completed by his pupil, Philipp Jarnach. Its admirers claim overwhelming grandeur and strength for its music, while being less happy with the libretto. It has been dubbed neo-classical and has an austere, intellectual vein, according to Edward Dent, who claimed nobility and beauty for it.

The post-war generation has seen *avant-garde* composers emerge in Italy, but despite several exciting occasions evoking the brave days of old, complete with scandals and demonstrations, the Modernists have failed to catch the public's love, or even real respect – in the sense of demanding regular revivals – any more than other post-*verismo* composers. These are facts of life and cannot be hidden under paeans of praise for adventurous talent and abuse of audiences for being reactionary.

The best known Modernists are Luigi Dallapiccola (1904–75), Luigi Nono (1924–) and Luciano Berio (1925–). The first, in spite of his advocacy of twelve-note technique, remembered the Italian love of the voice. His finest operas are *Volo di Notte* (1940) and the very moving *Il Prigioniero* (The Prisoner, 1950). Nono, a disciple of Webern, made his contribution to exposing the well-known evils of our society in his *Intolleranza 1960*, but Auber still remains the only composer who has actually started a revolution. Berio, Dallapiccola's pupil, is working in realms beyond the range of this book.

Others, like Nino Rota (1911–　) and Federico Ghedini (1892–1965), who wrote his version of *Billy Budd* (1949), have kept more in line with tradition. But let no one naïvely believe that the old days can be reborn. Such a rebirth is against all the facts of artistic life.

Germany

In Germany there is a tradition of adventurous audiences willing to sample new experiences. The operatic set-up helps in this, as there are some hundred opera houses in the two Germanys which are as much part of the local scene as public libraries are in Britain. But the problem remains the same. No one since Richard Strauss has achieved overwhelming acclaim.

Hans Pfitzner (1869–1949), like other contemporaries of Strauss, is little known outside Germany and Austria, though *Palestrina* (1917) is at least known to many by name. It concerns a legendary event in the life of the great Italian composer and its 'angelic' scene has been hailed by Pfitzner's champions as one of our century's supreme pieces of music. This Romantic nationalist and follower of Wagner wrote several other operas, including *Der Arme Heinrich* (Poor Henry, 1895).

Emil von Reznicek (1860–1945) is best remembered for his sparkling overture for *Donna Diana* (1894), a Viennese work for all its Spanish folk-themes, and Max von Schillings (1868–1933) is recalled for *Mona Lisa* (1915), a dramatic work about *the* Mona Lisa. Erich Korngold (1897–1957), a cult figure now for his masterly, rapidly-written scores for Warner Brothers' Errol Flynn films, had his greatest success with *Die Tote Stadt* (The Dead City, 1920). As befitted an embryo film-composer, he often sounds like Puccini and often like Strauss. Space forbids mention of all the German composers of the years between the wars, or just before them, but the magnificent score of *Notre Dame* (1914) by Franz Schmidt (1874–1939) deserves to be heard.

Better known abroad than any is Franz Lehár (1870–1948),

the Hungarian-born composer who changed from operas to operetta and overnight revived a flagging art-form in 1905 with *Die Lustige Witwe* (The Merry Widow). This is a masterpiece fit to rank with the classical operettas of the nineteenth century. After years of being treated as a musical comedy in Britain, complete with extra 'gags', its greatness was revealed when the Sadler's Wells Opera revived it in 1958. *Giuditta*, his only real opera, given its première at the Vienna State Opera, was the most successful of his later works, which included *Der Graf von Luxembourg*, *Gipsy Love* and *Das Land des Lächelns* (The Land of Smiles). The Mozartian tenor Richard Tauber helped Lehár's waning popularity in mid-career, though his temperamental nature closed the triumphant run of *The Land of Smiles* at Drury Lane long before it should have done.

Part of Lehár's strength lay in his frank admiration of Puccini (who returned that admiration) and Strauss (who did not), but his gift was his own. He paved the way for the final years of operetta proper with Oscar Strauss, Kálmán and Fall, but only great operetta is the concern of this book, and only with his *Widow* did Lehár, aided by the excellent libretto by Léon and Stein from Meilhac's *L'Attaché*, reach greatness in the strictest sense of the word. Never again did he achieve quite such a melodic feast, melodies that range from the sensuous and sweet to the deeply emotional (*Vilia*), from the uproarious (the March Septet) to the sophisticated and charming (Danilo's entrance number) – to mention but a handful of the riches.

Arnold Schoenberg (1874–1951) was in his 30s when the *Widow* was first given in his birthplace in 1905, and only four years later, he was to write one of the first works in which tonality was definitely abandoned – the very year that Richard Strauss seemed to be pushing the limits of music as far as they could go with his *Elektra*. The Schoenberg work was *Erwartung*.

Schoenberg's use of twelve-tone music and his invention of 'speech-song' have, with his great talent, made him widely admired within the musical world, not least because his influence has been immense; but it would be foolish to suggest that the ordinary opera-goer reaches a point beyond respect. Full houses at Covent Garden for *Moses und Aron* in 1965 were less to do with the work, or with Georg Solti and Peter Hall, than with mammoth publicity and dreams of debauchery on stage.

Erwartung, finally produced in 1924, is a monodrama, short and powerful, in which a woman looks for her lover in a forest and finds his dead body. With an excellent libretto by Marie Pappenheim, it gives a searing account of a frantic woman's mind, but without homework in advance the average opera-goer will be lost. *Die glückliche Hand* (The Lucky Hand, 1913; produced 1924) outdoes Strindberg at his most nightmarish, while *Von Heute auf Morgen* (From One Day to the Next, 1930) is the first comic opera to use the twelve-note system. Finally came *Moses and Aaron*, with its unfinished third act, which was first staged at Zürich in 1957. The words of the third act have been given with background music from Act 1, but this cannot be artistically right. It is an opera about communication between God and Man, and the way that God's truth, brought down from the mountain by Moses, is distorted by the eloquent Aaron. It would be idle to pretend that this is remotely 'easy' music, but repeated hearings should explain to even the sceptical listener why this opera is claimed as a masterpiece. It is a very serious work, and a tragedy with a most powerful impact. The composer, wishing to realise an ideal, made it difficult to mount and to sing and play, but it remains one of the few operas of the last half-century that many consider great.

Schoenberg's two pupils, Egon Wellesz (1885–1975) and Alban Berg (1885–1915) had dissimilar careers. The former in *Alkestis* (1924) followed his master, but was influenced by his studies of baroque opera. *Incognita* (1951) is less remarkable. Wellesz was for many years a lecturer at Oxford University. Berg, by far the more famous, achieved in *Wozzeck* (1925), from Georg Büchner's drama, one of the few modern operas that have created a considerable following. This is a *verismo* opera in the 'slice of life' sense, for the story tells how the anti-heroic Wozzeck, dull and put-upon and betrayed by his woman, Marie, kills her and afterwards drowns himself.

The drama is superb and the score, once it is mastered, is passionate and moving, a superb blend of modern techniques and older traditions. Sometimes it is harsh and nauseating, but so is the story. The construction is brilliant, with Berg providing his own libretto. Berg's feeling for humanity's lower depths makes the listener's worries about the complexities of the score less acute even at first hearing, and *Wozzeck*, without showing signs of becoming as popular as, say, *Salome* or *Elektra*, seems fairly certain to survive, no mean feat for any opera written since 1914. His *Lulu* was left unfinished, and first staged in Zürich in 1937. It is based on two plays by Wedekind and the heroine is a destructive *femme fatale* who is eventually killed by Jack the Ripper. It is even more highly admired by musicians than *Wozzeck*, though it has not the same hold on the public, who find little to identify within the lurid, albeit splendidly theatrical, tale.

Perhaps Béla Bartók (1881–1945) may be included here, since during the time he wrote his only opera, *Duke Blue-beard's Castle* (1911), this Hungarian was a citizen of the Austro-Hungarian Empire. It is in one act, and is too static to be an ideal work, but the score is both fascinating and tremendous, as door after door is opened by Bluebeard's wife Judith, leading her to her ruin. It is a disaster that this great composer did not turn again to opera.

Paul Hindemith (1895–1963) made his name with the tragic *Cardillac* (1926) from a Hoffmann story of a goldsmith who kills his clients to repossess his creations. In 1952, he successfully revived and improved it. *Neues vom Tage* (News of the Day, 1929) got him into trouble with the Gas Company, as the heroine of this satire on the Press sings in her bath that electric heating is better than gas. But his most impressive work is *Mathis der Maler* (Mathis the Painter, 1934, produced 1938) which resulted in exile, as Hindemith showed peasants rebelling on stage. The story is based on an actual painter and shows Hindemith's views on the artist's relation to society. Never a popular favourite, it is sufficiently respected to ensure revivals. *Die Harmonie der Welt* (The Harmony of the World, 1957), concerns the astronomer Kepler, while *Der lange Weinachtsmahl* (The Long Christmas Dinner), is from the play by Thornton Wilder. In Germany at least Hindemith is recognised as a major operatic figure.

Ernst Křenek (1900–), born in Austria, moved to the USA in 1938, but his finest work dates from before the move, including the famous jazz opera, *Jonny spielt auf* (Johnny strikes up, 1927). This well-made work, about a Negro who steals a violin and then conquers the world with his dance-music, created a sensation, though the 'serious' and jazz elements only rarely blend, and it has now lost its freshness. Earlier, in *Orpheus und Eurydike* (1926), Křenek had combined jazz and atonality. In *Leben des Orest* (The Life of Orestes, 1930) he tried to condense the *Oresteia* into a single evening, using neo-Schubertian music. *Karl V* (1938), a full-scale atonal music-drama, was banned by the Nazis, while *Pallas Athene Weint* (Pallas Athene Weeps, 1956) is a fierce twelve-tone work. Despite his modernist techniques, however, he has never ceased to strive for the popular touch. Many consider *Orpheus* musically his finest work.

Better known outside Germany are the operas of Kurt Weill (1900–50), partly because of his famous partnership with Bertold Brecht. Their first collaboration resulted in the highly influential *Die Dreigroschenoper* (The Threepenny Opera, 1928) in which this pupil of Busoni showed for the first time his uncomplicated, sourly romantic popular style. Based on *The Beggar's Opera*, it transferred the action to Edwardian London, and was followed by the more ambitious and far finer *The Rise and Fall of the City of Mahogonny* (1930), a searing satire by Brecht about an American city given over to material pleasure. This, and *Die Bürgschaft* (Hostage, 1932), to Caspar Neher's libretto, was political opera, and not surprisingly, Weill had to flee to America in 1935. In lighter vein there he wrote *Down in the Valley* (1948) and *Street Scene* (1949).

Weill's influence on the future of opera was indirect but, in the light of recent failure to make convincing modern music-dramas, significant, because he showed a popular way in which it could be done. Younger composers have used his techniques from time to time. His partnership with Brecht was uneasy owing to the old problem of the relative importance of words and music, but, especially in *Mahagonny*, the results were superb. The finest interpreter of Weill's songs was his wife Lotte Lenya.

Werner Egk (1901–) became popular in Germany via the radio, and by the time he came to write his first opera, *Die Zaubergeige* (The Magic Violin, 1935) he was very experienced. It was a truly popular opera, as was *Peer Gynt* (1938) after Hitler approved it. Other works have included *Columbus* (1941) an opera written originally for radio, but transformed, complete with narrators and splendid choruses, to the stage. The lightweight *Circe* (1948) was followed by the ambitious *Irische Legende* (1954) from a Yeats play, then *Der Revisor* (1957) an entertaining version of Gogol's *The Government Inspector*. Then came *Verlobung in San Domingo* (1963), '*verlobung*' meaning a betrothal. Egk has true theatrical instinct and is ready to use the skills of his predecessors, especially Stravinsky, to create his own popular style.

Carl Orff (1895–) solved the operatic problem more drastically in *Carmina Burana* (1937), his most widely known work, a cantata that is often enough staged to rank as an opera. It divides opinion fiercely, for to recapture the audiences estranged by modern music, he employed strong rhythms, exciting and often primitive effects and simple, instantly recognisable melodies. The mediaeval Minstrel Songs he uses are hymns to life, sexual love and nature, but critics have felt that Orff's treatment is inadequate: naïve percussive effects rather than a true reflection. It is up to the listener to decide. When the work is staged, the cast includes chorus and three soloists and dancers. *Der Mond* (The Moon, 1939) is even more tuneful and is a fairy-tale piece along the same lines, while *Catulli Carmina* (1943) is based on the life and work of the Roman poet and his love for Lesbia. With *Trionfi dell'Afrodite* (1953) and *Carmina Burana*, this became one of three cantatas of a triple bill, called *Trionfi*. *Antigonae* (1949) is a tragic opera and Orff has also written *Oedipus der Tyran* (1959), from Sophocles and what many consider his masterpiece, *Die Kluge* (The Clever Woman, 1943) from a story by the Brothers Grimm. The opera is once again simple, but also an amusing delight.

Rudolf Wagner-Regeny (1903–69), a Hungarian, later a German composer, had his greatest success with *Der Günstling* (The Favourite, 1935) to a Caspar Neher text, a violent story set in Mary Tudor's court, but with subdued music in effective formal style. A later success was *Prometheus* (1959).

Born the same year, Boris Blacher, who died in 1975, showed himself to be an original and ingenious composer, notably in *Die Flut* (The Tide, 1947), a chamber-opera for five wind instruments and a string quintet, and a strong plot about the effect on a small group of people of being cut off by the tide on a wreck they have been visiting. Other works that followed this one-act piece include a treatment of the story of the Captain of Köpenick, *Preussisches Märchen* (Prussian Fairy-tale). He also acted as librettist for his friend Gottfried von Einem (1918–), an Austrian who was Blacher's pupil. Von Einem's best-known works are taken from world-famous sources. *Dantons Tod* (Danton's Death, 1947) is a splendidly theatrical operatic version of Büchner's powerful French Revolutionary drama and *Der Prozess* (The Trial, 1953), comes from Kafka. In this Heinz von Cramer collaborated with Blacher on the libretto. *Die Bluthochzeit* (Blood Wedding) by Wolfgang Fortner (1907–) is yet another example of a famous play providing an opera, in this case a drama by Lorca.

This section will have indicated the sheer amount of new operatic activity in Germany since Richard Strauss and it has culminated in the work of Hans Werner Henze (1926–), one of the few living operatic composers who are internationally known. Before looking at his career, several other names must be noted, including Karl Hartmann (1905–63), whose chamber opera *Des Simplicius Simplicissimus Jugend* (The Youth of Simplicius . . ., 1948) made his name, as did Paul Dessau's (1894–) *Das Verhör des Lucullus* (The Trial of Lucullus, 1951). Giselher Klebe (1925–), a follower of Berg, first came to be known with *Die Räuber* (The Robbers, 1957), making his name with *Die Tödlichen Wünsche* (The Fatal Wishes, 1959), based on Balzac's *La Peau de Chagrin*. But neither he nor any other German composers of the day have the reputation of Henze.

In 1952, Henze's *Boulevard Solitude*, a treatment of the Manon Lescaut story, in which there is a notable amount of ballet, was a major success. A radio opera, *Das Ende einer Welt* (The End of a World, 1953) followed, in which this disciple of Schoenberg, albeit with a bias in favour of lyricism, first displayed his fascination with the artist in relation to himself and his fellow men and the responsibility between them. The story was a satire on the 'arty' set. *König Hirsch* (King Stag, 1956), with a libretto by Heinz von Cramer, is taken from Gozzi's *De Cervo*; in the opera a king turns into a stag, but seeing that his escape from life leads to no solution, he returns to his responsibilities. At this time Henze had come under the influence of a stay in Italy and the result was an intensification of his own exotic brand of lyrical writing. And meanwhile the opera divided opinion, unlike all too many modern operas which neither excite nor repel. *Der Prinz von Homburg* (1960), based on Kleist's play (adapted by Ingeborg Bachmann) found Henze taking in yet more musical influences – some say too many – in his portrait of a soldier dreamer, while *Elegy for Young Lovers* (1961), with an English text by W. H. Auden and Chester Kallman is about a major poet and his relation to society and, in particular, the way he devours his own group to help his art. The pair also adapted Euripides' *Bacchae* for Henze in his *The Bassarids* (1966), his richest and most substantial work to date. It runs for over two hours without a break and has a score alternatively magical and powerful. At the time of writing (1976) his *We Come to the River* is about to be given at the Royal Opera House, Covent Garden, which commissioned it. His political commitment since visiting Cuba (1966) is yet another influence on his art.

Spain

In Spain, Manuel de Falla (1876–1946) wrote his own brand of nationalistic impressionism in his early *La Vida Breve* (A Short Life, 1905, produced 1913). This is a superbly colourful work on two levels, Spanish popular life and strong drama, and the tragic heroine is a major creation. Later operas by the composer include *El Retablo de Maese Pedro* (1923) from *Don Quixote* and the posthumously produced *Atlantida* (1962), completed by Ernst Halffter. Enrique Granados (1867–1916) is remembered for *Goyescas* (1916).

France

In France, after Debussy's single masterpiece, another impressionist of genius, Maurice Ravel (1875–1937) turned to opera, but, alas, only wrote two short pieces. Both, however, were far more truly theatrical than *Pelléas*. *L'Heure Espagnole* (The Spanish Hour, 1911) is an entertaining, bawdy one-act work, which goes admirably with a good cast, while *L'Enfant et les Sortilèges* (The Child and the Enchantments, 1925) to a Colette text in which a naughty child gets his come-uppance from books, toys and furniture in part one and trees and animals in part two, until a good deed makes all well, is sheer delight.

The tradition of operetta started so superlatively by Offenbach, was continued in France by *La Fille de Madame Angot* (1872), by Charles Lecocq (1832–1918), *Les Cloches de Corneville* (1877) by Robert Planquette (1848–1903) and by André Messager (1853–1929), conductor of the first *Pelléas*, who wrote the delightful *Véronique* (1898), *Monsieur Beaucaire* (1919), and others.

Two years after this late operetta (for, as we have seen, the genre had almost faded despite Lehar, being diluted into musical comedy), Arthur Honegger (1892–1955) had a great success with his *Le Roi David* (1921). This major French composer, whose parents were Swiss, had conceived his *David* as an opera, but it appeared as a striking oratorio, with contrasting sections of simplicity and harsh modernity. *Judith* (1926) and *Antigone* (1927) were operas, and, after other works, he produced his best-known work, *Jeanne d'Arc au Bûcher* (Joan of Arc at the Stake, 1936). This has a speaking heroine and is part-oratorio, part-opera, and finely theatrical, for Honegger was able to fuse these different strands and make them convincing in a way few have ever achieved. The text by Paul Claudel was a key factor in the success of this 'opera in eleven scenes'. Later works included *L'Aiglon* (1937) in collaboration with Jacques Ibert.

Darius Milhaud (1892–1975) had an early success in collaboration with Jean Cocteau, with *Le Pauvre Matelot* (1927), a grim melodrama simply put across, unlike the vast *Christophe Colombe* (1930), with Claudel providing the text, and an assembly of nearly all the performing arts, film included. The music is clearer than some of the thought. *Bolivar* (1943) was praised without being a great success, but *David* (1950), another vast affair written to celebrate Israel's 3 000th anniversary, made a profound impression at La Scala and elsewhere.

Our last French composer, last, let it be recalled, of a long and honourable line, is Francis Poulenc (1899–1963) who, after a *comédie-bouffe*, *Le Gendarme Incompris* (1920) and the scintillating satire, *Les Mamelles de Tirésias* (1944) in which a husband and wife change sexes, produced the totally different *Dialogues des Carmelites* (1957), which is a sombre religious work set in the French Revolution, with a shattering scene at the Guillotine in the last act. It had a modest but real success in several countries. *La Voix Humaine* (1958) to a Cocteau text followed. This is a 45-minute monodrama for a soprano who speaks over the telephone to the lover who has jilted her.

Switzerland

Switzerland has a trio of modern composers to its credit, one of whom, Rolf Liebermann (1910–), after sterling work in charge of the Hamburg Opera from 1959, took over the Paris Opéra in the 1970s as noted earlier, and made it a great international house again, aided, amongst others, by Sir Georg Solti and an opera-loving President. His operas include *Leonore 40/45* (1952) about a German soldier and a Parisian girl in World War Two; *Penelope* (1954), and *The School for Wives* (1955). He uses twelve-note music, jazz and clever parodies to gain striking effects.

Heinrich Sutermeister (1910–) was a pupil of Orff and he made his name with *Romeo und Julia* (1940), a version of Shakespeare that concentrates almost entirely on the love-story. There is nothing complicated about his music and the opera has been widely performed, including at Sadler's Wells in the 1950s. *Die Zauberinsel* (The Magic Island, 1942), *Raskolnikoff* (Crime and Punishment, 1948), another major success, and *Titus Feuerfuchs* (1958) are among his other works.

Frank Martin (1890–1974) wrote the dramatic oratorio, *Le Vin Herbé* (The Love Potion, 1941), but only one true opera, *Der Sturm* (1956), an operatic version of *The Tempest*. Some of the verse is unaccompanied and some demands a *parlando* style of singing. It is a long work, as few cuts are made in the play.

Russia

It would be wrong to suggest that Igor Stravinsky (1882–1971) was a major opera composer, for he wrote only two full length operas in the strict sense of a not very strict word. *Le Rossignol* (The Nightingale, 1914), a spectacular and lush work, was started in 1908, and encompasses a change of style between the first act and the final two: Stravinsky, one of Diaghilev's brightest young men, was developing fast in those fabulous days. There followed a period when his works become hard to classify. *Les Noces* (The Marriage, 1914–17; produced 1923) is a ballet, yet it has choral and solo singing too. *Renard* (1922), the tale of a fox, has dancers on stage and male singers firmly in the orchestra pit while *Mavra* (1922) is a counterblast to Wagner in the form of a one-act *opera buffa* in the Italo-Russian style.

Oedipus Rex (1927), with a Latin text by Cocteau after Sophocles, plus a speaker, is a fiery opera-oratorio, neoclassical and passionate. Chorus and cast are masked in the ancient Greek fashion and movements are minimal, although the detachment of the speaker cannot conceal the fervour of the music. Other works had some slight links with opera, but in 1951 came the genuine article, *The Rake's Progress*, with a libretto by Auden and Kallman. The story is roughly that of the Hogarth engravings, and the exhilarating music is neo-Mozartian, *bel canto* Italian in places, but always Stravinskian as well. The Rake is finely drawn and the Bedlam Scene finds the composer, never one to wear his heart on his sleeve, in a most compassionately human vein. The score is for a classical orchestra, with no trombones and with recitatives supplied by a harpsichord. Naturally, the opera has admirers and detractors, as does nearly all the composer's pre-1914 music, but many consider it a masterpiece, while Stravinsky considered his libretto one of the best ever written.

After a brief spell when it looked as if the theatre and opera and ballet might be written off as bourgeois decadence, the Russian Revolution helped opera become more popular in the performing sense than ever before in Russia, for many more opera houses were built; but it had a dampening effect on composers, who were now expected to write suitable music, acceptable to the authorities. Censorship over music is particularly fatuous, especially when the safe way is to write post-Tchaikovsky works and stay out of trouble. As it happened, there were two men of genius at work in the Soviet Union, Sergey Prokofiev (1891–1953) and Dimitri Shostakovich (1960–75).

Prokofiev wrote his first opera at the age of nine. He was a pupil of Rimsky-Korsakov and he lived abroad from 1918 until 1934 after which his style, which had sometimes been, as Arthur Jacobs has put it, 'rather acid and iconoclastic', became simpler and more frankly popular. This did not prevent some of his music from being denounced by the authorities as being contaminated with 'formalism' – i.e. too clever, concerned with 'form' at the expense of 'content', or so the jargon went. It must be remembered that all Russian composers have laboured under the threat of some sort of denunciation for half a century, the degree depending on the period, and their native gift for opera has been sorely curbed.

Prokofiev's first surviving opera, *The Gambler*, after Dostoievsky, failed to be produced because of the Revolution and was finally given in Brussels in 1929. At once a major lyrical talent was evident to some, and the composer's examination of mental abnormality was a sign of things to come. *The Love of the Three Oranges* was very different and was first given in Chicago in 1921. Based on a Gozzi comedy, it is a highly unromantic fantasy and the music is high-spirited, sharp, stimulating and often bizarre. It is highly entertaining, if heartless.

There followed a totally different work, *The Fiery Angel*, written between 1922–5 and finally given at Venice in 1955. (Neither it nor its predecessor pleased the authorities back home. Both works were condemned for including 'parody' and 'expressionism'.) *The Fiery Angel* is based on a novel by Valery Bryusov (1908) about possession and sorcery. The composer thought it his finest opera and the few who have been able to hear it might well agree. The music is superbly romantic and often of great power and the exorcism rite in the last act, with hysteria mounting to a frenzy, is tremendous musictheatre. The role of the possessed Renata is a splendid one. Back in Russia the composer conformed sufficiently in *Semyon Kotko* (1940), a work suitably full of optimism, to please the guardians of taste and there is plenty of lyrical writing in the score which is set in the Ukraine during the Revolution. *The Duenna* (1940–41; produced 1946), based on Sheridan's play, is a delight, but *The Story of a Real Man* (1948), composed after the Zhdanov tribunal of official philistines had raised the bogey of formalism and other menaces to the state against a number of leading composers, was not liked by them.

War and Peace remains to be discussed. Most of this was written in 1941–42, but the composer was revising it up to his death. It had concert performances in 1944 and 1945 and part of it was given the next year. Then came the tribunal. Finally, it was given in Florence in 1953 and Leningrad in 1955.

This tremendous work assumes a knowledge of the Tolstoy masterpiece, for without it the opera is not easy to follow in detail, partly because of the sheer mass of characters. It was written when Russia was being attacked by Germany and is a patriotic epic suitable to those desperate days. Now a Soviet classic, it is not as fine a work of art as *The Fiery Angel*, but for many it solves – in spite of being a deeply romantic work – the problem of writing a modern opera for a mass audience without being deliberately reactionary. It needs all the resources of modern staging and can make a great effect, and much of the music of 'Peace' is beautiful. On the whole 'War' is more conventional, though nonetheless effective. Dramatically, many events are blurred because of lack of time in what in any event is an enormously long work, but however the individual opera-goer rates the work; it remains one of the few operas of the last forty years to impress itself on vast numbers of listeners – which is a cautious way of suggesting that it may almost be a popular masterpiece, if not so secure a one as *Turandot*.

Apart from a topical operetta on Moscow's housing, *Moscow Cheremushki* (1959), Shostakovich's operatic output was confined to two works, both of which got him into trouble, one of them so much that one can hardly blame him for not increasing his output. *The Nose* (1930) from Gogol was a satire on Tsarist times, but Authority decided that it was too musically eccentric for good citizens: the inclusion of 'eccentric effects of the onomatopoeic kind' was the crime. Then came his masterpiece, *Lady Macbeth of the Mtsensk District* (1934). It was acclaimed as a model of Soviet realism, but two years later *Pravda* savagely attacked it in an article entitled 'Confusion instead of Music'. A revised version (the revisions being mainly textual) was renamed *Katerina Ismailova*, and in 1963 it returned to the Russian repertory, having been quite well known abroad for many years before that. The heroine Katerina who takes a lover and, with him, murders her husband, is memorably and sympathetically drawn, many of the other characters being satirically portrayed. The new version of this powerful and passionate work is minus some passages in the libretto of 'crudely erotic character' (Martin Cooper). Its history is curious and – for the composer and for art – tragic.

Other Soviet operas have run into trouble down the years, but none have made a mark outside Russia. Many are of purely local interest and reflect a long pre-Revolution tradition. For instance, the first Azerbaidjan opera, *Leili i Medzhun* (1907) by Uzir Gadzhibekov, which uses local instruments, was written as long ago as 1907. *Prince Igor* was given in Moscow in 1960 by a Mongolian troupe singing in their own language, rather than Russian. Modern Soviet operas include *The Quiet Don* (1935) by Dzerzhinsky, while Kabalevsky, Shaporin and Khrennikov are among those who have attempted to write major works within the system. Whatever one may think of official interference with composers, one must ruefully note that even in countries where there is no state interference few have managed to solve the problem of writing modern operas that appeal to the public.

Czechoslovakia

To the near despair of his admirers, the operas of Leoš Janáček (1854–1928) make tortoise-like progress towards general acceptance. He is no more 'difficult' musically than Richard Strauss, and *Jenufa* could hardly strain a Puccinian. True, his subject-matter is somewhat alienating to those who like conventional operatic plots, while his orchestration is sometimes (happily) unusual, though hardly complex. His words are tightly allied to the Czech language – which rarely makes for completely successful translations – but that is no new thing in opera. It must be admitted, though, that it is sometimes hard to catch crucially important phrases because of the level of sound. Yet when all these alleged objections have been paraded, the lack of appreciation remains startling, for these operas are enjoyable and most of them are excellent theatre.

Janáček made his name with *Jenufa* (1904), a dramatic and tragic opera with superbly lyrical passages and stirring use of native folk idiom, though the composer said there was not a single folk-tune in it. Despite passages of searing beauty, there is no romantic gloss over the score, and two characters, Jenufa and her step-mother, the Kostelnička, who murders Jenufa's child, are major creations of a humanist whose love of life, people, and nature, played so great a part in his career.

Jenufa was the turning point, for his first opera, *Sarka*, dating back to 1887, was not heard until 1925, and his second, *The Beginning of a Romance* (1894) was watered-down Smetana. In *Jenufa*, Janáček wrote his own libretto from a play by Gabriela Preissová, but it was followed by *Osud* (Fate) which was fatally weakened by its libretto and was not seen until 1958. Not until 1920 did Janáček return to the opera house with *The Excursions of Mr Brouček*. This is in two parts, *Mr Brouček's Excursion to the Moon*, which gave him much trouble, and *Mr Brouček's Excursion to the Fifteenth Century*. A masterpiece followed this interesting work, *Káta Kabanová* (1921) after Ostrovsky's *The Storm*. It is a strong, passionate tragedy and the portrait of its heroine is superb. Interestingly, the play made little impression when given at Britain's National Theatre, but the effect of the opera on its audiences is tremendous. *The Cunning Little Vixen* (1924) is a paean of praise to nature. It has production problems (most of the cast are animals) but none that cannot be solved, as was shown by Felsenstein in East Berlin and Jonathan Miller at Glyndebourne. The music is delightful, and, at the end of the opera, ravishingly beautiful, worthy to be set beside that other pantheistic masterpiece, Beethoven's Pastoral Symphony. Yet neither of its two productions in Britain have caught the public imagination. *The Makropoulos Case* (1926) from the play by Capek, has had more success, but for all its theatrical qualities, has not become widely loved. The heroine possesses the secret of eternal life, for she has lived for some 300 years and remains a beauty, but longs to find the formula to end her intolerable existence. Though the first act has almost too much plot and has to be followed very closely, the star role is a tremendous one and the ending of the opera, when the heroine ages and dies, is even finer musical theatre than his other operas.

Lastly came *From the House of the Dead* (1930) from Dostoievsky's novel of his experiences in a Siberian labour camp. From its haunting prelude, it is a riveting work, though some people are understandably (though mistakenly) put off by the subject matter. Again, the opera is vividly theatrical, though so episodic that sometimes the tension relaxes too much, and parts of it are very moving. At the start of the score Janáček wrote, 'In every human being there is a divine spark' and here all men are brothers. Enormously popular in his own intensely operatic country, his works seem to be gaining headway abroad, if slowly. Some critics alienate potential converts by foolishly praising him at the expense of Puccini and Strauss: he should be praised on his own merits as one of the masters of the twentieth century, and some day his popularity may be as high as his reputation.

Great Britain

Because Benjamin Britten's *Peter Grimes* (1945) made so memorable an impact at its première and remains one of the most astonishing first operas in history (for surely we do not have to include the fascinating early operetta, *Paul Bunyan* (1941) given at Aldeburgh in 1976, and spoil a good point), it did not create modern English opera overnight. There had even been some modest foreign adventures for British works. English (or British) opera in the early nineteenth century was, as we have seen, not very national.

Balfe and his contemporaries were pale imitations of the

Italian masters, and none the worse for that. Sir Charles Villiers Stanford (1852–1924), an Irishman, fought hard to establish English opera, writing ten completed works, while championing the art of opera at a time when Parry and his disciples were abusing it. His *The Critic* (1916) and, especially, *Shamus O'Brien* (1896) and *The Travelling Companion* (1925) were all worthy and enjoyable efforts. The last of these was given at Sadler's Wells, where Lilian Baylis (1874–1937) reigned from 1931 as she had at the Old Vic from 1914. This glorious, ill-educated, God-intoxicated, inspired, earthy, invincible woman created, without subsidy, but with plenty of prayer and push, what became the Old Vic Theatre Company, the Royal Ballet and the Sadler's Wells Opera, now the English National Opera. In other words, she created three national theatres. But before her day the English renaissance, exemplified by Edward Elgar, who loved opera but alas did not write one, produced some minor but fine works.

The redoubtable Dame Ethel Smyth (1858–1944) wrote six operas, the best of which, *The Wreckers* (1906) and *The Boatswain's Mate* (1916) reflect her German training, but also her essential Englishness. The former was first given in Leipzig. Beecham, who spent a fortune on giving his countrymen high-class opera, was a champion of this remarkable supporter of Women's Rights, who actually composed the Suffragettes' anthem, and he championed even more fervently Fredrick Delius (1862–1934). By far the most successful opera by this Bradford-born composer of German-Scandinavian descent (who trained in Leipzig, and later lived in France, having been for a while an orange-planter in Florida) is *A Village Romeo and Juliet* (1900–1, produced 1907). It was given in Berlin before Beecham presented it at Covent Garden in 1910 and its intermezzo, 'The Walk to the Paradise Garden', is a concert-hall favourite. *Irmelin* (1890–2, produced 1953), *Koanga* (1895–7, produced 1904) and *Fennimore and Gerda* (1900–10, produced 1919) are scarcely known despite Beecham's efforts.

Nor are the operas of Gustav Holst (1874–1934) ever likely

to challenge the popularity of his suite *The Planets*, though his one-act *The Perfect Fool* (1923), best known for its ballet music, has some nice parodies of opera, notably of Verdi and Wagner. *Savitri* (1916) is admired, being a one-act chamber opera reflecting Holst's interest in India and Sanskrit. He also wrote the Falstaffian *At the Boar's Head* (1925) and *The Tale of the Wandering Scholar* (1934), a comedy.

That most English of composers of our century, Ralph Vaughan Williams (1872–1958) had more success, though it seems that none of his operas is destined to enter even the irregular repertory. This is particularly hard on *Hugh the Drover* (1924), a splendid ballad opera revived as late as the 50s at Sadler's Wells. Set in Napoleonic times, its first act shows the composer at his most enjoyable, as exhilarating as it is tuneful, and the second act is only comparatively less successful. *Riders to the Sea* (1937) follows J. M. Synge's tragedy word for word and this one-act piece is probably his finest opera. For the rest, *Sir John in Love* (1929), the Falstaff of the *Merry Wives*, is enjoyably vigorous and lyrical, but is not helped by comparison with Verdi's *Falstaff*, while *The Poisoned Kiss* (1936) with a brilliant and satiric score has a sub-Gilbertian libretto that does it no favours. The one-act *The Shepherds of the Delectable Mountains* (1922) was later included in *The Pilgrim's Progress* (1951), which will always attract lovers of the composer, even though it is, as it states, a Morality, not an opera.

Rutland Boughton (1878–1960) longed to make Glastonbury in Somerset an English Bayreuth, but the operas of this Wagnerian have been forgotten except for *The Immortal Hour* (1922), which had a huge success in the commercial theatre and is now a theatre legend weakened by an inadequate revival at Sadler's Wells in the 1950s.

This, then, was the situation when *Grimes* burst on the scene – a certain amount of native activity over a period of half a century by the listed composers and a few more, an outlet for some of them at Sadler's Wells (which was bombed in the war), and precious little place for English opera in the short international and other seasons at Covent Garden between the wars. Covent Garden was used as a dance hall in World War Two, a sure indication of the fragility of opera's hold.

Benjamin Britten (1913–76) was far and away the most successful operatic composer in British history, and he is genuinely popular, liked and loved in the way many of the great figures in this book were loved in their own lifetime. It would be untrue to suggest that his public is Verdian or Puccinian in its size, but it is considerable, and not just in Britain. After the triumph of *Peter Grimes* by the Royal Opera, Covent Garden, at La Scala in 1976 Harold Rosenthal bluntly stated in *Opera* that it 'proved we have produced the greatest operatic composer of the post-war period'.

Its hero, an outsider like so many of Britten's, is less stark than the Grimes of George Crabbe's poem, used as the basis of Montague Slater's libretto. In the scene in the Boar tavern with a storm raging outside, Crabbe's Grimes could never suddenly sing so hauntingly of the stars and Fate in 'Now the Great Bear and Pleiades', a visionary time-stopping moment in a busy, dangerous scene. Characterisation throughout the opera is masterly. Grimes is misunderstood, an object of hatred to otherwise ordinary, kindly people, but we know why they feel as they do, and suffer the more when he alienates his one true friend, Ellen Orford, whose impassioned 'Let her among you without fault' is only the first of many lyrical treasures. The choral music reveals total mastery, and the pauses between the great cries of 'Peter Grimes' when the townspeople have turned into a mob are themselves enough to proclaim a major talent, as are the interludes. The Moonlight Prelude before Act 3 is simple, powerful, beautiful and shattering – after which we go straight into an entertaining scene on the beach with a dance in the background in the Moot Hall. We are in Britten's beloved Aldeburgh (called 'the Borough') around 1830 and the sea is very much part of this score – a virile, mystical, gentle and thrilling score, and as professional a first opera as any in operatic history.

No excuse need be made for the amount of space devoted

here to *Grimes* because it is important to stress its impact, which so overwhelmed its first audiences (who saw Peter Pears as Grimes and Joan Cross as Ellen). In the modern British theatre only the impact of John Osborne's *Look Back in Anger* (1956) can be compared to it. Many writers looked to the theatre after Osborne's explosive play and Britten's opera similarly transformed the whole operatic scene. That a school of popular operatic composers has not resulted – as opposed to a number of fine individual ones – is due to the difficulty of communicating in the musical language of today. With Britten, however, there is no real difficulty for anyone with open ears who is prepared to listen and listen again.

Britten founded the English Opera Group in 1946 (with John Piper and Eric Crozier) to create and perform new operas and encourage poets and playwrights to write librettos in collaboration with composers. *The Rape of Lucretia* (1946) was a notably successful result, scored for a twelve-piece orchestra, while *Albert Herring* (1947) in which Eric Crozier transferred a Maupassant story to Suffolk complete with local types and a hero whose virtue gets him elected King of the May, is at once delightful, totally assured technically, and genuinely funny. Britten's version of *The Beggar's Opera* (1948) is an inventive, though not final, solution to the problem of presenting the famous old piece.

There followed *Let's Make an Opera* (1949), with a first part in which children and adults rehearse an opera, *The Little Sweep*, with the audience's help. This first half is in play form, then the opera is given. The entire proceedings are a delight. In 1951, Britten, a devoted Purcellian, gave his realisation of Purcell's *Dido and Aeneas*, then returned to full-scale opera with *Billy Budd*, E. M. Forster providing a libretto from Herman Melville's classic story of the good young sailor destroyed by evil. Even more sea-haunted than *Grimes*, this deeply impressive and finally emotionally shattering work was originally in three acts, but is now reduced to two. It has an all-male cast, which may have held it back in popularity, though it has been widely admired, and was a success on television. Billy's characterisation is superb, which in itself is a triumph in view of the problem of presenting sheer goodness in musical terms, while Captain 'Starry' Vere, sensitive but duty-bound, is another major creation. Although the evil Claggart is not totally convincing, the way in which the difficulties of setting it aboard a Man-o'-War are overcome is astonishing; and for many the opera is Britten's most compelling.

Gloriana (1953), written for the Coronation, suffered at its première from an audience who rarely went to opera, let alone a modern one, and the unknowing might have imagined that Britten had committed high treason with what was in fact a deeply compassionate version of the story of Elizabeth and Essex. Britten, besides, was so successful that, like others before him, he was attracting hostility. Though the characterisation is not as fine as usual, with the exception of the two principals, and though the pageantry is alleged to weaken the dramatic flow, it is a superb and often ravishing score, and since the Sadler's Wells revival in the 1960s has become greatly loved. It was liked from the start by many, though legend has it otherwise. The Queen has some glorious music. *The Turn of the Screw* (1954) saw a return to chamber-opera, with innocence again corrupted. The integration of this haunting, powerful work is total, while *Noyes Fludde* (1958), from one of the Chester cycle of Mystery Plays, is surely the finest work for children since *Hansel and Gretel*, or the finest of any period. That children take so notable a part in it has helped make it the most widely known and loved of all Britten's works.

A Midsummer Night's Dream (1960) can be given in its chamber-opera form or as a full-scale piece. Peter Pears adapted half the play and Britten provided a *Dream* of sheer magic in the traditional (as opposed to Peter Brook/Royal Shakespeare Company) sense. He gave each of the three worlds, Fairies, Lovers, Mechanicals, their own brand of music and musical colour and the result is, for many, another masterpiece. The Pyramus and Thisbe scene is a Donizettian pastiche complete with mad scene and only purists have objected to it. For everyone else it is a riotous triumph, while the ending of the opera, with children's voices used sublimely, would melt a heart of granite. For the record, Oberon is a counter-tenor part and Puck is spoken.

There followed the 'Parables for Church Performance', *Curlew River* (1964) and *The Burning Fiery Furnace* (1966) and *The Prodigal Son* (1968), then *Owen Wingrave* (1971), originally given on television. From a Henry James story, this drama of a pacifist in a military family showed yet another advance musically, for Britten never ceased to experiment in sound, but the dice are too loaded in favour of the hero, his monstrous family being so unsympathetically drawn that the opera is weakened artistically. There is no such weakness in *Death in Venice* (1973) from Thomas Mann's novel. Though the structure of the opera has divided opinion and the use of dance has been questioned, it has been hailed as yet another masterpiece. The score is dazzling in its inventiveness, and the central character, created unforgettably by Peter Pears in his 60s, is a triumph. Unfortunately ill-health afflicted Britten in the 1970s, and his death in 1976 ended hopes of yet more triumphant solutions to the very real problems of modern opera.

Sir William Walton (1902–   ) has written two operas, *Troilus and Cressida* (1954), containing some fine romantic music and a notable characterisation in Pandarus, and the one-act *The Bear* (1967) from the Chekhov farce, an entertaining, zestful piece. Sir Michael Tippett (1905–   ) has written three operas, *The Midsummer Marriage* (1955), *King Priam* (1962) and *The Knot Garden* (1970), all with librettos by himself. The first was thought to have failed because of its rather tortuous allegorical libretto, but revivals and a recording have attracted a growing band of enthusiasts whose love of the music – much of it beautiful and all of it the product of a truly musical mind – has caused them to hail it as a masterpiece. *King Priam*, a sparser score set in the Trojan War is about 'the mysterious nature of human choice' and has not yet been so acclaimed, though there are fine musical and theatrical moments in it. *The Knot Garden* is a richer score and concerns human nature and the need to reconcile its darker and lighter sides so that peace and full maturity may result.

Other British composers have produced operas with varying degrees of success. Lennox Berkeley (1903–) wrote *Nelson* (1953), an interesting attempt at portraying the hero, though somewhat handicapped by its structure, whereas his one-act *A Dinner Engagement* (1954), with a witty libretto by Paul Dehn, is a delight. Others have been *Ruth* (1956) and *The Castaway* (1967), both for the English Opera Group. Alan Bush (1900–) has had a number of operas successfully staged in East Germany, the subjects reflecting his political beliefs. They include *Wat Tyler* (1950) and *The Men of Blackmoor* (1955). Arthur Benjamin (1893–1960), an Australian, wrote several operas including the entertaining *Prima Donna* (1933, produced 1949) and *A Tale of Two Cities* (1949–50), which last, though it won a Festival of Britain Award, was not given until 1957, a sure indication of the difficulties opera composers have suffered in England. Another Australian, Malcolm Williamson (1931–) now the Master of the Queen's Musick, has written operas in what some critics believe is a reactionary vein, complete with 'obvious' tunes. *Our Man in Havana* (1963) was much abused for this, but gave pleasure and *The Violins of St Jacques* (1966) a finer opera, gave even more.

Richard Rodney Bennett (1936–) made his name with the very dramatic *The Mines of Sulphur* (1965) and also wrote *A Penny for a Song* (1967) and *Victory* (1970) from Conrad's novel. Eschewing obvious melody in his operas (alas), he is probably the most promising of the younger operatic composers. Other composers who make up the growing band working in the opera house from time to time include Humphrey Searle (*Hamlet*), Alexander Goehr (the powerful *Arden Must Die*), Iain Hamilton (*The Catiline Conspiracy*), Alun Hoddinott (*The Beach of Falesa*) and Nicholas Maw (the entertaining *The Rising of the Moon*). Inflation permitting, the future is perhaps not so bleak, though the public has taken no British composer to its heart except – as has been indicated – Benjamin Britten.

The United States

The United States is better known for a long line of fine singers than for its native operatic composers. Early operas include *The Archers*, or *Mountaineers of Switzerland* (1796) by a Mr Carr, some of whose music survives, and the first publicly performed opera by an American was Fry's *Leonora* (1845). Frederick Converse's *Pipe of Desire* (1910) was the first American work to be given at the Metropolitan, New York, and among other operas of the first decades of the century is *Peter Ibbetson* (1931) by Deems Taylor (1885–1966) which was a success at the Met.

It was in the 1930s that a native American idiom began to be heard in opera, the most famous and finest example being *Porgy and Bess* (1935) by George Gershwin. As the years go by its reputation, always considerable, grows. Mixing jazz and 'serious' music without blending them and without apology, Gershwin created the American national opera, full of superb characterisation, drama, humour, vitality, local colour and haunting melody. Set in Catfish Row, a Black tenement in South Carolina in the late nineteenth century, its libretto is by Du Bose Hayward and Ira Gershwin after *Porgy*, a drama by Du Bose and Dorothy Heyward. The cripple Porgy and his unfaithful sweetheart Bess, the dope-pedlar Sportin' Life, and Serena are among the legendary characters, and it is the last of these that sings 'Summertime', a simple, haunting masterpiece, magnificent even by Gershwin's standards.

Samuel Barber (1910–   ) has written two operas, *Vanessa* (1958) with a libretto by Menotti, which was produced at the Met. and at Salzburg and had a respectful hearing, and *Antony and Cleopatra* (1966) which opened the new Met. in 1966 and was swamped by the occasion and by the over-active production, complete with stage machinery, of Franco Zeffirelli at his most exuberant. Menotti has been discussed in Chapter 8, but though born in Italy, he ranks as American, and for all the critical savagery launched at him, remains America's most successful operatic composer, even if none of his work approaches the quality of *Porgy*.

A famous opera between the wars, unheard now, but highly regarded by many was *Four Saints in Three Acts* (1928, produced 1934) by Virgil Thomson (1896–) with a text by Gertrude Stein, who also provided one for his *The Mother of us All* (1947). The former's score has charm as well as sophistication and its composer is also a notable critic. Aaron Copland (1900–) is far better known for his wonderful ballet scores than for his operas. *The Second Hurricane* (1937) is a 'play opera' for schools. *The Tender Land* (1954) set in the mid-West in the Depression is an often beautiful and hauntingly evocative drama.

The most politically minded American operatic composer was Marc Blitzstein (1905–64), whose *The Cradle will Rock* (1937), produced by Orson Welles, is a fiercely anti-capitalist opera, claimed by the theatre critic Brooks Atkinson to be 'the most versatile triumph of the political insurgent theatre'. It was not liked by the authorities, and nor was his *No for an Answer* (1941). *Regina* (1949) was a musical version of *The Little Foxes*, and his adaptation of *The Threepenny Opera* (1954) ran for 2 250 performances.

Thanks to the money available for the arts in American universities and colleges, whose theatrical departments are often richly endowed, there is an enormous amount of operatic activity today, and apparently more than 1 000 American operas were written between 1930–67. As yet, and despite many notable efforts, the United States has no more solved the problem of making modern opera truly popular than has any other country. Yet with barriers crumbling between theatre artforms, and with the endless vigour of the American Musical, the solution may well be found in the USA. Leonard Bernstein (1918–), that exceptionally gifted composer-conductor, wrote in *Candide* (1956) a superb parody of opera and operetta which in many ways was also operetta and opera, while his *West Side Story* (1957) showed how all the theatre arts could be amalgamated on the highest level (given a fine cast). As yet his only true opera is *Trouble in Tahiti* (1952), but he, or someone inspired by him, might produce a modern opera that has wide appeal without falling back on old methods.

Yet if opera is doomed to become 'Museum Art', as the language of music grows steadily more complex, and composers, even with large grants, feel that opera as we know it is not for them, then opera-goers should relax and make the most of what is in the Museum. With foundations built on Mozart, Verdi and Wagner and a score of lesser masters, the opera-lover may well ask: 'What is wrong with a museum?'

Appendix I

An ABC of Opera – some definitions and descriptions

(Many are more fully explained in the text. See Index.)

Aria
The elaborate song-form of opera and oratorio, from the Italian for 'air'.

Arietta
A shorter, simpler aria.

Arioso
An aria-like vocal form, roughly half way between an aria and recitative.

Baritone
The male voice between tenor and bass.

Bass
The deepest male voice. Several countries have sub-divisions of this and other voices, for which see *The Concise Oxford Dictionary of Opera*, etc.

Bass-baritone
Not, as might be supposed, simply a voice between bass and baritone, but the voice required for certain parts – Wotan, Hans Sachs, Boris, etc. – demanding lyricism and the depths of a *basso profondo*.

Bel Canto
A rather imprecise term meaning beautiful singing or beautiful song. *Bel Canto* flourished in Italy from the seventeenth to nineteenth centuries, with the stress on lovely tone, perfect technique and smooth phrasing. Drama was less in evidence than in the German style, yet the most admired artists of the early nineteenth century who used the Italian style, Pasta and Malibran, were intensely dramatic, as was Callas when she did so much in the 1950s to revive the art of Bel Canto. And a major Verdian role with-

out dramatic singing as well as beautiful tone is a negation of what the composer intended.

Brindisi   A drinking song, from the Italian 'far brindisi,' meaning 'to drink one's health'.

Buffo   A singer of comic roles, as in 'basso buffo'. From the Italian for 'gust' or 'puff'.

Cabaletta   Though this can mean a short simple aria with repeats, as used by Rossini and others, or a recurring passage in an aria, the opera-goer is most likely to meet it as the brilliant, usually swift, last section of an aria. Verdi's raised the form to fiery, often electrifying, heights.

Cadenza   A virtuoso display by a singer (or instrumentalist) at the end of an aria, notably in eighteenth-century music. It could be dragged out far beyond legitimate ornamentation, as indeed some pianists do to this day.

Cantelina   Vocal writing that is smooth and tuneful, or an indication by a composer that such singing is required.

Canzone   A song in an opera that is not part of the action, a famous example being the Veil Song in *Don Carlo*, sung by Eboli.

Castrato   Though this sad subject is dealt with in Chapter 1, it may be amplified a little. Castrati entered opera because there was a shortage of trained women singers, while some countries banned females on stage (as did England until the Restoration). Long after opera abandoned them – though as late as the 1820s Meyerbeer wrote a a role for Velluti the last great castrato in *Il Crociato in Egitto* – the Vatican continued using male sopranos and altos, castrated before puberty.

Cavatina   A short aria.

Claque   Hired applauders, who strangely do more good than harm, whatever the essential fraudulence of their 'profession'. Many are students and indigent music-lovers and they merely get free tickets, as opposed to their leader who is paid. A good leader can transform a dull audience in Italy, Vienna, etc, by carefully-timed expressions of joy – as opposed to anti-claques who are basically hired assassins out to wreck, as has happened to Callas and others in our own times. The most notable example of the artistic integrity of a claque occurred at Parma, that rugged hot-bed of passionate enthusiasm, where once the local claque returned a tenor's fee to him and proceeded to boo his every performance until he fled the town.

Coloratura   Elaborate ornament of a melody, from the German 'Koloratur', hence the *coloratura* soprano.

Comprimario   The small part artists in opera: Barbarina in *Figaro* and Spoletta in *Tosca* are both *comprimario* roles, though the former is often a stepping-stone to larger roles, whereas the *comprimario* singer is normally a specialist in such parts.

Conductor   The key figure in any operatic performance, however distinguished the singers, however glamorous and/or talented the producer. Conducting an opera is inevitably a more arduous and responsible job than conducting a symphony orchestra, for the forces under the conductor's command in the opera house are so much vaster and the opportunity for disaster so much more considerable. Not until the present century was the conductor given the respect he deserved – assuming he had talent – though exceptions in the nineteenth century included Hans Richter and Hans von Bülow, both notable Wagnerians, and Franco Faccio, who conducted the first *Otello* and ranks as the first great modern Italian opera conductor. Space forbids a list of the elect, but no roster, however select, could leave out Arturo Toscanini, Gustav Mahler, Bruno Walter, Thomas Beecham, Erich Kleiber, Clemens Krauss, Tullio Serafin, Vittorio Gui, Otto Klemperer, Hans Knappertsbusch, Felix

Weingartner and Rudolf Kempe from the past, and Georg Solti, Herbert von Karajan, Carlos Kleiber, Reginald Goodall (in Wagner) Leonard Bernstein, Claudio Abbado, James Levine and Colin Davis (in Berlioz) and Karl Böhm from the present. Carlo Maria Giulini, alas, has virtually abandoned opera.

Contralto   The lowest women's voice.

Continuo   A part played throughout a work in the bass line, on the harpsichord, organ, etc.

Contrapuntal   It is the adjective of counterpoint, which is the method of combining two or more melodies simultaneously, yet making musical sense out of them.

Counter-tenor   A voice higher than a tenor's using an exceptional amount of head resonance. It is not a falsetto voice and is not to be confused with a castrato. The most notable part written for it is Oberon in Britten's *A Midsummer Night's Dream*. Few counter-tenors have enough power for a large opera house, an exception being James Bowman.

Csardas   A Hungarian national dance, though, as in Rosalinda's Csardas in Act 2 of *Die Fledermaus*, the term can be applied to a song.

Da Capo aria   An aria in three sections, the third being a repeat of the first. In use from *c* 1650–1790.

Dramma Giocoso   Mozart so described *Don Giovanni*. The term was used mainly in the eighteenth century to describe a comic opera with serious or tragic scenes.

Dramma per musica   A term used in the seventeenth and eighteenth centuries to describe a libretto and its serious operatic treatment.

Festivals   The oldest European opera festival is Bayreuth's, which began in 1876 with the first complete *Ring*. Many so-called festivals, however enjoyable, are really a glamorous part of the ordinary opera season, but the truest festivals have an identity of their own. Among them are Salzburg, which has been famous since its start in the 1920s, not simply for its Mozart, but for Strauss, Verdi, etc, and many modern works. A new Festspielhaus was built in 1960, which houses the Easter Festival, the creation of von Karajan, whose Wagnerian performances during it are famous. Perhaps the most legendary performances were given under Toscanini from 1935 to 1937, including *Falstaff, Fidelio, Zauberflöte* and *Meistersinger*. The greatest open air festival is in the Verona Arena, greatest in locale, size of audiences and performance standards. Other notable festivals include Glyndebourne (1934) Edinburgh (1947), Spoleto (1958), Florence (1933), Santa Fé (1957), Aix-en-Provence (1948), Aldeburgh (1948), and Wexford (1951). Some have super-stars, other stars in the making, some are tourist traps. Cinncinnati's (1920) takes place in a zoo, Bregenz's (1946) on a 'floating stage' on Lake Constance. Inflation is putting many festivals out of bounds for the ordinary operatic traveller, but if he lives in or near such operatic centres as London or Munich (which has its own late summer festival) there is opera to be had most nights of the year. The real advantage of a good festival, its location apart, is that rehearsals are normally adequate, which all too often is not the case in the average opera house.

Fioritura The decoration added to a melody, either with written or improvised figures, the word being the Italian for flowering. From the seventeenth to the early nineteenth centuries adding *fioriture* was traditional practice, though sometimes it was so abused by singers that composers could not recognise their own music. Yet when a great or good artist added such ornaments, the result enhanced the music. Joan Sutherland in roles like

Lucia di Lammermoor has discreetly and brilliantly revived the old skill, but it can come as a shock to a modern audience in, say, *Figaro*, to hear ornaments in the second verse of 'Voi che sapete', however historically correct. Even an *appogiatura*, where the main note is delayed by a grace-note, can be startling to those not used to hearing them in, say, a Mozart aria.

Grand opera   In Anglo-American countries, another word for opera, though officially it means serious opera without spoken dialogue. However, in France grand opera means a large-scale work, with chorus and ballet, in four or five acts, as exemplified in the operas of Meyerbeer.

Intermezzo   The historical intermezzo was discussed in Chapter 1. The more usual use of the word means a short piece between scenes, as in *Cavalleria Rusticana*; in other words, it is an interlude, either of original music, or developing themes that have already been heard, as in *Manon Lescaut*.

Leitmotiv   Meaning 'leading motive' in German, it is a short musical phrase which characterises a person, idea or thing. Wagner was its chief and most brilliant exponent.

Maestro   The Italian's descriptive name for composers and conductors. In Germany the conductor is called a Kapellmeister, though this once meant the choir-master of a Court chapel. The Italian equivalent was *maestro di capella*.

Mezza voce   Singing at half power, from the Italian for half-voice.

Mezzo-soprano   The middle female voice.

Opera buffa   The term for eighteenth century Italian comic opera, as opposed to *opera seria* (see below).

Opéra comique Though this signifies comic opera in French, it has two meanings. The first refers to eighteenth-century French comic operas with spoken dialogue, the second to nineteenth-century French operas with spoken dialogue, comic or not. So serious operas like *Carmen* and *Faust* rank as *opéra comique*.

Opera seria Though the term simply means 'serious' opera, it normally refers to the Italian operas of the eighteenth century with their mythological or heroic plots, formal music and (lack of) drama, sometimes tortuous librettos and regular use of *castrati* singers (see above). Mozart's *Idomeneo* (1781) is proof that the stultifying form could occasionally be transcended. Technically superb singers of great influence allowed it to survive so long, as did their audiences. Rossini's *Semiramide* (1823) is a final example.

Parlando The singer, directed by the composer, lets the voice sound approximately like speech. A famous example occurs in Act 2 of *Tosca* when the heroine has killed Scarpia and rejoices in amazement: 'E avanti a lui tremeva tutta Roma!' – 'And all Rome trembled before him!'.

Prima donna is the leading female singer in an opera, or the star soprano of a company.

Producer The English word for the man or woman who stages an opera. The theatre has sensibly switched to the American 'Director' which is more accurate, though in America the opera producer is known as the (General Stage) Director. In France and elsewhere including Germany, he is known as the *Régisseur*, in Germany also, the *Spielleiter* and in Italy the *Regista*. Producers as such entered opera in the early years of the century, before which conductors, composers and singers did the job, with varying degrees of success, one may assume. Wagner was surely the best of the composer-producers and

Mahler on evidence was a fine conductor-
producer. Max Reinhardt (1873–1943) was one
of the first theatre directors to turn to opera (and
it should be noted that there were few theatre
directors until some 70 years ago), but the first
great opera producer was possibly Carl Ebert
(1887–   ), especially in his work at John
Christie's Glyndebourne before and after World
War Two with Fritz Busch (1890–1951), the co-
founder of the Festival in 1934. Ébert was an ex-
actor and man of the theatre and, unlike some
producers who try their hand at opera, truly
musical. So is Peter Hall, one of the the world's
greatest directors of plays who is also a superb
director of opera.

Other great names of the post-war years are,
or have been, Luchino Visconti, whose collaboration at La Scala with Callas in the 1950s produced supreme art; Franco Zeffirelli, a Renaissance man of our day and one of the finest
exponents of operatic realism; Giorgio Strehler,
a great director who has opened Italian eyes to
advanced theatrical ideas in the opera house; and
Walter Felsenstein whose work at the Berlin
Komische Oper from 1947 showed just what
could be done in the opera house with months
of rehearsal under a genius. At Bayreuth, as has
been noted, Wolfgang and, especially, Wieland
Wagner transformed Wagnerian productions
from fossilisation to artistic brilliance.

And what must the operatic director do, apart
from sincerely carrying out the composer's in-
tentions as he sees them? He must, through the
music, stage the opera in a totally professional
manner and, as part of this, he must get every
singer – if he is given adequate rehearsal time –
to act, relax and look as if he or she belongs on a
stage. Any director who cannot do this should
not be in the opera house, for Zeffirelli for one
has proved that any singer can act, given en-

couragement. In opera, as in the theatre, there is good acting and bad acting: there is ideally no such thing as operatic acting. Of course, Wagner is slow-paced with flashes of sudden action, compared with *Falstaff*, which is quicksilver, just as a Feydeau farce is quicksilver compared with Ibsen. But one can only repeat, there is only acting, good or bad, whatever the medium, and despite the fact that the opera singer is paced by the music in a way that a straight actor is not.

The producer can be too powerful, but he is essential to a well-realised opera. Not that the public would now stand for concerts-in-costume. It has experienced Visconti's *Traviata* with Callas, his *Don Carlos* at Covent Garden, Strehler's *Simone Boccanegra*, Zeffirelli's *Cav and Pag*, Wieland Wagner's *Ring*, Felsenstein's *The Cunning Little Vixen*, Hall's *Figaro*, to name but a few brilliant productions.

Répétiteur His job is to coach the singers in their roles and he may conduct off-stage bands, etc. in performance. Many conductors have started in this post, which is called *solo répétiteur* in Germany and *maestro collaboratore* in Italy.

Scena A dramatic solo less formal than an aria, often less lyrical, a supreme example being Leonore's 'Abscheulicher' in *Fidelio*.

Singers Time has a way of erasing even the names of famous singers, but a handful of them survive as legends of past glories. Only specialists in operatic history recall the names of pre-nineteenth-century stars, and perhaps the first whose glamour still lasts, not least because the music they sang has been so successfully revived in our own generation are Giuditta Pasta (1798–1865), Maria Malibran (1808–36) and Wilhelmine Schröder-Devrient (1804–60), all three of whom have already appeared in this book.

Pasta, a soprano of striking classical looks, dramatic fire vocally, and superb gifts as an actress, was immortalised by Stendhal, amongst others; Malibran, the fiery young comet, a mezzo-contralto with the range of a soprano, and even more exciting dramatic gifts, was the queen of the Romantic era, the more so because she died so tragically young. As for Schröder-Devrient, 'the Queen of Tears', her part in Wagner's career has been described.

Who, regardless of fame in their own time, truly survives in the operatic folk-consciousness from the remainder of the century? Pauline Viardot-Garcia perhaps (1821–1910), Malibran's sister and the friend of Turgenev; Adelina Patti (1843–1919), the super-star soprano whose contracts had a no-rehearsal clause; Jenny Lind (1820–87); Giovanni Rubini (1794–1854), the incomparable tenor; Giovanni Mario (1810–83) his true successor; Giulia Grisi (1811–69) his wife, who created Elvira in *Puritani* and Norina; Luigi Lablache (1794–1858), a giant bass in every way. All these are beyond living memory as artists except Patti, but the gramophone will see to it that later stars are never totally forgotten.

This section is an exercise in nostalgia as well as history and to keep this entry to reasonable proportions, here are some names that fifty years from now should still shine bright. Enrico Caruso (1873–1921), the century's most famous singer; Nellie Melba (1861–1931), a *prima donna assoluta* indeed; Jean de Reszke (1850–1925), the princely tenor who never recorded; Feodor Chaliapin (1873–1938), greatest of all actor-singers; Frida Leider (1888–1975), Kirsten Flagstad (1895–1962) and Birgit Nilsson (1918–), three Wagnerian goddesses; Hans Hotter (1909–), their match as a god; Lotte Lehmann (1888–), the most famous Marschallin in

Rosenkavalier; Ezio Pinza (1892–1957), the in-comparable Don Giovanni who became a Broadway super-star; Rosa Ponselle (1897–); Giovanni Martinelli (1885–1969): Lauritz Mel-chior (1890–197); Elizabeth Schumann (1885–1952); Jussi Björling (1907–60); Maria Callas (1923–), La Divina who changed the course of operatic history; Joan Sutherland (1926–) La Stupenda; Boris Chrìstoff (1918–); Tito Gobbi (1915–); Jon Vickers (1926–); Ren-ata Tebaldi (1922–); Leontyne Price (1927–).

Clearly a dozen others could have been chosen, some of them more 'perfect' singers. And for reasons of space no prophecies can be made from the ranks of today's younger singers. But perhaps several other twentieth-century names may be listed simply by their surnames. If the fairly recent newcomer to opera instantly recog-nises them, the chances are that they, too, will be remembered a century hence: Sills, Domingo, Evans, Bumbry, Baker, Verrett, Pears, Merill, della Casa, Schwarzkopf, Milnes, Milanov, Carreras. To name but a few . . .

Singspiel	A German form of English ballad opera and French *opéra comique*, which developed in the eighteenth century.
Soubrette	The word means 'cunning' in French and opera-tically refers to clever servant girls like Despina and Susanna, though it may also mean a light soprano comedienne role like Adèle in *Fleder-maus*.
Soprano	The highest female voice. There are too many sub-divisions to list here, but two words which often appear in reviews may be noted. Desde-mona in *Otello* is a *soprano lirico spinto* role, and 'spinto' means urged or pushed on, while Norina in *Don Pasquale* is a *soprano leggiero*, the latter word meaning 'light' or 'lightly'.
Sprechgesang	'Speech-song', originated by Schoenberg and used by Berg, in which the singer emits, but

does not sustain, the note. It is a blend of speech and song, but is not the same as *parlando* (see above).

Stage design Its early days were traced in Chapter 1, and later periods continued the tradition of scenic grandeur. The Italian opera house shape dominated Europe until well into the twentieth century and designers were particularly drawn to La Scala, Milan (1778–). Nineteenth-century Italy gloried in sumptuously pictorial scenery, sets being moved, like earlier ones, sideways in grooves. Not until the 1920s did La Scala fly sets from 'towers'.

Meanwhile, the French delighted in bigger and better scenery, while German design, as has been noted, went through a poor period of dull pictorial realism that even held Wagner back. Apolphe Appia (1862–1928) was appalled by what he saw at Bayreuth and anticipated the reforms of Wagner's grandsons with his symbolic approach: as little scenery as possible and the utmost use of lighting. Gordon Craig, Ellen Terry's son, was also working towards a new vision of opera.

Between the wars, Caspar Neher and Alfred Roller continued Appia's revolution, and today, even the most conservative of opera-goers – and no theatre-goers are more conservative visually – are timidly accepting advanced designs. A sign of the times is the success in London and Milan of a *Peter Grimes* (1975) produced by Elijah Moshinsky and designed by Timothy O'Brien and Tazeena Firth of the Royal Shakespeare Theatre, simply, starkly, effectively – and unrealistically. Yet so committed was this almost Brechtian staging that the sea and the shore and the life of the fisherfolk – strikingly sombre costumes, vivid props – were more 'real' than in any previous production. It would be a sorry sight if every opera in the repertoire was produced in this way, but every opera *could* be done (and cheaply) like this.

Stagione The Italian word for season, but in its widest sense, it has an important meaning. A *stagione* opera house like La Scala, or Covent Garden since the early 1950s, gives a limited number of performances of certain operas, some of them new productions, and all with as few cast changes as possible. These productions may or may not be revived later. This raises standards considerably even if not so many operas are on display as there are in a repertory house like the Vienna State Opera. A vast number of productions may be seen in such a house, with many cast changes, and the result is that, except at festival times, standards are overall lower than at a *stagione* house. Artistically, *stagione* must rank as the finer system.

Tenor The highest male voice (but see Counter-tenors). Most of the variations explain themselves, such as the vivid *tenore di forza*, which admirably describes the role of Otello.

Tessitura The average range of an aria in relation to the voice for which it has been written. Turandot's 'In questa reggia' for instance has a notoriously high tessitura. The term can also be used of a singer's voice.

Tonadilla Spanish entertainment using a few singers.

Transposition Some singers transpose an aria down to be able to cope better with high notes, though only those with perfect pitch can be sure of catching them out if the transposition is minimal. A singer can transpose up as well.

Travesti Breeches-roles in opera such as Cherubino in *Figaro*, Octavian in *Rosenkavalier*, etc, the male characters being taken by women.

Twelve-note music Music based on all the twelve (black and white) notes of the scale as opposed to the seven notes of the diatonic scale. (*Note*: there is no simple way of describing the above.)

Verismo   Meaning 'realism' in Italian, it is used to describe the realistic school that began with Mascagni's *Cavalleria Rusticana* (1890). But see p. 131 for a discussion of the word 'realism'.

Zarzuela.   A popular style of Spanish *opera buffa*, usually in one act. It has been popular for several centuries and deals with, and sometimes satirises, subjects close to the people. Improvisation and audience participation are features of the genre, along with easily enjoyable music.

Appendix 2

A short chronology of opera

1597	Peri's *Dafne*, the first opera stemming from the meetings of the Camerata
1607	Monteverdi's *Orfeo*
1637	First public opera house, the Teatro San Cassiano, opened in Venice
1643	Death of Monteverdi
1656	Davenant's *The Siege of Rhodes*
1662	Lully becomes master of Court music to Louis XIV
1669	Founding of L'Académie Royale de Musique, later the Opéra
1689–90	Purcell's *Dido and Aeneas*
1705	An Italian opera, Franceschini's *Arsinoe*, heard in England
1711	*Rinaldo*, Handel's first *opera seria* in England
1728	John Gay's *The Beggar's Opera*
1733	Pergolesi's influential *La Serva Padrona*, Rameau's first opera, *Hippolyte et Aricie*
1740	Frederick the Great opens his opera house in Berlin
1746	*La Serva Padrona* reaches Paris
1753	The Residenztheater, Munich, opened
1752–4	The *Guerre des Bouffons* in Paris
1756	Birth of Mozart
1762	Gluck's *Orfeo ed Euridice*
1767	Gluck's *Alceste* plus important preface
1778	La Scala, Milan, built
1781	Mozart's *Idomeneo*, his first great opera
1791	Mozart's last supreme masterpiece, *Die Zauberflöte*. Death of Mozart

1805	Beethoven's *Fidelio* (Final revision, 1814)
1813	Verdi and Wagner born. Rossini's *Tancredi* makes his makes his name outside Italy
1821	Weber's *Der Frieschütz*
1829	Rossini's *Guillaume Tell*, after which he retires
1831	Bellini's *Norma*
1835	Death of Bellini. Donizetti's *Lucia di Lammermoor*
1836	Death of Maria Malibran. Meyerbeer's *Les Huguenots*, Glinka's *A Life for the Tsar*
1838	Berlioz's *Benvenuto Cellini*
1842	Verdi's *Nabucco*. Wagner's *Rienzi*
1843	Wagner's *Der Fliegende Holländer* at Dresden
1850	Wagner's *Lohengrin* given by Liszt at Weimar
1851	Verdi's *Rigoletto* triumphs in Venice
1858	Royal Opera House Covent Garden rebuilt, after fire
1859	Gounod's *Faust*. Verdi's *Un Ballo in Maschera*
1863	Berlioz's *La Prise de Troie* given at Théatre-Lyrique
1864	Wagner meets King Ludwig
1865	Wagner's *Tristan und Isolde*
1866	Smetana's *The Bartered Bride*
1868	Boito's *Mefistofele*
1871	Verdi's *Aida*
1874	Strauss' *Die Fledermaus*. Mussorgsky's *Boris Godunov*
1875	Bizet's *Carmen* and death
1876	First Bayreuth Festival and first complete *Ring*
1877	Saint-Saëns' *Samson et Dalila*
1879	Tchaikovsky's *Eugene Onegin*
1881	Offenbach's *Les Contes d'Hoffmann*
1882	Wagner's *Parsifal*
1883	Wagner dies in Venice. Metropolitan Opera House, New York, opens
1884	Massenet's *Manon*
1885	Gilbert and Sullivan's *The Mikado*
1887	Verdi's *Otello*
1890	Mascagni's *Cavalleria Rusticana*
1893	Puccini's *Manon Lescaut*. Verdi's *Falstaff*
1896	Puccini's *La Bohème*
1897–1907	Mahler at Vienna
1898	Toscaninj first made principal conductor of La Scala
1900	Death of Sir Arthur Sullivan

1901	Death of Verdi
1902	Debussy's *Pelléas et Mélisande*
1904	Janáček's *Jenufa*
1905	Richard Strauss's *Salome*. Lehár's *The Merry Widow*
1909	Rimsky-Korsákov's *The Golden Cockerel*
1911	Richard Strauss's *Der Rosenkavalier*
1917	Pfitzner's *Palestrina*
1919	Strauss's *Die Frau ohne Schatten*
1921	Death of Caruso. Prokofiev's *The Love of the Three Oranges*. Honegger's *Le Roi David*
1924	Death of Puccini
1925	Berg's *Wozzeck*
1926	Puccini's *Turandot* at La Scala. Hindemith's *Cardillac*
1927	Stravinsky's *Oedipus Rex*
1930	Weill and Brecht's *Mahogonny*. Milhaud's *Christophe Colombe*
1932–9	Beecham in charge at Covent Garden
1933	Strauss's *Arabella*
1934	Shostakovich's *Lady Macbeth of the Mtsensk District*. First Glyndebourne Festival
1935	Gershwin's *Porgy and Bess*
1937	Orff's *Carmina Burana*
1938	Hindemith's *Mathis de Maler* produced
1945	Britten's *Peter Grimes*
1946	Founding of Covent Garden Opera Company, now the Royal Opera. Reopening of La Scala after war damage
1949	Death of Richard Strauss. Callas the talk of Italy after singing Brünnhilde and Elvira (taken over at short notice) the same week in Venice
1950	La Scala visits Covent Garden
1951	Stravinsky's *The Rake's Progress*. Reopening of Bayreuth Festival under Wagner's grandsons
1952	Première of Strauss's *Die Liebe der Danae* at Salzburg
1955	Reopening of the rebuilt Vienna State Opera. Première (after 30 years) of Prokofiev's *The Fiery Angel* at Venice. Marian Anderson, the first Negro to sing at the Met. in New York
1957	*The Trojans* at Covent Garden

1959	Sutherland's first Lucia. Sarah Caldwell begins famous era at Boston
1961	Death of Sir Thomas Beecham
1962	Death of Kirsten Flagstad. Scottish Opera founded
1963	Karajan-Zeffirelli *Bohème* at La Scala
1964	Callas, Gobbi, Zeffirelli *Tosca* at Covent Garden. La Scala visits Moscow
1965	Schoenberg's *Moses and Aaron* at Covent Garden (Solti/Peter Hall). Giorgio Strehler's famous production of Mozart's *Die Entführung* at Salzburg. Sutherland's Company tour Australia
1966	New Metropolitan Opera opens at Lincoln Center, New York. Henze's *The Bassarids*
1967	Notable Canadian opera, *Louis Riel*, by Harry Somers
1969	*The Trojans* given in its entirety by Scottish Opera and Covent Garden
1970	Sir David Webster retires from Covent Garden after 25 years in charge
1971	Fourth post-war *Ring* at Bayreuth
1972	Rudolf Bing retires from Met. after 22 years in charge
1973	Britten's *Death in Venice*. Opening of Sydney Opera House. Rolf Liebermann takes over Paris Opera. English National Opera's *Ring*
1974	*La Gioconda* with copies of original sets makes tremendous impact at the Deutsche Oper, West Berlin
1975	Paris Opéra centenary. Death of Vittorio Gui
1976	Death of Luchino Visconti. Exchange visits between La Scala and Royal Opera House, Covent Garden
	Death of Benjamin Britten

Appendix 3

The world's repertoire – a selection of composers and works

Albert, Eugene d'Albert (1864–1932) *Tiefland* (1903)

Bartók, Béla (1881–1945) *Duke Bluebeard's Castle* (1911, produced 1918)

Beethoven, Ludwig van (1770–1827) *Fidelio* (1805/1806/1814)

Bellini, Vincenzo (1801–35) *Il Pirata* (1827), *I Capuletti ed i Montecchi* (1830), *La Sonnambula* (1831), *Norma* (1831), *Beatrice di Tenda* (1833), *I Puritani* (1835)

Berg, Alban (1885–1935) *Wozzeck* (1925), *Lulu* (unfinished, produced 1937)

Berlioz, Hector (1803–69) *Benvenuto Cellini* (1838), *Les Troyens* (Part 2, 1863/Parts 1 and 2, 1890), *Béatrice et Bénédict* (1862)

Bizet, Georges (1838–75) *Les Pêcheurs de Perles* (1863), *Carmen* (1875)

Boito, Arrigo (1842–1918) *Mefistofele* (1868)

Borodin, Alexander (1833–87) *Prince Igor* (produced 1890)

Britten, Benjamin (1913–) *Peter Grimes* (1945), *The Rape of Lucretia* (1946), *Albert Herring* (1947), *Let's Make an Opera* (1949), *Billy Budd* (1951), *Gloriana* (1953), *The Turn of the Screw* (1954), *Noyes Fludde* (1958), *A Midsummer Night's Dream* (1960), *Owen Wingrave* (1971), *Death in Venice* (1973)

Catalani, Alfredo (1854–93) *La Wally* (1892)

Cavalli, Pier (1602–76) *L'Ormindo* (1644), *Calisto* (1651)

Charpentier, Gustave (1860–1956) *Louise* (1900)

Cherubini, Luigi (1760–1842). *Médée* (1797)

Cilea, Francesco (1866–1950) *Adriana Lecouvreur* (1902)

Cimarosa, Domenico (1749–1801) *Il Matrimonio Segreto* (1792)
Cornelius, Peter (1824–74) *Der Barbier von Bagdad* (1858)

Dallapiccola, Luigi (1904–75) *Il Prigioniero* (1950)
Debussy, Claude (1862–1918) *Pelléas et Mélisande* (1902)
Delibes, Léo (1836–91) *Lakmé* (1883)
Donizetti, Gaetano (1797–1848) *Anna Bolena* (1830), *L'Élisir d'Amore* (1832), *Lucia di Lammermoor* (1835), *Maria Stuarda* (1835), *La Fille du Régiment* (1840), *La Favorite* (1840), *Don Pasquale* (1843)
Dvořák, Anton (1841–1904) *Rusalka* (1901)

Falla, Manuel de (1876–1946) *La Vida Breve* (1905)

Gershwin, George (1898–1937) *Porgy and Bess* (1935)
Giordano, Umberto (1867–1948) *Andrea Chénier* (1896)
Glinka, Mikhail (1804–57) *A Life for the Tsar/Ivan Susanin* (1834–6), *Ruslan and Ludmila* (1838–41)
Gluck, Christoph (1714–87) *Orfeo ed Euridice* (1762), *Alceste* (1767), *Iphigénie en Aulide* (1773), *Armide* (1777), *Iphigénie en Tauride* (1779)
Gounod, Charles (1818–93) *Faust* (1859), *Roméo et Juliette* (1867)

Handel, George Frederic (1685–1759) *Acis and Galatea* (1720?) *Alcina* (1735) *Serse* (1738), *Samson* (1743, staged oratorio), *Semele* (1744, staged oratorio)
Haydn, Joseph (1732–1809) *Il Mondo della Luna* (1777)
Henze, Hans Werner (1926–　) *Boulevard Solitude* (1952), *König Hirsh* (1956) *Der Prinz von Homburg* (1960), *Elegy for Young Lovers* (1961), *The Bassarids* (1966)
Hindemith, Paul (1895–1963) *Mathis de Maler* (1938)
Honegger, Arthur (1892–1955) *Jeanne d'Arc au Bûcher* (1936)
Humperdinck, Engelbert (1854–1921) *Hänsel und Gretel* (1893)

Janáček, Leos (1854–1928) *Jenufa* (1904), *Katya Kabanová* (1921), *The Cunning Little Vixen* (1924), *The Makropoulos Case* (1926), *From the House of the Dead* (1930)

Kodály, Zoltán (1882–1967) *Hary Janos* (1926)
Lehár, Franz (1870–1948) *Die lustige Witwe* (1905), *Der Graf von Luxembourg* (1909), *Das Land des Lächelns* (1929)

Leoncavallo, Ruggiero (1858–1919) *Pagliacci* (1892), *La Bohème* (1897), *Zaza* (1900)

Lortzing, Albert (1801–51) *Zar und Zimmermann* (1837), *Der Wildschütz* (1842)

Mascagni, Pietro (1863–1945) *Cavalleria Rusticana* (1890), *L'Amico Fritz* (1891), *Iris* (1898)

Massenet, Jules (1842–1912) *Hérodiade* (1881), *Manon* (1884), *Werther* (1892), *Thaïs* (1894), *Le Jongleur de Notre-Dame* (1902), *Don Quichotte* (1910)

Menotti, Gian Carlo (1911–   ), *The Medium* (1946), *The Telephone* (1947), *The Consul* (1950), *Amahl and the Night Visitors* (1951)

Messager, André (1853–1929) *Véronique* (1898), *Monsieur Beaucaire* (1919)

Meyerbeer, Giacomo (1791–1864) *Robert le Diable* (1831), *Les Huguenots* (1836), *Le Prophète* (1849), *L'Africaine* (1865)

Milhaud, Darius (1892–1975) *Christophe Colomb* (1930), *David* (1954)

Millöcker, Karl (1842–99) *Der Bettelstudent* (1882)

Monisuzko, Stanislaw (1819–72) *Halka* (1848)

Monteverdi, Claudio (1567?–1643) *La Favola d'Orfeo* (1607), *Il Ritorno d'Ulisse in Patria* (1641), *L'Incoronazione di Poppea* (1642)

Mozart, Wolfgang Amadeus (1756–91) *Idomeneo* (1781), *Die Entführung aus dem Serail* (1782), *Der Schauspieldirektor* (1786), *Le Nozze di Figaro* (1786), *Don Giovanni* (1787), *Così fan tutte* (1790), *Die Zauberflöte* (1791), *La Clemenza di Tito* (1791)

Mussorgsky, Modest (1839–81) *Boris Godunov* (1873/4), *Khovanshchina* (post 1886), *Sorochinsky Fair* (unfinished, produced 1913)

Nicolai, Otto (1819–49) *Die lustigen Weiber von Windsor* (1849)

Offenbach, Jacques (1819–80) *Orphée aux Enfers* (1858), *La Belle Hélène* (1864), *La Vie Parisienne* (1866), *La Grande Duchesse de Gérolstein* (1867), *La Périchole* (1868), *Les Contes d'Hoffmann* (post 1881)

Orff, Carl (1895–   ) *Carmina Burana* (1937), *Der Mond* (1939), *Die Kluge* (1943)

Pfitzner, Hans (1869–1949) *Palestrina* (1917)
Pizzetti, Ildebrando (1880–1968) *Debora e Jaele* (1922), *La Figlia di Jorio* (1954), *L'Assassino nella Cattedrale* (1958)
Planquette, Robert (1848–1903) *Les Cloches de Corneville* (1877)
Ponchielli, Amilcare (1834–86) *La Gioconda* (1876)
Prokofiev, Sergey (1891–1953) *The Love of Three Oranges* (1921), *War and Peace* (produced 1946), *The Fiery Angel* (produced 1955)
Puccini, Giacomo (1858–1924) *Manon Lescaut* (1893), *La Bohème* (1896), *Tosca* (1900), *Madama Butterfly* (1904), *La Fanciulla del West* (1910), *La Rondine* (1917), *Il Trittico* (1918), *Turandot* (post 1926)
Purcell, Henry (*c.* 1659–95) *Dido and Aeneas* (?1689)

Rameau, Jean-Phillipe (1683–1764) *Les Indes Galantes* (1735)
Ravel, Maurice (1875–1937) *L'Heure Espagnole* (1907), *L'Enfant et les Sortilèges* (1925)
Rezniček, Emil (1860–1945) *Donna Diana* (1894)
Rimsky-Korsakov, Nikolay (1844–1904) *The Snow Maiden* (1882), *Sadko* (1898), *The Golden Cockerel* (1909)
Rossini, Gioacchino (1792–1868) *Tancredi* (1813), *L'Italiana in Algeri* (1813), *Il Barbier di Siviglia* (1816), *La Cenerentola* (1817), *La Gazza Ladra* (1817), *Mosè in Egitto* (1818, as *Moïse*, 1827), *Semiramide* (1823), *Le Comte Ory* (1823), *Guillaume Tell* (1829)

Saint-Saëns, Camille (1835–1921) *Samson et Dalila* (1877)
Schoenberg, Arnold (1874–1951) *Erwartung* (1909, produced 1924), *Moses und Aron* (unfinished, produced 1957)
Shostakovich, Dimitri (1906–75) *Lady Macbeth of Mtsensk* (Katerina Ismailova) (1934).
Smetana, Bedrich (1824–84) *The Bartered Bride* (1866), *Dalibor* (1868), *The Two Widows* (1874), *The Secret* (1878)
Spontini, Gasparo (1774–1851) *La Vestale* (1807)
Strauss, Johann (II) (1825–99) *Die Fledermaus* (1874), *Eine Nacht in Venedig* (1883), *Der Zigeunerbaron* (1885)
Strauss, Richard (1864–1949) *Salome* (1905), *Elektra* (1909),

Der Rosenkavalier (1911), *Ariadne auf Naxos* (1st version, 1912; 2nd, 1916), *Die Frau ohne Schatten* (1919), *Intermezzo* (1924), *Arabella* (1933), *Die schweigsame Frau* (1935), *Capriccio* (1942)

Stravinsky, Igor (1882–1971) *The Nightingale* (1914), *Oedipus Rex* (1927), *The Rake's Progress* (1951)

Sullivan, Arthur (1842–1900) From *Trial by Jury* (1875): there are too many of equal merit to list here.

Tchaikovsky, Petr (1840–93) *Eugene Onegin* (1879), *The Queen of Spades* (1890)

Thomas, Ambroise (1811–96) *Mignon* (1866)

Tippett, Michael (1905–   ) *The Midsummer Marriage* (1955), *King Priam* (1962), *The Knot Garden* (1970)

Vaughan Williams, Ralph (1872–1958) *Hugh the Drover* (1924), *Riders to the Sea* (1937)

Verdi, Giuseppe (1813–1901) *Nabucco* (1842), *I Lombardi* (1843), *Ernani* (1844), *I due Foscari* (1844), *Attila* (1846), *Macbeth* (1847, revised 1865), *La Battaglia di Legnano* (1849), *Luisa Miller* (1849), *Rigoletto* (1851), *Il Trovatore* (1853), *La Traviata* (1853), *Les Vespres Siciliennes* (1855), *Simone Boccanegra* (1857, revised 1881), *Un Ballo in Maschera* (1859), *La Forza del Destino* (1862), *Don Carlos* (1867), *Aida* (1871), *Otello* (1887), *Falstaff* (1893)

Wagner, Richard (1813–1883) *Der fliegende Holländer* (1843), *Tannhäuser* (1845, revised 1861), *Lohengrin* (1850), *Tristan und Isolde* (1865), *Die Meistersinger* (1868), *Das Rheingold* (1869), *Die Walküre* (1870), *Siegfried* (1876), *Götterdämmerung* (1876), *Parsifal* (1882)

Weber, Carl Maria von (1786–1826) *Der Freischütz* (1821)

Weill, Kurt (1900–50) *Die Dreigroschenoper* (1928), *Mahogonny* (1930)

Wolf-Ferrari, Ermanno (1876–1948) *I Quatro Rusteghi* (1906), *Il Segreto di Susanna* (1909)

Further Reading: a select list

General

Wallace Brockway and Herbert Weinstock: *The World of Opera* (Methuen, 1963)

Edward J. Dent: *Opera* (Penguin, 1949)

Philip Hope-Wallace: *A Picture History of Opera* (Hulton, 1959)

Arthur Jacobs and Stanley Sadie: *The Opera Guide* (Hamish Hamilton, 1964)

Gustave Kobbé: *The Complete Opera Book* (revised and enlarged by Lord Harewood, Cassell, 1976)

Leslie Orrey: *A Concise History of Opera* (Thames and Hudson, 1972)

Harold Rosenthal and John Warrack: *Concise Oxford Dictionary of Opera* (OUP, 1973)

Opera Magazine (monthly)

Composers

Eric Blom: *Mozart* (Dent, 1952)

David Cairns (ed.): *The Memoirs of Hector Berlioz* (Gollancz, 1969)

M. D. Calvocoressi: *Modeste Mussorgsky* (Rockliff, 1956)

Mosco Carner: *Puccini* (Duckworth, 1958)

Mina Curtiss: *Bizet and his World* (Secker and Warburg, 1959)

Robert Donnington: *Wagner's Ring and its Symbols* (Faber, 1963)

Patricia Howard: *Gluck and the Birth of Modern Opera* (Barrie and Rockcliff, 1963)

Spike Hughes: *Famous Puccini Operas* (Hale, 1959)

William S. Mann: *Richard Strauss: A Critical Study of his Operas* (Cassell, 1964)

Ernest Newman: *The Life of Richard Wagner* (Cassell, 1933–47)
Leslie Orrey: *Bellini* (Dent, 1969)
Stanley Sadie: *Handel* (Calder, 1962)
Stendhal: *Life of Rossini* (Calder, 1956)
Francis Toye: *Rossini: a Study in Tragi-Comedy* (Barker, 1959)
Francis Toye: *Verdi* (Gollancz, 1962)
Frank Walker: *The Man Verdi* (Dent, 1962)
John Warrack: *Tchaikovsky* (Hamish Hamilton, 1974)
John Warrack: *Weber* (Hamish Hamilton, 1968)
Herbert Weinstock: *Donizetti* (Methuen, 1964)
Eric Walter White: *Benjamin Britten* (Faber, 1970)

Some particular subjects

Dennis Arundell: *The Story of Sadler's Wells* (Hamish Hamilton, 1965)
Rudolf Bing: *5000 Nights at the Opera* (Hamish Hamilton, 1972)
Carlo Gatti: *Il Teatro alla Scala* (Milan, 1964)
Spike Hughes: *Glyndebourne* (Methuen, 1965)
Colonel J. H. Mapleson: *The Mapleson Memoirs* (Ed. Rosenthal, Putnam, 1966)
Frank Merkling and John Freeman: *The Golden Horseshoe* (Secker & Warburg, 1965)
Marcel Prawy: *The Vienna Opera* (Weidenfeld and Nicolson, 1970)
Harold Rosenthal: *Two Centuries of Opera at Covent Garden* (Putnam, 1958)
Simon Worsthorne: *Venetian Opera in the Seventeenth Century* (OUP, 1954)

Selective Index

For reasons of space the following is essentially a list of composers and operas, though a handful of other names and subjects are included. Operatic terms and professions – singers, conductors etc, – can be found in Appendix I. The names of operas in the standard repertory are mainly given in translation below, except for those like *La Traviata* which are never translated. Less well-known works are not translated. There is a certain amount of cross-referencing.